INDIA'S PAST

INDIA'S PAST

A SURVEY OF HER LITERATURES
RELIGIONS, LANGUAGES AND ANTIQUITIES

A. A. MACDONELL

GYAN

Published by

Gyan Publishing House
5, Ansari Road
Daryaganj, New Delhi-110002
Phone: 011-47034999, 9811692060
E-mail: books@gyanbooks.com

Distribution Network
gyanbooks.com
India, USA, Canada, UK, Australia, France

ISBN : 978-81-212-3625-6 (PB)
First Published, Oxfor, 1927

2nd Impression 2020

Printed at: Gyan Press, Delhi.

India's Past
Author: A. A. Macdonell

INDIA'S PAST

A SURVEY *of her* LITERATURES RELIGIONS, LANGUAGES *and* ANTIQUITIES

By

A. A. MACDONELL

Emeritus Professor of Sanskrit in the University of Oxford

OXFORD

AT THE CLARENDON PRESS

1927

EAST GATEWAY OF GREAT STŪPA, SĀNCHĪ

(*see p. 65*)

PREFACE

THIS work summarizes India's intellectual history, which in its various aspects has been the subject of my studies for slightly more than half a century (1875 to 1926). It sets forth in nine chapters the mental development of the most easterly branch of Aryan civilization since it entered India by land till it came in contact by sea with the most westerly branch of the same civilization after a separation of at least 3,000 years. The four centuries that have since elapsed (1498 to 1926) are here touched upon only as showing the most recent distribution of the Indian vernaculars and the rise of their literatures, as well as the process by which the development of the purely indigenous period gradually became known to the new-comers from the west. This process was so slow that three centuries passed before the alien arrivals recognized that they themselves were the inheritors of a civilization which was the same in origin as that of the recently occupied eastern land. An account of the influence of this western civilization on that prevailing in modern India, I have left to the political history of the last four centuries; for it would in any case have proved too extensive as well as unsuitable for inclusion in this volume. All such matter will be found in *The Oxford History of India* by the late Dr. Vincent Smith. The actual ground covered by the present volume is this. The introductory chapter describes the physical aspects of India and their resulting effect on migrations of population into this area. The next chapter tells of the language, the literature, and the religion of the earliest period of the Aryans in India. Then follows an account of the later

Vedic period and the introduction of writing. The fourth chapter describes the early post-Vedic age, including the rise of Jainism and Buddhism as well as their art. The next chapter deals with the epic and classical literature of India. The sixth chapter is concerned with Indian stories, fairy tales, and fables, together with their important place in world literature. The seventh chapter treats of the various aspects of technical literature such as grammar, lexicography, philosophy, law, practical arts, medicine, astronomy, and mathematics. The next chapter embraces the vernacular languages of India and their literatures. The final chapter shows how Europeans became acquainted with India's past by a study of her early literature, her inscriptions, her archaeology, and her coinage, pointing out the most efficient means of extracting from these sources further facts relating to the past. It also gives some account of the labours of those scholars by whom India's bygone history has been recovered.

Each chapter concludes with a selected bibliography including works that supply further references. For the range of our knowledge of India's past is now so extensive that the information supplied by this book could only cover the main and essential points, the selected bibliography being intended to serve as an up-to-date and trustworthy guide for both the general reader and the student in whichever direction further details are sought. Its contents are meant, within a small compass, to direct both the English and the Indian reader through the long tract of time from the beginning of the Vedic age down to the epoch when the modern European became acquainted with the Indo-Aryan. These two civilizations, starting from a common source, have after a separation of at least 3,000 years again become united during the last four centuries, representing together a quarter of the total of the earth's inhabitants. During these four centuries the new-comers from the west have gained acquaintance with and recovered the history of India's past mental development. All this, as set forth in the following pages, will, I trust, contribute something to clearer mutual understanding by two civilizations which in their origin were one and the same.

A. A. MACDONELL.

20 BARDWELL ROAD,
OXFORD,
Jan. 1, 1927.

CONTENTS

LIST OF ILLUSTRATIONS

MAPS

I

INTRODUCTION

Physical characteristics of India — Two great triangular areas: Hindustān, continental, shut off by mountain ranges; Deccan, maritime, shut off by the sea — Land access by migration practicable on north-west only — Three great river systems of Hindustān — Early trade between Mesopotamia and west coast of Deccan — Arabian coasting trade — Discovery of maritime route from Europe to India in 1498 — Its results — Recent archaeological discoveries in the Indus valley — Their interpretation as yet uncertain.

A GLANCE at the physical map of the world suffices to show that no country forming part of the old continents, in which the civilization of mankind has been evolved, is so isolated by nature as India. Rhomboidal in outline or roughly diamond-shaped, it extends from its northern angle in Kashmīr to Cape Comorin[1] as its southernmost extremity; and from the mouths of the Indus in the west to somewhat beyond the estuary of the Brahmaputra in the east, its utmost length, some 1,900 miles, being about equal to its greatest breadth. Its total area, which, excluding Burma, covers a surface of rather more than one million and a half square miles, is somewhat larger than fifteen times that of Great Britain. It is divided by the tropic of Cancer (23° N. lat.) into a northern and a southern triangle. These are separated from west to east across the greater width of the peninsula by the Vindhya and other

[1] This is a name of great antiquity, being a corruption of the Sanskrit *kumārī*, 'maiden', an epithet of the goddess Durgā, to whom a temple was dedicated at the extreme point of the peninsula. It is mentioned in the *Periplus*, *c.* 70 A. D., and by Ptolemy, *c.* 150 A. D.

connected ranges that lie between the longitude of Mount Abu (73° E.) and Pārasnāth Hill (87° E.). The northern triangle consists of an alluvial plain, which in an earlier geological age formed the floor of the ocean, but in later, though still prehistoric, times became raised above the level of the sea. It is continental in character, being surrounded by mountain ranges on all sides. On the west it is shut off from the neighbouring countries of Asia by high mountains. On the east it is separated from Burma by a series of high hills and by impenetrable jungle. On the north it is bounded by the most stupendous range in the world, at least 1,400 miles in length and about 19,000 ft. in height, its peaks varying from 25,000 to 29,000 ft. In this great barrier there are some mountain tracks by which men have found their way to India. Such are the passes from the Pāmirs by Gilgit, as well as those from Tibet by Leh, by the gorge of the Sutlej, and by Sikkim. But these are not highways by which migrations or invasions from the north have reached or could reach southwards to India. Nor has the eastern frontier, protected by hills and jungles, ever been exposed to hostile attack. It is only on the western side, though even this is guarded by almost continuous ranges of lofty hills, that from time immemorial immigration, conquest, and commerce made their way before 1500 A.D. by narrow roads into India. Access can here be gained either from southern Balochistān by the rocky track leading to the Indus delta, or from Afghānistān by the Bolān, the Tochi, and the Khaibar passes, as well as by the river valleys of the Gomal, the Kurram, and the Kābul, to the banks of the Indus farther north.

Only through the western gateways have passed the two great invasions that have vitally affected the fortunes of India. By this way came in prehistoric times the wave of

Aryan migration that overspread India with its civilization from that day to this. It was perhaps two thousand years or more afterwards that the Semitic conquest by Islām began on the western frontier, about 700 A.D. A considerable part of India was held under this alien despotic sway for more than seven hundred years, down to the middle of the eighteenth century. This dominion, though unifying India politically, did not essentially modify its civilization, in spite of the fact that one-fifth of the entire population professes Islām at the present day. With the exception of the Greeks, from 326 B.C. till about 200 A.D., only Asiatics have come in contact with the continental half of India by land.

This great northern plain is enclosed not only by mountain ranges but by rivers on every side. Two of the three largest of these rise close together in Tibet, near the great Kailāsa group of peaks and the Mānasarowar lake at the back and about the middle of the Himālayan barrier. The Indus in the first half of its course follows a north-westerly direction; then, bending round the extremity of the Himālayan chain, it flows southward till it falls into the Arabian Sea just north of the tropic of Cancer. Its whole course is about 1,500 miles in length. The Brahmaputra, rising slightly to the east of Lake Mānasarowar (*c.* 82° E.), after an easterly course of many hundreds of miles through Tibet, turns southward at the end of the Himālayan range (*c.* 96° E.), and, flowing slightly westward of Dacca, finally enters the Bay of Bengal somewhat to the south of the tropic of Cancer, almost opposite the mouths of the Indus on the other side of India. Its whole length is about 1,800 miles.

The third great river of northern India. the Ganges (in Sanskrit Gaṅgā), which is about 1,540 miles long, rises (*c.* 80° E.) somewhat to the south-west of the sources of the Indus and the Brahmaputra. Breaking through the southern range of the central Himālaya, it flows in a south-easterly direction through the eastern half of the alluvial plain of Hindustān. At Goālanda it joins the Meghnā, the largest and most easterly estuary of the Brahmaputra. Between this and the Hūgli, the most westerly and main branch of the Ganges, lies the combined delta of the two mighty rivers.

Parallel to the southern slopes of the Vindhya range, which shuts off the northern plain, flows the Narbadā river from its source at Amarkantak (82° E.) with a slight northerly trend past Jabalpur (80°E.) and then westward, by Broach[1] (thirty miles from its mouth) to the Bay of Cambay.

The area of the great alluvial plain of northern India is called by the Persian name of Hindustān,[2] the 'country of the Indus', the river on the western side of the country, with which foreigners first became acquainted.

The area of the great alluvial plain of Hindustān is shut off by the Vindhya range, which forms the northern buttress of the Deccan,[3] the name of southern India, the whole of which lies within the tropics south of the Narbadā river. It is a rocky plateau, bounded on both sides by high ridges of hills called Ghāts,[4] which are separated by narrow strips of lowland on the west from the

[1] Anglicized form of Bharōch, an ancient, still surviving city, the original Sanskrit of which is Bhṛgukaccha, 'Bhṛigu-bank', mentioned by Strabo (*c.* 20 B.C.) as Bargozē, and in the *Periplus* (*c.* 70 A.D.) as Barygaza.

[2] From *hindū*, the Persian equivalent of the Sanskrit *sindhu*, 'the river', 'the Indus', and *stān*, corresponding to *sthāna*, 'land'.

[3] The anglicized form of the vernacular Dakkin or Dakkhan, from the Sanskrit *dakṣiṇa*, 'right hand (country)', so called because the ancient Indians faced the rising sun in naming the points of the compass.

[4] From the vernacular 'mountain pass', then 'mountain range'.

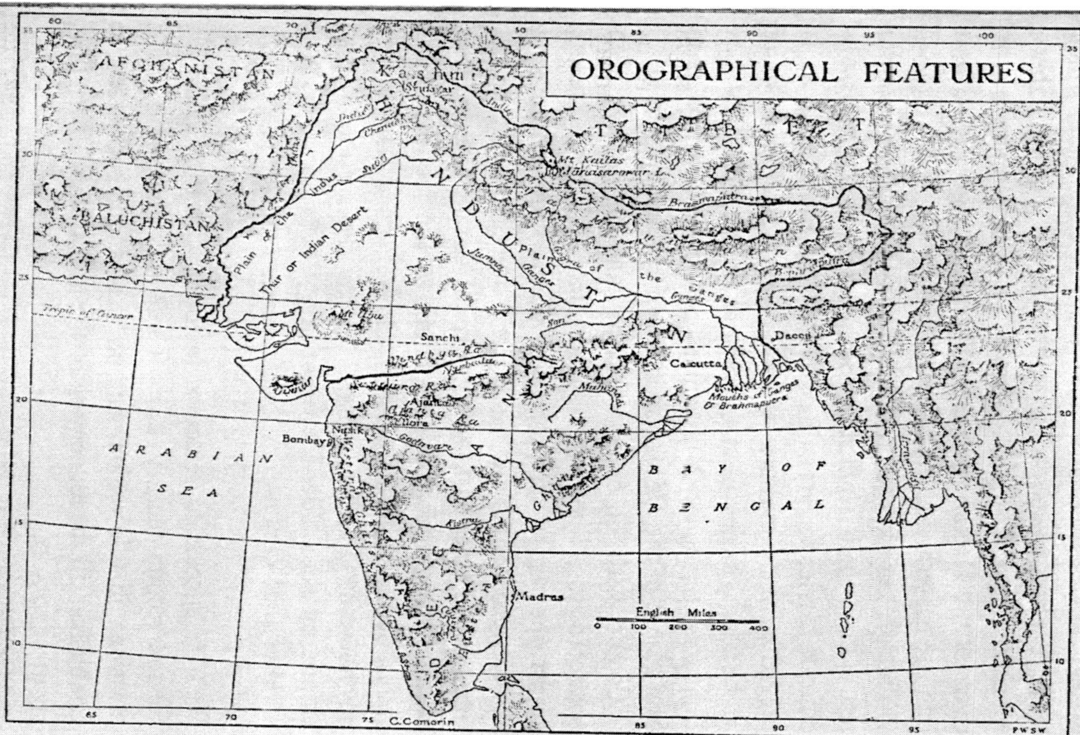

OROGRAPHICAL FEATURES
AFGHANISTAN
BALUCHISTAN
Kashmir
Srinagar
Indus
Jhelum
Chenab
Sutlej
HINDUSTAN
TIBET
Mt Kailas
Manasarowar L.
Brahmaputra
Plain of the Indus
Thar or Indian Desert
Plain of the Ganges
Jumna
Ganges
Tropic of Cancer
Mt Abu
Sanchi
Vindhya Ra.
Narbada
Ajanta
Ellora
Nasik
Bombay
Godavari
Mahanadi
Kistna
Calcutta
Dacca
Mouths of Ganges & Brahmaputra
Madras
C. Comorin
ARABIAN SEA
BAY OF BENGAL
English Miles
0 100 200 300 400
PWSW

Arabian Sea, and on the east from the Bay of Bengal. The plateau slopes gradually from the western Ghāts, which average about 3,000 ft. in height, to the eastern Ghāts, which are 1,500 ft. high. Owing to this fact many of the rivers of the Deccan rise near its western edge and all fall into the eastern sea.

Though less exposed to migration and conquest from the rest of Asia than Hindustān, the Deccan did not oppose a difficult barrier to Aryan incursion within India itself, as is proved by the occurrence of Indo-Aryan inscriptions quite in the south, dating from as early as the third century B.C. But at a later period Muhammadan rule did not acquire so firm a hold of the Deccan as it did of Hindustān.

Contact with the outer world by land has always been restricted to Hindustān. More than 500 years before Christ the region on both sides of the Indus, comprising the western Panjāb and Sindh, from the district in ancient times called Gandhāra (with its capital Taxila, twenty miles north of the modern Rāwal Pindi) to the mouths of the Indus, became (from 530 B.C.) and remained part of the neighbouring Persian Empire till the destruction of that empire by Alexander the Great in 331 B.C.

After that conqueror's brief invasion of the Panjāb in 326 B.C., and his death at Babylon in 323 B.C., his Graeco-Bactrian successors remained in touch with the north-west till the second century A.D. There followed some minor invasions in this region, but no permanent conquest was established till the foundation of the Muhammadan Empire, about 1200 A.D.

The Deccan was really more completely isolated from the rest of the world by the sea than Hindustān by its mountain barriers, till little more than four centuries ago. While every cape and bay of the Mediterranean and East

2. ALEXANDER THE GREAT

3. VASCO DA GAMA

Africa were known to the Phoenicians, the coasts of India seem to have remained unknown to them. But the evidence available warrants the belief that maritime commerce between India and Babylon by the Persian Gulf flourished from about 700 to 480 B.C. Specially Indian products—rice, peacocks, and sandalwood—were known in the west by their Tamil designations. That they must have been imported from the west coast of India into Babylon by sea is an inference to be drawn from an early Buddhist book, dating from perhaps 400 B.C.

The Indian products must have been first imported not later than the sixth century B.C., because direct intercourse between Babylon and India practically ceased after 480 B.C., and because rice and peacocks must have reached Greece at the latest by about 460 B.C., so as to become familiar at Athens in the time of Sophocles (495–406 B.C.). Corroboration of the date of the early trade between Mesopotamia and India is supplied by the alphabetical Phoenician writing, which was introduced into India and must have been in use there not later than about 700 B.C. A similar conclusion is indicated by numismatic evidence: the oblong silver coins bearing no legend and known as *purāṇas*, which are the oldest coinage of India and are represented on Buddhist bas-reliefs of the second century B.C., resemble the coins of Babylon of about 500 B.C. and are not improbably an imitation of them.

When Babylon and Egypt declined, the merchants of Yemen in South Arabia entered into the commercial inheritance of those two countries, and the greater part of the trade with India, as well as with equatorial Africa, passed into their hands. But the Arabs do not seem to have been among the early sea-going races, though southern Arabian tribes were from remote ages the carriers of the East. Their caravans traversed the Arabian peninsula in every direction, but their traffic was by land and not by sea.

With the establishment of Islām, in 622 A. D., the trade of the Arabs spread not only on land over a great part of Asia Minor, the Black Sea region, northern Africa and south-western Europe, but also acquired control of the harbours of the Arabian Sea and the African coasts, as well as of the maritime route from the Persian Gulf to India and China.

Contact with the rest of Asia by sea thus remained restricted to the coasting trade on the western side of India down to the end of the fifteenth century A. D. Then for the first time India became known to the nations of Europe by maritime intercourse. The discovery of the ocean route to India by Vasco da Gama, in 1498, brought India not only within the range of world commerce, but under the influence of Western civilization. It has led to the establishment of a new empire which, though like that of Rome in being incorporated and ruled from the centre, is gradually being trained to progress and the attainment of autonomous powers. The result is that India has already been more westernized on the surface than any other Asiatic country. This European influence, superficial though it still may be, is bound, in the inevitable march of progress, to modify with increasing rapidity its indigenous civilization in all its aspects: political, economic, social, educational, intellectual, religious, and moral.

In the new era the European settlers, whose chief interest was commercial, became acquainted, though in a very imperfect manner, with the latest forms of Indian language, custom, and religion. But after the consolidation of British rule, in the middle of the eighteenth century, administrators and scholars began to study with increasing intensity India's past in all its aspects—literary, linguistic, religious, archaeological. The result of their aggregate researches is that the history of Indian civilization has in every direction been reconstructed and revealed to the modern world. It can now be presented to the reader as a whole, not only as a picture of the past, but as a guide for the days that are to come.

After Alexander's invasion, in 326 B.C., we have from about 300 B.C. fairly clear archaeological evidence of man's activities in India. This supplies the basis on which the early political history of India has been established. But before the third century B.C. we have only glimmerings of what happened on Indian soil. We have had nothing more than prehistoric graves in the south and some cyclopean walls at Rājagṛiha in the north to throw uncertain light on the remoter past. Suddenly there has been revealed by the operations of the archaeological survey of India, quite recently, a new class of objects which may illuminate much better the prehistoric period of the country. At present (1926), however, they furnish insufficient evidence to establish their age and origin. These finds lie at two sites in the Indus region, 400 miles apart, at Harappa in the lower Panjāb, about half-way between Multān and Lahore on the railway, and at Mohenjo-daro in the Lārkhāna district of Sindh on the Indus. At both sites there are numerous artificial mounds rising as much as sixty feet above the plain, and especially conspicuous along dried-up beds of the main stream of the Indus. There is little doubt that this region will prove a valuable area for systematic archaeological exploration. At Mohenjo-daro has been found in the dry bed of the river a Buddhist *stūpa* of the second century A.D. Below this have been excavated at least two other strata containing brick structures, the character and age of which can as yet only be conjectured. The remains at these two sites consist of pottery painted and plain, some hand-made, some turned on the wheel; terracottas; new types of coins; dice and chessmen; a number of engraved and inscribed seals. The legends on the stone seals are engraved in an unknown script, the figures and style being different from anything in Indian art; but they show a certain general affinity to the picto-graphs of the Mycenaean age. The coins here found may turn out to be the oldest in existence, the earliest as yet known being the Lydian coins of the seventh century B.C. Iron is found only in the latest layer of these deposits. The culture here revealed must have extended over many centuries, but seems to have come to an end not long before the rise of the Maurya dynasty (320 B.C.).

Nothing very definite can yet be said about this newly discovered forgotten civilization. It may have developed in the Indus valley and have died out without any influence on the civilization of India proper. Similarity has already been discovered between plaques found here and tablets found at Susa. This similarity may point to intercourse between Susa and north-western India. It is possible that the people who made these seals were in close contact with Sumerian civilization, and borrowed their artistic style and the elements of their writing from the Sumerians at some period about 3000–2800 B.C. We must, however, await the results of careful research before being able to decide what light, if any, these recent discoveries can throw on the early civilization of India. Though the excavations began to be made some four years ago, nothing about them was known in England till the appearance of some articles and letters regarding them by Sir John Marshall and others in the last quarter of 1924.

The Cambridge History of India, Cambridge, 1922: vol. i, ch. i, pp. 1–34; ch. ii, pp. 37–62; ch. xiv, pp. 319–41. Holdich, *India*, London, 1904: map facing title page. *Imperial Gazetteer of India*, vol. xxvi, p. 66, map. iv, Oxford, 1909. Bartholomew, *Oxford Advanced Atlas*, maps lviii–lxiv. J. Kennedy, 'The Early Commerce of Babylon with India', *Journal of the Royal Asiatic Society*, 1898, pp. 241–88. Harappa and Mohen-Jo-daro Excavations: Sir J. Marshall, *Illustrated London News*, Sept. 20, 1924. Prof. Sayce, ibid., Sept. 27, 1924. C. J. Gadd and Sidney Smith, ibid., Oct. 4, 1924. C. J. Gadd, *Discovery*, v, No. 60, Dec. 1924. S. K. Chatterji, *Modern Review*, Dec. 1924.

II

THE ANCIENT OR VEDIC PERIOD

Relationship of Vedic to European languages — Habitat of Vedic Indians — Importance of Vedic language and literature — The four Vedas — Three literary strata in Vedic period — Arrangement of the Ṛigveda — Its relation to other Vedas — High authenticity of the Ṛigvedic text — Textual safeguards — Vedic accent, metre, interpretation — Religion of the Ṛigveda — Gods of the Ṛigveda — Hymns to Dawn and to Indra — Verses to the Maruts and to Parjanya — Terrestrial deities — Abstract gods — Prajāpati — Deified objects — Demons — Magical, funeral, and didactic hymns — Secular data in the hymns — Literary merit of the Ṛigveda — The Atharvaveda — Some of its spells translated — Hymn to Varuṇa — Selected bibliography.

WE are able to infer safely from the evidence of the earliest phase of Indian literature that in remote prehistoric times certain warlike tribes invaded India from the north-west, and, gradually spreading first to the east and then to the south, subjected the aborigines and imposed both their speech and their civilization on almost the entire country. The approximate date of this invasion remains conjectural, but there are good grounds for regarding the fourteenth century B.C. as not improbable.

The language spoken by the conquerors was the earliest form of Sanskrit preserved in the hymns that the poet-priests of the invaders began to compose after they had entered the country. It was not known till little more than a century ago that this language is closely allied to Persian, Greek, Latin, Teutonic, Celtic, and Slavonic.

Their relationship is illustrated by such words as Sanskrit *mātár*, Greek *μήτηρ*, Latin *māter*, Old Irish *māthir*,

English *mother*; Skt. *sūnú*, Lithuanian *sūnŭ*, Old High German *sunu*, English *son*. Known at an earlier stage than any of the others, the ancient Indian branch has been of prime importance in the history of philology. The evidence indicating the region where the invading Aryans entered India consists mainly of geographical data to be found in the early hymns. From the names of the rivers there mentioned it may safely be concluded that the area occupied by the newcomers lay between the Indus and the Sutlej, bounded on the north by the Himālaya, with a fringe of settlements to the east and west of these limits. This evidence is corroborated by that of the fauna and flora referred to in the earliest period. The lion, to whose habits western India is well adapted, is familiar, but the tiger is never mentioned. Rice, the natural habitat of which is in the south-east, is unknown.

The ancient Aryan language has been minutely examined, and the historical evidence contained in its literature extracted. The final result has been that the two sources have taken an important place both in the history of Indian civilization and in the foundation and development of four branches of Western study. For they are respectively the basis not only of nearly all the vernaculars and of the indigenous religions of modern India, but have also originated in the Western world of scholarship several new sciences, Comparative Philology, Comparative Mythology, Comparative Religion, and Comparative Literature, which between them have made a large contribution to the culture and enlightenment of the world.

The oldest book of the ancient period is, for various reasons, the most important work of Indian literature. It is the earliest product not only of Indian, but of Indo-European literature. It is therefore capable of shedding light in various directions on prehistoric phases of language (such as inflexion, accent, and metre), of religion, and of civilization in general. Many of these problems would be insoluble without its evidence. The investigation of its religion led in the second half of last century to the foundation of the sciences of Comparative Mythology and Comparative Religion. The Indian religion of Buddhism could not be fully understood by one not knowing this Veda, for its relation to the latter is like that of the New Testament to the Old. Finally, it has been the authoritative sacred book, for over 3,000 years, of myriads of Hindus: prayers derived from it are uttered by them even at the present day.

The word 'Veda', primarily meaning 'knowledge' (from *vid*, 'to know'), virtually signifies 'sacred knowledge or scripture', and expresses the whole character of the ancient period of Indian literature, which bears an exclusively religious stamp: even the latest productions of that age, though not directly religious, were ancillary to Vedic religion. In the Vedic period three literary strata can be clearly distinguished: the first is that of the four Vedas, which consist of hymns, prayers, and spells addressed to the gods; the second, that of the Brāhmaṇas or ritual treatises; the third, that of the Upanishads or theosophical works, the basis of much of the later Indian philosophy.

The most ancient of the four Vedas is the *Ṛigveaa*, 'the Veda of verses' (*ṛic*), which consists chiefly of lyrics in praise of various gods. It may be called the 'book of psalms' as describing its contents most characteristically. From this Veda the other three largely borrow their subject-matter. The *Sāmaveda* has no independent importance, for it consists almost entirely of stanzas taken from the *Ṛigveda* for the ritual of the Soma sacrifice. The verses of the *Yajurveda* are for the most part also derived from the *Ṛigveda*; but about half of its contents, consisting of prose formulas, are original. Its subject-matter being arranged in the order in which it is employed in various sacrificial rites, it is characteristically the 'Veda of sacrificial spells' (*yajus*). For a considerable time these three Vedas alone were recognized as canonical scriptures, being in the next literary phase described as the 'threefold knowledge' (*trayī vidyā*, Pāli *tevijja*). The *Atharvaveda* came to be recognized as canonical only a good deal later than the other three; it is similar in form to the *Ṛigveda*, from which many of its hymns are taken; but the evidence both of its language and of its matter show that it was formed into a collection subsequently to the *Ṛigveda*. In spirit also it differs entirely from that Veda. For it does not deal with the higher gods, but for the most part with the demon world, being concerned with primitive ideas of witchcraft. It may appropriately be called the 'book of magical spells'. As these two, the *Atharvaveda* and the *Ṛigveda*, record an earlier phase than any other sacred literature, they are of very high value to the student of the evolution of religious ideas. The arrangement of the *Ṛigveda*, unlike that of the *Sāma*- and the *Yajur-veda*, was an historical one, for the intention of its ancient editors was simply to preserve this heritage of the past from change and destruction. The 1,028 hymns contained in it are grouped in ten books called *maṇḍalas*, or cycles of varying length, except that the tenth embraces the same number as the first. Six of these books (ii–vii) are homogenous, inasmuch as they are the work of the descendants of different Ṛishis, or seers. The hymns in these books all follow a uniform arrangement differing from that of the rest. They probably formed the nucleus to which the others were successively added. It seems likely that the earliest addition to the 'family' books was the second part of Book i (51–191), because it resembles the 'family' books in its internal arrangement. The eighth book has a character of its own, and the first part of Book i (1–50) resembles it in some ways: it is therefore probable that these two formed the next addition. Book ix is of a peculiar type, as consisting entirely of Soma hymns, though these were evidently composed by authors of the same families as the hymns of Books ii–vii, as appears from their having the same characteristic refrains. It evidently did not come into being as a collection till after the first eight books had already been combined into a whole. For it was clearly formed into a homogeneous group of hymns addressed to the same deity by extracting all the Soma hymns from the eight books (which retain altogether only three) and then placing this uniform combination at the end of Book viii. Though the Soma hymns in a collected form are thus comparatively late, there is good reason to believe that the composition of the individual Soma hymns as a whole belongs to an early part of the Vedic period, because it deals with a ritual going back to Indo-Iranian times. The hymns of the tenth book clearly date from a later period than those of the first nine, because their composers were evidently familiar with the latter. That it is a collection of supplementary hymns is indicated by their being made up to the number (191) of those in the first book. It bears the general stamp of lateness, of which there is internal evidence of various kinds. The subject-matter, the mythology, and the language all show signs of a later age.

The passages taken from the *Ṛigveda* that appear in the other Vedas furnish evidence akin to various readings. They indicate that the text of the *Ṛigveda* is more original than the text of the others and that it has been handed down, with a remarkably high standard of integrity, from a time hardly later than 1000 B.C. There is good reason to believe that in the period lapsing between the composition of the hymns of the *Ṛigveda* and the constitution, by grammatical editors, of the extant phonetic text called *Saṃhitā*, a very high level of verbal authenticity was maintained, though some unmistakable corruptions in detail can be detected. The most minute irregularities in the way of accent or alternate forms, which might have been removed with the utmost ease, have been retained unmodified. Hence it may be said that in the Saṃhitā text the actual words used by the ancient seers remain the same: thus *sumna* would not be substituted for *dyumna*; the changes would only apply to the phonetic forms required by the rules prevailing in the later phase of the Sanskrit language at the time when the sacred text was edited. Thus the old form of the words *tuam hi agne* would appear as *tvaṃ hy agne*, 'for thou, O Agni'. But such modernization is only partial and not consistently applied. These modern phonetic changes are often in conflict with the metre; if read in accordance with the metre the actual words in the form used by the ancient seers would be restored except when there are corruptions due to mistakes of tradition in the earlier period, or to errors arising from grammatical theories in the later.

The statements of the Brāhmaṇas justify the conclusion that the Saṃhitā text was not constituted till after those treatises were completed, but the somewhat later manuals called Āraṇyakas and Upanishads contain evidence that the Saṃhitā text of the *Ṛigveda* came into being before the post-Vedic ancillary literature concerned with Vedic grammar, phonetics, and other subjects arose, that is, about 600 B.C.

Soon after the constitution of the Saṃhitā text various means were devised to preserve that text intact. These devices have secured a faithfulness of tradition unparalleled in any other ancient literature. The first measure of this kind was the formation of a new text in which the Saṃhitā is analysed in such a way as to restore every single word to its independent phonetically unmodified form, and to separate compounds into their elements. Thus *tvaṃ hy agne* here appears as *tvam* | *hi* | *agne* |; and the compound *uṣarbudh* as *uṣaḥ·bhut*. This text, which is of a grammatically analytical character, is called the *Pada-pāṭha* or 'word-text'. Though it seems to have been composed soon after the Saṃhitā text, it yet contains some analyses that are certainly erroneous. Another measure for guarding the text of the *Ṛigveda* with still greater safety was the *Krama-pāṭha* or 'step-text': here every word of the *Padapāṭha* occurs twice, being pronounced both after the preceding and before the following one. Thus *a b c d*, as representing the first four words, would be read as *ab*, *bc*, *cd*. There are some still more complex texts of this type, the sole purpose of which was to preserve the sacred book from loss or change. The phonetic treatises called *Prātiśākhyas* were also of the nature of safeguards, as they set forth, with examples, the euphonic modifications necessary for turning the Pada into the Saṃhitā text.

Lastly, a class of supplementary works called Anukramaṇīs, or, 'Indexes', was compiled for the purpose of safeguarding the *Ṛigveda*, by stating the number of the hymns, verses, words, and even syllables contained in the sacred text.

The four Vedas and three works of the Brāhmaṇa period have been preserved in an accented form. Owing to the necessity of reciting the sacred texts with absolute correctness, the marking of the accent was of great importance. The Vedic accent was a musical one, dependent on the pitch of the voice, like the ancient Greek accent; and it retained this character till long after the time of the grammarian Pāṇini. But as the Greek, so the Vedic accent was, some time after the beginning of our era, transformed into a stress accent. While, however, in Greek the new stress accent remained on the same syllable as bore the old musical accent, the modern Sanskrit accent has no connexion with the ancient Vedic one, but depends on the quantity of the last two or three syllables, as in Latin. Thus the last syllable but one, if long, is stressed, e. g. *Kālidā́sa*; or the third from the end, if long, and followed by a short syllable, e. g. *brā́hmaṇa* or *himā́laya* ('abode of snow'). This change was brought about by the influence of Prākrit, or vernacular language, in which the stress can be traced to a time long antecedent to our era.

The most important Vedic accent is the *ud-ātta* ('raised') equivalent to the Greek acute. The evidence of comparative philology proves that in the Vedic language the same syllable of a particular word bears it as that syllable did in proto-Aryan. For it is in the same place as in cognate Greek words, except where a new restrictive law of accentuation interferes, as in *heptá*, which is identical with the Vedic *saptá*, 'seven'; but *pherómenos*, Skt. *bháramāṇaḥ*.

The hymns of the *Ṛigveda* are composed in stanzas, generally of four lines, each hymn on the average containing about ten. The number of metres is fifteen, but three are by far the commonest, as four-fifths of the total number of stanzas are composed in them. The metrical unit is not, as in Greek, the foot (of two or three syllables), but the line, which by a curious coincidence is also called 'foot' (*pāda*).[1] The rhythm of the Vedic line is more elastic than that of Classical Sanskrit, for in the former the rhythm of only the last four or five syllables, while in the latter the whole line is metrically regulated, except in one metre. The main metrical principle in the Veda is the number of syllables in the line. In Indo-Iranian prosody this must have been the sole principle; for the *Avesta*, which forms stanzas containing lines of eight or eleven syllables, ignores quantity altogether. In Sanskrit, on the other hand, the quantity of each syllable was fixed in every metre except the loose octosyllabic iambic line of the epic stanza called *śloka*. Thus the metrical regulation of the line beginning with its last syllables first appeared in the Vedic period, and extended in Classical Sanskrit to every syllable. The rhythmical end of the Vedic line is called *vṛtta*, 'turn', which corresponds etymologically to the Latin *versus*.

The metre is a valuable aid in restoring the original form of the line, because the phonetic combination of later times applied between the finals and initials of contiguous words in the Saṃhitā text reduces the number of syllables in the metrical line.

The commonest metre but one in the *Ṛigveda*, though it entirely disappeared in later Sanskrit, is the *gāyatrī*, which consists of three octosyllabic lines ending in two iambics, and forms one-fourth of all the stanzas in the *Ṛigveda*, e.g.:

sá naḥ pitéva sūnáve,
Ágne, sūpāyanó bhava;
sácasvā naḥ suastáye.

To us, as father to his son,
O Agni, be accessible:
Do thou abide with us for weal.

[1] Metaphorically 'quarter', stanzas having, on the analogy of quadrupeds, four feet or lines.

The *triṣṭubh* stanza is the commonest, two-fifths of the *Ṛigveda* being composed in this metre. It consists of four lines of eleven syllables ending trochaically (– ᴗ – ᴗ). The following is an example:

Víṣṇor nú kaṃ vīrlāṇi prá vocaṃ
yáḥ pā́rthivāni vimamé rájāṃsi
yó áskabhāyad úttaraṃ sadhástham,
vicakramāṇás trayadhórugāyáḥ.

I'll now proclaim the heroic powers of Vishṇu,
Of him who measured out the earthly spaces,
Who has made firm the upper gathering station;
Who triply has stepped out, the widely striding.

The *jagatī* stanza consists of four lines in which the final rhythm of the *triṣṭubh* is increased by one syllable. This produces an iambic cadence:

Ví vṛkṣā́n hanti utá hanti rakṣáso:
víśvaṃ bibhāya bhúvanaṃ mahā́vadhāt.
utā́nāgā īṣate vṛ́ṣṇiāvato,
yát Parjányaḥ standáyan hánti duṣkṛ́taḥ.

The trees he shatters and he strikes the demons down;
The whole world quakes in terror of his mighty strokes.
The very sinless man before the strong one flees,
When thundering Parjanya smites the miscreants.

When European scholars first became acquainted with the *Ṛigveda*, they knew only the language and literature of Classical Sanskrit. They were thus confronted with the difficulty of interpreting poetry which dated from the remotest period of Indian civilization, which was composed in an ancient and isolated dialect, and which represented a world very different from the world known to them. Fortunately there existed a voluminous Sanskrit commentary to the *Ṛigveda* which explains every word of its hymns and which was written in the fourteenth century by a learned Vedic scholar named Sāyaṇa. As the latter continually refers to ancient authorities, all that was considered necessary about 1850 was to translate the *Ṛigveda* according to his interpretations. But Roth, the founder of Vedic philology, pointed out that Sāyaṇa often gives several inconsistent explanations of a word in his comment on a single passage, as well as of the same word occurring in different passages. Even the interpretations of the numerous predecessors whom Yāska, the earliest Vedic commentator (*c.* 500 B.C.), mentions are often conflicting. One of them even asserted that the science of Vedic exposition was useless, the Vedic hymns being obscure, unmeaning, or mutually contradictory. Roth, in fact, declared that there was no continuity of interpretation going back to the time of the poets themselves, because interpretation could only arise when the meaning of the hymns had become uncertain. The commentators, he said, only preserved attempts at solving difficulties, and indeed betrayed a tendency to misinterpret both the language and ideas of a bygone age by the scholastic notions prevailing in their own. Roth consequently rejected the commentators as our chief guides in the interpretation of the Veda, holding that in its more obscure passages it must be self-interpreting. He accordingly proceeded to subject the *Ṛigveda* to an historical treatment within the range of Sanskrit, by carefully comparing all passages parallel in form and matter, and by paying special regard to context, grammar, and etymology, as well as consulting, though perhaps insufficiently, traditional interpretations. He also availed himself of the help supplied not only by the *Avesta*, which has such close affinities with the *Ṛigveda* in language and matter, but also by comparative philology, aids unknown to the traditional Indian scholar. The results of his labours are laid down in the great St. Petersburg Sanskrit Dictionary. Vedic scholars now all follow Roth's methods in the scientific investigation of the *Ṛigveda*. But they exploit more fully the aid supplied by native traditional scholarship. By close adherence to the critical method and by admitting all available evidence, many of the obscurities and difficulties still confronting the interpreter will, there is good reason to hope, ultimately vanish. In the generation that has passed since Roth's labours came to an end, many works and investigations have been published, such as books on anthropology and comparative religion, articles on grammar, metre, textual criticism, ritual, which when worked up as a whole, will contribute to decide numerous points of detail that are at present still obscure. A work like Prof. Bloomfield's *Rig-veda Repetitions*, which enumerates something like 5,000 lines that recur in the *Ṛigveda*, will without doubt greatly advance the precision of translation, because hitherto the rendering of repeated passages has varied greatly owing to the translator overlooking the fact that he has been dealing with a repetition. There are other points in which this book will supply aid in the work of interpretation. Considering the accumulation of exegetical material during the last thirty years, the time seems to have arrived for summing up these results in a new translation of the *Ṛigveda*. Such a one has, in fact, already begun to be published in German, and there is some prospect of a critical rendering appearing in English at no very distant date.

It may be said that the religion embodied in the *Ṛigveda* is a more important subject of study for the investigator of the history of religion than the religion of any other ancient sacred book; for here we see the development of mythology and religion from the most primitive to an advanced stage, and gods coming into being before our very eyes: a transition being evolved from the animistic to the polytheistic stage, from that in which natural phenomena are thought to be possessed of a soul like living beings to one in which they are personified, deified, and anthropomorphized as a polytheistic group, which is finally unified in a pantheistic sense. We see deification here in all its phases, from the beginning to the end of the scale. Thus the sky has only just begun to be touched by personification. In others it is more advanced, as in the case of Sūrya, the Sun, or Agni, Fire, who are much more anthropomorphic: their rays or flames, for instance, are called hands or tongues, though the poet can hardly imagine them apart from the actual phenomena of the solar orb or the actual element whose names they bear.

Others, like Indra, as an inheritance from a pre-Vedic period, are completely anthropomorphized, and can only conjecturally be identified with the phenomena that formed their starting-point. In later hymns we find some quite abstract figures showing no traces of connexion with concrete phenomena, such as Prajāpati, 'Lord of Creatures', or personifications of pure abstractions, such as Śraddhā, 'Faith'. Finally, there appears in the last book of the *Ṛigveda* a tendency to arrive at the conception of a deity embracing all the gods as well as nature, that is, a single world-soul, though this is a conception not to be found fully developed till the period of the Upanishads.

The religion of the *Ṛigveda*, then, is a polytheistic one, concerned with the worship of gods, the great majority of whom are personifications of phenomena or powers of nature. The hymns are mainly invocations of these gods, meant to accompany the oblation of Soma juice and the offering of melted butter in the sacrificial fire. Many of the hymns no doubt originally arose independently of the sacrificial ritual and some of them came only secondarily to be applied to it. The number of the gods is stated in the *Ṛigveda* to be thirty-three, though there are a few groups that obviously cannot be included in this total. Only about twenty are, however, frequently invoked. The best known of them are the following: Dyaus and Varuṇa, gods of the sky; Sūrya, Mitra, Savitar, Pūshan, Vishṇu, solar divinities; the Aśvins (the two horsemen) and Ushas (Dawn), deities of the morning; Indra, Apāṃ napāt, Rudra, Maruts (Storm-gods), Vāyu (Wind), Parjanya (Rain), Āpas (Waters), gods of the air; Pṛithivī (Earth), Agni (Fire), Soma (draught of immortality), terrestrial deities; and Sindhu (Indus), Vipāś (Beäs), Śutudrī (Sutlej), Sarasvatī (Sarsūti), Rivers of the Panjāb. When fully personified the gods are conceived as human in form; but their bodily parts are still often merely figurative terms: thus the arms of the Sun are nothing more than his rays; and the tongue and limbs of Agni are simply his flames. Some of the gods, especially Indra and the Maruts, appear as warriors; others are described as priests, as Agni and Bṛihaspati. All of them drive in celestial cars, drawn as a rule by two horses. Their food is the same as the favourite food of men: milk, butter, grain, and the flesh of sheep, goats, and cattle. This food is offered to them in the sacrifice, which is conveyed to them in heaven by the god of Fire, or which they come down in their cars to enjoy on the sacrificial ground. Their drink is the exhilarating Soma juice, cheered by draughts of which they live a life of bliss in heaven.

The most prominent characteristic of the gods is power: they regulate the order of nature and vanquish the agencies of evil; they hold sway over all creatures; their laws cannot be thwarted; and they alone can fulfil desires. Another trait is their benevolence, for they bestow good gifts on men.

They are also true and not deceitful, protecting the righteous and punishing the guilty. As the gods are nearly always conceived in connexion with the natural phenomena which they represent, their anthropomorphism is hardly ever complete, and each deity has few distinctive attributes, while many general divine qualities, such as power, brilliance, beneficence, and wisdom, are common to them all. They are therefore indefinite in outline, and may easily be identified one with another. Thus a poet addressing the Fire-god exclaims: 'Thou at thy birth, O Agni, art Varuṇa; when kindled thou becomest Mitra; in thee, O son of might, all gods are centred; thou art Indra to the worshipper.' In late hymns the idea is even expressed that various gods are only different forms of a single divinity. Thus we find the verse: 'The one being priests speak of in many ways; they call it Agni, Yama, Mātariśvan' (i. 64); and another: 'Priests and poets make into many the bird (i.e. the sun) which is but one' (x. 114). This idea, however, never ended in monotheism. In other late hymns the deities Aditi and Prajāpati are identified not only with all the gods, but with nature as well. This germ of pantheism developed in the later Vedic literature of the Upanishads till it reached its final form in the Vedānta philosophy, which has remained the most popular system of the Hindus down to the present day.

The gods are regarded as immortal, but not as originally having been so. Their physical aspect is human, for face, arms, hands, fingers, and other anthropomorphic parts are attributed to them. But their shapes are shadowy. Thus of Vāyu, Wind, it is said: 'His sound is heard, but his form is never seen'. Hence it is easy to understand that the *Ṛigveda* contains no mention of images of the gods, still less of temples, which imply images. No reference to idols is to be found in the literature till two or three centuries before our era, in the Sūtra period, and divine figures begin to appear in Buddhist sculptures from the second century B.C. onwards.

Goddesses play an insignificant role in the *Ṛigveda*: the only one to whom more than one or two hymns are addressed is Ushas, Dawn. She is, in fact, the only important goddess, for she is celebrated in about twenty hymns, which are the most beautiful in the *Ṛigveda*. Though Ushas, unlike most other divinities, receives no share of the Soma offering, the thoughts of the Vedic poets love to dwell on the beauties of the dawn, sometimes with a touch of sadness suggested by the eternally recurring phenomena of early morning in contrast with the fleeting nature of human life. The following translation, in which the *triṣṭubh* metre of the original is imitated, may perhaps reflect some of the beautiful imagery occurring in these ancient hymns.

This light has come, of all the lights the fairest;
This brilliant brightness has been born, far-shining;
Urged onward for god Savitar's uprising,
Night now has yielded up her place to morning.

The sisters' pathway is the same, unending;
Taught by the gods, alternately they tread it.
Fair-shaped, of form diverse, yet single-minded,
Morning and night clash not, nor do they tarry.

Now Heaven's Daughter has appeared before us,
A maiden shining in resplendent garments.
Thou sovran lady of all earthly treasure,
Auspicious Dawn, shine here to-day upon us.

In the sky's framework she has gleamed with brightness:
The goddess has cast off the robe of darkness.
Rousing the world from sleep, with ruddy horses,
Dawn in her well-yoked chariot is arriving.

Bringing upon it many bounteous blessings,
Brightly she shines and spreads her brilliant lustre.
Last of innumerable morns departed,
First of bright morns to come has Dawn arisen.

Again and again newly born though ancient,
Decking her beauty with the self-same colours,
The goddess wastes away the life of mortals,
Like wealth diminished by the skilful player.

Gone are the mortals who in former ages
Beheld the flushing of the earlier morning.
We living men now look upon her shining;
Those will be born who shall hereafter see her.

The twin gods of morning, called Aśvins or Horsemen, are the most frequently invoked among the deities of celestial light. They are the sons of Heaven, eternally young and handsome, at the yoking of whose car Ushas is born.

The importance of Indra, the favourite and national god of the Vedic Indian, is indicated by the fact that more than one-fourth of the *Ṛigveda* sings the praises of his greatness. Primarily a thunder-god, he constantly appears as vanquishing the demon of drought and darkness called Vṛitra, 'the Obstructor', setting free the waters or winning the light. This is the essence of the mythology of which he is the centre. The following stanzas illustrate his fight with the dragon.

I will proclaim the manly deeds of Indra,
The first that he performed, the lightning-wielder.
He smote the dragon, then discharged the waters,
And cleft the caverns of the lofty mountains.

Him lightning then availèd not, nor thunder,
Nor mist, nor hailstorm that he spread around him.
When Indra and the dragon strove in battle,
The Bounteous god gained victory for ever.

Plunged in the midst of never-ceasing torrents,
That stand not still, but ever hasten onward,
The waters bore off Vṛitra's hidden body:
Indra's fierce foe sank down to lasting darkness.

Indra thus became the god of battle who aided the invading Aryans in their conflicts with the aborigines. His combats are often called *gav-iṣṭi* (literally 'desire of cows'), equivalent in meaning to 'cattle-raid'.

The following is a stanza celebrating Indra's greatness:

Both Heaven and Earth themselves bow down before him;
Before his might the very mountains tremble.
Who, known as Soma-drinker, armed with lightning,
Is wielder of the bolt: he, men, is Indra.

Though historically the most important of the solar deities, because in his later development he became one of the two chief gods of modern Hinduism, Vishṇu occupies a very subordinate position in the *Ṛigveda*. He is invoked in few hymns, and little is said about him except that he takes three strides. This action is his characteristic trait, which doubtless represents the course of the sun through the three divisions of the universe. Later, in the Brāhmaṇas, can be traced the development of the trait of benevolence, which culminates in the doctrine of his Avatars ('descents to earth') or incarnations which he assumed for the good of humanity.

The god Rudra occupies a curiously parallel position to Vishṇu in the history of Indian religion. For while he is invoked as seldom as Vishṇu in the *Ṛigveda*, he later becomes the other chief god in Hinduism. But while the goodwill of Vishṇu is conspicuous, Rudra is the only god whose malevolence is already characteristic, and later becomes even more prominent. The hymns addressed to him mainly express fear of his terrible shafts and deprecation of his anger. In the post-Vedic period he appears under the regular name of Śiva, a euphemistic epithet meaning 'auspicious', and already applied to him in the *Ṛigveda*. Rudra is, of course, not purely malevolent like a demon. For he is besought not only to preserve from calamity, but to bestow welfare and healing on man and beast. This is, no doubt, only a euphemistic way of alluding to the injurious side of his activities.

His sons are the Maruts, or Storm-gods, a group of youthful warriors, variously referred to as twenty-one or sixty in number, the track of whose car is brilliant with lightnings:

They gleam with armlets as the heavens are decked with stars;
Like cloud-born lightnings shine the torrents of their rain.

Their onset is terrible when they cause the hills to quake:

The Maruts spread the mist abroad
And make the mountains rock and reel,
When with the winds they speed along;

and shatter the forests:

Before you, fierce ones, even woods bow down in fear,
The Earth herself, the very mountains tremble.

Parjanya, whose name in several passages simply means 'rain-cloud', and whose rudimentary personification is closely connected with the phenomena of the rain-storm, is characteristically a shedder of rain:

Like charioteer, his horses lashing with a whip,
The god makes manifest his messengers of rain.
From far away the roaring of the lion sounds,
What time Parjanya veils the firmament with rain.

The winds blow forth; to earth the quivering lightnings fall.
The plants shoot up; with moisture streams the realm of light.
For all the world abundant nourishment is born,
When by Parjanya Earth is fertilized with seed.

The Waters (Āpas), who are regarded as aerial, not terrestrial divinities, are goddesses that come to the sacrifice and bestow boons. They are described as young wives, especially of Agni, the 'son of (the celestial) waters'. They cleanse not only from deflement,but even from moral guilt, bestowing remedies, long life, and immortality.

Agni is by far the most important of the terrestrial deities. Next to Indra, he is the most frequently invoked of the Vedic gods, for about one-fifth of the hymns of the *Ṛigveda* are addressed to him. Since the priestly singers were in such close touch with him in his elemental form as the centre of the Vedic ritual, his anthropomorphism is still somewhat undeveloped. His name, too, Agni (Lat. *igni-s*), being the ordinary designation of the element, would naturally retard that process. His bodily parts are clearly connected with the various aspects of fire; thus, he is 'flame-haired'; and his teeth, jaws, and tongues evidently allude to the action of burning. He rides on a brilliant car, for he is the charioteer of sacrifice. The poets constantly dwell on his ritual aspects: thus, they often allude to his daily production from the two fire-sticks by means of friction. They are his parents who generate him as a new-born infant hard to catch. From the dry wood the god is born living; the child as soon as born devours his parents.

Reference is often made to Agni's threefold character or origin on earth (terrestrial fire), in the atmosphere (lightning), and in heaven (the sun). This Vedic triad may be the historical progenitor of the later Hindu Trinity of Brahmā, Vishṇu, and Śiva. It may also have suggested the division of a single sacrificial fire into the three which form an essential feature of the cult of the Brāhmaṇas.

As perpetually concerned with the sacrifice, Agni is mythologically the great priest, just as Indra is the great warrior.

A feature more characteristic of Agni than of any other Vedic deity is that of warding off evil spirits and hostile magic. As the Soma sacrifice forms, beside the fire-cult, a main feature in the ritual of the *Ṛigveda*, the personified Soma plant is naturally one of its leading deities. Judged by the number of hymns addressed to him (120), he comes next in importance to Agni. Since the Soma plant and its juice are pressed and offered by the priests as they invoke the god, the personification of Soma is undeveloped, as in the case of Agni. He is called the king of plants, and is often referred to as growing on the mountains. But heaven is regarded as his original and true home; and the myth of his having been brought down from thence by an eagle is frequently mentioned.

The hymns to Soma consist mostly of incantations chanted while the stalks of the plant are being pounded with stones, and the juice, as it passes through woollen strainers, flows into wooden vats, in which it is offered to the gods on the sacred grass. These processes are described with endless variety in obscure and mystical imagery. In a few of the latest hymns of the *Ṛigveda* Soma begins to be mystically identified with the moon. In several passages of the *Atharvaveda* Soma actually means the moon. This identification is a commonplace of the Brāhmaṇas, which explain the waning of the moon as the result of the ambrosia of which it consists being consumed by the gods and fathers. In post-Vedic literature Soma is a regular name of the moon. The starting-point of this remarkable development of meaning is doubtless to be found in the exaggerated terms with which the poets of the *Ṛigveda* describe the celestial nature and the brilliance of Soma.

Because of the mental exaltation produced by the beverage, Soma is regarded as a drink bestowing immortal life and is called the draught of immortality (*amṛta*). The god is thus described as an awakener of eager thought, as a generator of hymns, a leader of poets.

The following stanzas illustrate the stimulating aspect of this ritual divinity:

I have partaken wisely of the sweet food,
That stirs good thoughts, best banisher of trouble,
The food round which all deities and mortals,
Calling it honey-mead, collect together.

We have drunk Soma and become immortal;
We have attained the light the gods discovered.
What can hostility now do against us?
And what, immortal god, the spite of mortals?

Of this thy juice, pressed out with mind devoted,
We would partake as of paternal riches.
Prolong the years of life for us, king Soma,
As Sūrya lengthens out the days of spring-time.

Soma was not a creation of Vedic ritual. For both the plant and its deification were important features of the cult and mythology of the Indo-Iranian period, as there are many points of agreement in these respects between the *Ṛigveda* and the *Avesta*.

The belief in an intoxicating divine beverage, the home of which was in heaven, goes back, in fact, to the Indo-European period, when it must have been regarded as a kind of honey-mead (Sanskrit *mádhu*, honey ; Greek *μέθυ*, wine ; Anglo-Saxon *medu*, mead).

Towards the end of the Rigvedic period the thought of the singers shows a tendency to advance from the concrete to the abstract. This movement resulted in the creation of abstract deities, of which some seven or eight, being personifications of abstract nouns, are found in the last book of the *Ṛigveda.* Such are Śraddhā, 'Faith', and Manyu, 'Wrath'. These become commoner in the later Vedas. Thus, in the *Atharvaveda* appears the personification Kāma, 'Desire', who in post-Vedic mythology becomes the Hindu Cupid, the flower-arrowed god of love.

Another and more numerous class seems to have originated in epithets which were applicable to older deities, but which acquired an independent value as the want of a god exercising the particular activity in question made itself felt. Such is Prajāpati, 'Lord of Creatures', originally an epithet of gods like Savitar and Soma, who appears, in a later verse of the last book of the *Ṛigveda*, as a distinct deity in the character of a creator. He is, in the *Atharvaveda* and the *Yajurveda* often, and in the Brāhmaṇas regularly, recognized as the chief god. In the Sūtras he is identified with Brahmā, who becomes his successor in the post-Vedic age.

A peculiarity of the Vedic religion is the invocation of pairs of deities whose names are associated in the form of dual compounds. There are about twenty-four of these pairs in the *Ṛigveda*, as *Mitrā-Varuṇā*, that is, 'Mitra and Varuṇa'. The prototype of this class was probably *Dyāvā-Pṛithivī*, or 'Heaven and Earth', the universal parents.

Some deities appear in groups. The most numerous of these are the Maruts, who have already been mentioned. Another group consists of the Ādityas, the sons of Aditi, seven or eight in number, whose chief is Varuṇa. There are besides some other colourless groups, such as the Vasus.

In addition to the higher gods, a number of lesser divinities appear in the *Ṛigveda*. The most prominent of these are the Ṛibhus, a deft-handed trio, who by their marvellous feats acquired immortality.

Not only do we find the great phenomena of nature invoked as divine powers in the *Ṛigveda*, but also various features of the earth's surface, as well as artificial objects. Besides Rivers and Waters, Mountains are often addressed as divinities, but only along with other natural objects or in association with gods. Plants are invoked as divine, chiefly with reference to their healing powers. Ritual implements, too, are deified, the most prominent among them being the sacrificial post and the pressing stones. Weapons also are sometimes addressed as divine.

Beside the celestial gods, demons often play a part in the *Ṛigveda*. Among these, two classes must be distinguished. The higher and more powerful kind fight against the gods in aerial combat. The typical conflict is that between Indra and the demon of drought Vṛitra, the 'encompasser' of the waters, who is often described as a serpent (*ahi*). The lower class comprises terrestrial goblins, the enemies of men. They are usually called *rakṣas* and appear as obstructors of the sacrifice.

About thirty hymns of the *Ṛigveda* are not concerned with the worship of gods or deified objects. Some twelve of these, nearly all occurring in the last book, are magical in character, like those of the *Atharvaveda*, such as spells directed against disease. One of them is addressed to frogs as bringers of rain. Here are two of its stanzas:

Resting in silence for a year,
Like Brahmins practising a vow,
The Frogs have lifted up their voice,
Excited by Parjanya's call.

As Brahmins at the mighty Soma offering
Sit round the large and brimming vessel talking:
So throng ye all around the pool to hallow
This annual day that, Frogs, begins the rain-time.

Hardly a score of the hymns are concerned with secular matters. They are of much interest as illustrating, apart from the religious hymns, the earliest thought and social life of India. One of the most important is a long wedding hymn. The following is one of its stanzas:

Free from the evil eye, thy husband hurting not,
Kind to our beasts, be friendly, full of energy;
Bear heroes, love the gods, and live in happiness;
Bring welfare to our bipeds and our quadrupeds.

One of the five funeral hymns is quite secular in tone, though a few of its stanzas mention the names of two or three of the gods. It supplies a good deal of information about the funeral customs of early Vedic India. Here are two of its stanzas:

Depart, O Death, along the furthest pathway,
Which is thine own, not that by mortals trodden.
I speak to thee that hast both sight and hearing:
Do not our offspring injure nor our heroes.

From the dead hand I take the bow he wielded,
To win for us dominion, might and glory.
Thou there, we here, rich in heroic offspring,
Will vanquish all assaults of every foeman.

Four hymns are didactic in character. One of them is a striking poem, in which a gambler laments the ruin brought on him by the irresistible lure of the dice. The following are three of its stanzas:

Downward they roll, then swiftly springing upward,
They overcome the man with hands, though handless;

Cast on the board like magic bits of charcoal,
Though cold themselves, they burn the heart to ashes.

It pains the gambler when he sees a woman,
Another's wife, and their well-ordered household.
He yokes those brown steeds early in the morning,
And when the fire is low sinks down a beggar.

'Play not with dice, but cultivate thy cornfield,
Enjoy thy riches, deeming them sufficient;
There are thy cows, there is thy wife, O Gambler':
This counsel Savitar the noble gives me.

The other three didactic hymns are forerunners of the sententious poetry for which post-Vedic literature is noted. The subject-matter of two other hymns is expressed in the form of riddles. One of these, for instance, speaks of the wheel of order with twelve spokes revolving round the heavens and containing within it, in couples, 720 sons. The allusion is evidently to the solar year with its twelve months comprising 360 days and 360 nights.

Besides what we learn from the comparatively few secular poems regarding the life and thought of those ancient times, the vast bulk of the hymns give us, as we have seen, a detailed account of the religious beliefs and practices of the earliest Indo-Aryans. But there are also many data incidentally scattered throughout these hymns, from which other information can be collected about their country and their manner of life. Thus, we can infer with certainty what was the geographical area inhabited by the Indo-Aryans when the hymns of the *Ṛigveda* were composed. Of the twenty-five streams mentioned, only two or three did not belong to the Indus river-system. Their western boundary was evidently the Indus, if some of its western tributaries, such as the Kubhā (Kābul) with its affluent the Suvāstu

(Swāt) and the Gomatī (Gomal) are included. On the east they extended to the Yamunā (Jumna), the most westerly branch of the Gangetic system, though the Gaṅgā (Ganges) itself was hardly known. On the north they were bounded by the mountains of the Himālaya, but on the south they

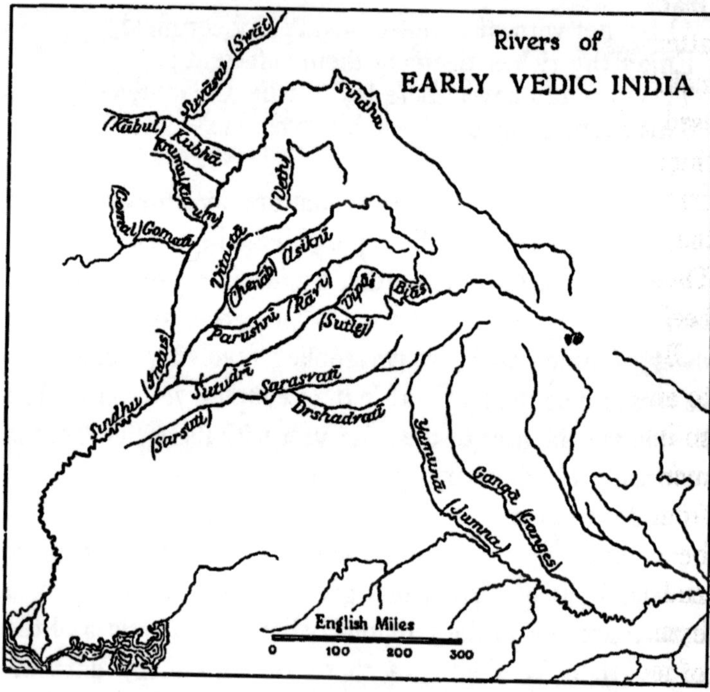

had not yet spread to the Vindhya hills and the river Narmadā (Narbadā), which separate Hindustān from the southern triangle of the Deccan.

The evidence of rivers and mountains is corroborated by that of the flora and fauna mentioned. Thus the lotus, the names of which permeate the later Sanskrit poetry, is not used by the Vedic seers in their similes. The banyan tree and rice, so characteristic of eastern India, are unknown to the poets of the *Ṛigveda.* The lion is familiar, but the tiger is not mentioned in the hymns. The elephant, as its name, 'the animal with the hand' (*mṛga hastin*), indicates, was still a novelty.

The Indo-Aryans were still moving eastwards, as conquering invaders, calling the aborigines unbelievers and 'black-skins'. As the cities and the great wealth of the latter are spoken of, they cannot have been nomads. The main occupation of the Aryans was warfare, in which they used chariots, bows and arrows, spears and axes. Their chief source of livelihood was cattle-breeding, but they practised agriculture also. For the eastern Panjāb, where they chiefly dwelt, abounds in pastoral and agrarian land. Their food was mainly vegetarian. They ate meat, chiefly beef, but only when animals were sacrificed.

Before leaving the *Ṛigveda* we may pause for a moment to answer the question that naturally arises: Is this work, so important in other respects, characterized by any literary merit worth mentioning? The answer is, that regarded from this aspect alone, its value is considerable. As is to be expected from its great antiquity, its diction is simpler and more natural than that of post-Vedic Sanskrit. Its hymns as a whole are composed with a surprising degree of metrical skill and command of language. As they were produced by a sacerdotal class, and were in general intended to accompany a ritual no longer primitive, their poetry is often impaired by conceits and mysticism, particularly where the two specifically ritual deities Agni and Soma are concerned. Yet the hymns contain much genuine poetry often expressed in beautiful and even noble imagery, as may perhaps be gathered from the few specimens translated above.

The *Sāma-* and the *Yajur-veda* may be passed over,

because the former, with the exception of a few verses, is entirely, and the latter as to more than one-fourth of its contents, derived from the *Ṛigveda*, and because both are concerned with the great sacrificial ceremonial. But the *Atharvaveda* calls for some attention. Its most salient feature is sorcery, which is directed mainly against hostile agencies, though a good many of its spells are also of an auspicious character, intended to secure health, long life, prosperity, and luck at gambling.

Contrasted with the *Ṛigveda*, the *Atharvaveda* consists for the most part of spells embodying popular magical notions that are concerned with demoniac powers and are of great antiquity. It also contains a large amount of theosophic and pantheistic matter representing a later stage of thought than the *Ṛigveda* does. With its 730 hymns and about 6,000 stanzas, its bulk amounts to not much more than one-half that of the *Ṛigveda*. A considerable part of the *Atharvaveda*, about one-sixth, is, as is also the case with the *Yajurveda*, written in prose.

Linguistically the *Atharvaveda* is decidedly later than the *Ṛigveda*, but earlier than the Brāhmaṇas. It seems probable that its hymns, though some of them must be very old in matter, were not edited till after the Brāhmaṇas of the *Ṛigveda* were composed.

The hostile charms of the *Atharvaveda* are largely directed against different diseases, or the demons supposed to cause them. These charms are accompanied by the employment of suitable herbs.

Hence the *Atharvaveda* is the oldest source of Indian medicine. The following is a charm against cough:

> Just as the arrow sharpened well
> Swift to a distance flies away,
> So even thou, O cough, fly forth
> Along the broad expanse of earth.

Another is meant to cure leprosy by the use of a dark-coloured plant:

> Born in the night wast thou, O herb,
> Dark-coloured, sable, black of hue:
> Rich-tinted, tinge this leprosy,
> And stain away its spots of grey!

A good many of these spells are imprecations against foes and sorcerers:

> Avoid and pass us by, O curse,
> Even as a burning fire a pond.
> Here strike him down that curses us,
> As Heaven's lightning smites the tree.

Of the auspicious charms, many aim at the prolongation of life:

> Rise up, O man, from here, and straightway casting
> Death's fetters from thy feet, depart not downward;
> From life upon this earth be not yet severed,
> Nor from the sight of Agni and the sunlight.

Here is a spell to secure luck at play:

> As at all times the lightning-stroke
> Smites irresistibly the tree:
> So gamesters with the dice would I
> Beat irresistibly to-day.

The following stanzas are meant to secure victory in battle:

> Arise and arm, ye spectral forms,
> Followed by meteoric flames;
> Ye serpents, spirits of the deep,
> Demons of night, pursue our foes!
>
> As birds start back affrighted at the falcon's cry,
> As, day and night, they tremble at the lion's roar:
> So thou, O drum, resound against our enemies,
> Scare them away in terror, and confound their aims.

This is a stanza from a hymn meant to command a woman's affection by the agency of Kāma, god of desire:

> With longing feathered, tipped with love,
> Its shaft is formed of fixed desire:
> With this his arrow levelled well
> Shall Kāma pierce thee to the heart.

There is one hymn which, though ending in two spells of the usual Atharvan type, describes in its preceding stanzas the omniscience of the god Varuṇa in an exalted strain, doubtless to emphasize the impossibility of any foe's escaping his vigilance:

> This earth is all King Varuṇa's dominion,
> And that broad sky whose boundaries are distant.
> The loins of Varuṇa are these two oceans;
> Yet in this drop of water he is hidden.
>
> He that would flee afar beyond the heavens,
> Could not escape King Varuṇa's attention:
> His spies come hither, from the sky descending,
> With all their thousand eyes the earth surveying.
>
> King Varuṇa discerns all things existent
> Between the earth and sky, and all beyond them.
> The winkings of men's eyes by him are counted.
> As gamesters dice, so he lays down his statutes.

History of Sanskrit Studies: Benfey, *Geschichte der Sprachwissenschaft*, Munich, 1869. Windisch, *Geschichte der Sanskrit-Philologie*, in Bühler's *Encyclopaedia of Indo-Aryan Research*, 1917–20. General History of Indian Literature: Macdonell, *History of Sanskrit Literature*, 1900 (especially pp. 438–41). Winternitz, *Geschichte der indischen Litteratur*, i, pp. 47–163. Pischel, *Indische Literatur*, 1925, pp. 170–223. Text: Aufrecht, *Die Hymnen des Ṛigveda* (in Roman characters), Bonn, 1877. Macdonell, *A Vedic Reader*, Oxford, 1917. Bloomfield, *A Vedic Concordance*, *Harvard Oriental Series*, vol. x; *Rig-veda Repetitions*, H.O.S., vols. xx and xxiv. Grammar: Macdonell, *A Vedic Grammar for Students*, Oxford, 1916; *Vedic Grammar*, in Bühler's *Encyclopaedia*, 1910. Dictionary: Grassmann, *Wörterbuch zum Ṛigveda*, Leipzig, 1873. Mythology: Macdonell, *Vedic Mythology*, in Bühler's *Encyclopaedia*, 1897. Hillebrandt, *Vedische Mythologie*, Breslau, 1902. Religion: Oldenberg, *Die Religion des Veda*, Berlin, 1894. Bergaigne, *La Religion Védique*, Paris, 1878–83. Philosophy: Deussen, *Die Philosophie des Veda*, Leipzig, 1894. Subject-matter: Macdonell and Keith, *Vedic Index*, London, 1912. Interpretation: Macdonell, in *Bhandarkar Commemorative Volume*, Poona, 1917. Oldenberg, *Ṛgveda-Noten*, Berlin, 1909–12. Translation: Grassmann, Leipzig, 1876–7. Ludwig, Prag, 1876–88. Griffith, Benares, 1896–7. Geldner, Books i–iv, Göttingen, 1923. *Sāmaveda*: Benfey, Leipzig, 1848. Griffith, Benares, 1893. *Yajurveda*: VS., Griffith, Benares, 1899. TS.: Keith, *Harvard Oriental Series*, xviii, xix. *Atharvaveda*: Whitney, in *Harvard Oriental Series*, vii, viii. Bloomfield, SBE., xlii. Subject-matter: Bloomfield, *The Atharva-veda*, in Bühler's *Encyclopaedia*, 1899.

III

THE LATER VEDIC PERIOD

Brāhmaṇas: ritual — Upanishads: theosophic — A new religion opposed to sacrificial ceremonial — The Absolute (brahma) — Cosmical illusion (māyā) — Fundamental doctrine of the Upanishads: tat tvam asi — Rise of the theory of transmigration (saṃsāra) — The doctrine of retribution (karma) — Probable date of the Brāhmaṇas — Rise of vernaculars — Introduction of writing — Earliest Indian alphabet — Its source — Its arrangement — Vedic texts handed down by memory — Late use of writing explained — Age of Indian manuscripts — Palm-leaves old Indian writing material — Use of paper after 1000 A.D. — Rise of libraries — Three linguistic periods of Indian literature — Selected bibliography.

THE poetical and creative period of the Vedas was followed by that of the Brāhmaṇas, several of which are attached to the Vedas, but in both form and matter constitute an entirely different type of literature. Written throughout in prose of a clumsy kind, they are notable as representing the earliest Indo-European prose-writing, which is specially valuable in tracing the history of syntax. They are theological treatises analogous to the Hebrew Talmud as compared with the Old Testament. Being expositions of the sacrificial ceremonial, they explain it in minute detail, illustrating its value with numerous myths and speculations on its origin. As the most ancient literature on ritual, they contain much interesting material both for the student of the history of religion and of the history of Indian civilization. In these works we find a definite development of the system of the four castes which form the basis of the almost innumerable castes and sub-castes into which the Hindu society of to-day is divided. In this system the priesthood, as the holders of the secret of the all-powerful sacrifice, gained the dominating position. These works also show the growth of a sacrificial ceremonial more elaborate and complex than any other the world has ever seen. They thus shed much light on the sacerdotalism of ancient India. One or more Brāhmaṇas are attached to each Veda. They vary in age, as is shown by their internal linguistic evidence. The most important of them all is that which is attached to the White *Yajurveda*: the *Śatapatha Brāhmaṇa*, or 'Brāhmaṇa of the Hundred Paths'. It is, next to the *Ṛigveda* and the *Atharvaveda*, the most valuable product of the Vedic age.

A later development of the Brāhmaṇas are the Āraṇyakas or 'Forest Treatises', which constitute their concluding portions and are partly theosophic in character. They form a transition to the Upanishads, which are usually their final part. These Upanishads, or esoteric treatises, mark the last stage in the development of the Brāhmaṇa literature, being entirely concerned with theosophical speculations on the nature of things. The subject-matter of all the old Upanishads is essentially the same, consisting of speculations on the nature of the Supreme soul (*Ātmā* or *Brahma*).

That the Upanishads represent the latest phase of Vedic literature is corroborated by the fact that their language very closely approximates to the Classical Sanskrit of the post-Vedic age, which may be said to have assumed its permanent form about 500 B.C. The two most important of the Upanishads are the *Chāndogya* of the *Sāmaveda* and the *Bṛhadāraṇyaka* of the White *Yajurveda*. About a dozen Upanishads stand out as the best, but there are many others of less value.

The Upanishads generally form a continuation of the Brāhmaṇas on their speculative as contrasted with their ritual side. But they really expound a new religion which is opposed to the sacrificial ceremonial and has virtually represented the philosophic aspect of Hinduism for 2,500 years. They do not aim at securing earthly and afterwards heavenly bliss in the abode of Yama by sacrificing correctly to the gods, but at obtaining deliverance from mundane existence by the absorption of the individual soul in the world-soul through correct knowledge. Here, therefore, ritual appears as useless, and saving knowledge as all-important. The Upanishad conception of the world-soul (*Ātmā*) is the final development of the personal creator Prajāpati, who has become the impersonal source of all being, Brahma. *Ātman* in the *Ṛigveda* means only 'breath'; in the Brāhmaṇas it came to mean 'soul' and even to be attributed to the Universe, being said to 'pervade this Universe'. *Brahma* (neuter) in the *Ṛigveda* meant nothing more than 'devotion', 'prayer'; even in the oldest Brāhmaṇas it already has the sense of 'universal holiness'; in the Upanishads, finally, it signifies the holy principle animating nature. Having a long subsequent development, this term is a very epitome of the evolution of religious thought in India. Ātmā and Brahma usually appear as synonyms in the Upanishads; but strictly speaking Brahma is the cosmical principle pervading the universe, while Ātmā is the psychical principle in man. The *Bṛhadāraṇyaka Upanishad* describes Brahma negatively in an exhaustive manner, as without physical or other qualities, as immortal thinker and knower, as the eternal in which space is woven, and which is interwoven in it. Here for the first time in the history of human thought the Absolute is grasped and definitely expressed.

The following is an account of the Ātman from a metrical Upanishad:

> Its form can never be to sight apparent,
> Not any one may with his eye behold it:
> By heart and mind and soul alone they grasp it,
> And those who know it thus, become immortal.
>
> Since not by speech and not by thought,
> Not by the eye can it be reached:
> How else may it be understood
> But only when one says 'it is'?

The notion that the material world is an illusion (*māyā*), familiar in the later Vedānta philosophical system, is first met with in the *Śvetāśvatara*, one of the later Upanishads, though it is inherent even in the oldest. This is virtually identical with the teaching of Kant, that the things of experience are only phenomena of the thing in itself.

The fundamental doctrine of the Upanishads is the identity of the individual *ātman* with the world *Ātman*. It is expressed in the *Chāndogya Upaniṣad* thus: 'This whole world consists of it: that is the real, that is the soul, that art thou, O Śvetaketu.' All the teachings of the Upanishads are summed up in that famous formula, 'That art thou' (*tat tvam asi*).

Many metaphors are used to make clear the nature of the pantheistic self. Here is one: 'As a lump of salt, thrown into the water, would dissolve and could not be taken out again, while the water, wherever tasted, would be salt, so is this great being endless, unlimited, simply compacted of cognition. Arising out of these elements, it disappears again in them. After death there is no consciousness.' This is further explained to mean that when the duality on which consciousness is based disappears, consciousness must necessarily cease.

Parallel with the doctrine of salvation depending on the knowledge that the individual soul is identical with the world soul was developed the theory of transmigration. In its earliest form it appears in the *Śatapatha Brāhmaṇa*, where the notion occurs that retribution is inflicted in the next world in the guise of repeated births and deaths. It is developed in the Upanishads, where the fullest account given of it is this. The forest ascetic possessed of true knowledge enters, after death, the 'path of the gods', which leads to absorption in Brahma. But the householder who has performed sacrifice and good works goes by the 'path of the fathers' to the moon, where he remains till the results of his actions are exhausted. Then he returns to earth, where he is first born as a plant and afterwards as a man of one of the three highest castes. This is a double retribution: first in the celestial, then by transmigration in the terrestrial world. The former is a survival of the old Vedic belief regarding the future life, but it continues throughout later Hinduism along with terrestrial transmigration.

The theory of transmigration must have been firmly established by the time when Buddhism arose (*c.* 500 B.C.), for Buddha accepted it without question. A curious thing, however, is that he also adopted the doctrine of *karma* or 'action', which regulates the new birth as dependent on a man's own previous deeds, although he denied the existence of soul altogether; he thus assumed that *karma* continued to operate from one birth to another, though there was no soul to pass between them.

There are indications of a chronological nature that the latest Brāhmaṇas were produced not long before the rise of Buddhism. The general evidence of the geographical data contained in the Brāhmaṇa literature points to its having grown up in the land of the Kuru-Pañchālas, the region around the upper courses of the Jumna and the Ganges. But the *Śatapatha Brāhmaṇa* indicates that the Brāhmanical system by the time this book was composed had spread to the east of Madhyadeśa, the Midland, to Kosala with its capital Ayodhyā (Oudh), and to Videha (Tirhut) with its capital Mithilā. There is some probability that the White *Yajurveda* was edited in this eastern region. Some allusions it contains indicate that the *Śatapatha Brāhmaṇa* came into being shortly before Buddhism and the germs of the Sanskrit Epics arose. Internal evidence also shows that it belongs to a late period of the Brāhmaṇa age. For its style is more lucid, its treatment of the sacrificial ritual is more methodical, and the idea of the unity of the universe is more developed than in any other Brāhmaṇa, while its Upanishad, the *Bṛhadāraṇyaka*, is the finest outcome of Vedic philosophy.

The Vedic period had now reached its final stage, the Upanishad literature of which supplies the unclarified theosophic doctrines that in the post-Vedic period developed into the pantheistic system called Vedānta, which has ever since remained the predominant philosophy of India. To the hymn collections of the four Vedas and their Brāhmaṇas the expression Veda is alone applicable. These two literary phases combined correspond to what the Old Testament was among the Jews. They were regarded as authoritative, as the ultimate appeal, by all Hindu sects and systems of philosophy. They were after the close of the Vedic period thought to be revealed, and were called by the name of *Śruti* or 'hearing' because the sacred texts were not written, but recited and heard. They were believed to have been emitted by the god Brahma and 'seen' (not composed) by the seers of old.

During the whole of the Vedic period there was, apart from the non-Aryan tongues that must have prevailed in the area of India, only one Aryan, the Vedic language, at least as preserved in literary records. This language remains almost changeless, as far as its phonetic aspect is concerned, throughout the Vedic period. But in grammar and vocabulary considerable change may be traced between the beginning and the end of this period. The wealth and variety of nominal and verbal forms tended to diminish and to approach the greater uniformity and regularity of Classical Sanskrit. Not only, however, do the Vedic texts furnish traces of the existence of contemporary vernacular words cognate to the literary language, but the knowledge that Buddha by the end of the Vedic period already used a vernacular dialect in order to be understood by the people, besides the evidence of the Aśoka inscriptions from *c.* 250 B.C., show that popular Aryan dialects must have been developing long before 500 B.C.

The hymns of the Vedas composed in the earliest form of Sanskrit were handed down orally for many centuries by families of priestly singers. It was not till towards the end of the Vedic period that writing became known in India. There is no proof of its existence there till the third century B.C. in the reign of the Buddhist king Aśoka, who caused religious edicts to be inscribed on rocks and pillars all over the country. Many of these have been discovered, deciphered, and published. Minute palaeographical investigations made towards the end of last century have shown that the script here used is derived from the oldest form of northern Semitic writing that appears in Phoenician inscriptions and on the Moabite stone which was inscribed about

890 B.C. This may have been introduced by traders perhaps as early as 800 B.C., but its use was doubtless long limited to commercial requirements such as accounts, and was then employed in the chancelleries for documents of various kinds. But the writing of the third century shows that it must have undergone a long-continued elaboration by grammarians who adapted an alphabet of twenty-two letters to the phonetic needs of Sanskrit which already had forty-four sounds. The right-to-left direction of the Semitic script had been reversed in the Aśoka inscriptions. By the fourth century B.C. at the latest, the letters of this alphabet had already been arranged and classified phonetically, as we know from the great Sanskrit grammar of Pāṇini, whose work cannot be dated later than the fourth century. Here the vowels come first (*a*, *i*, *u*, &c.), then the consonants in groups according to the organ (guttural, palatal, &c.) with which they are pronounced. The same Semitic writing is the source of the Greek alphabet which, through Latin, has come down to us, and which still retains the unscientific order of the letters derived from the Semitic script. The Latin name of the list of letters, *alphabetum*, which we have adopted, represents the first two Greek, borrowed from the first two Semitic letters *aleph* (hieroglyphic for ox = *a*) and *beth* (hieroglyphic for house = *b*). Thus our own word *alphabet* contains perhaps more of the history of civilization than any other word in the language. From this early Sanskrit writing are derived all the numerous other scripts prevalent in India, however much they may differ at the present day.

We do not know when the alphabet first began to be used in India to write down texts. In the whole of ancient (Vedic) literature no evidence can be produced that writing was known. Buddhism arose about 500 B.C., and its sacred canon was probably completed by 400 B.C. But though we here find a good deal to prove a knowledge of writing and of its extensive use at that time, there is no mention of manuscripts nor of the reading or copying of sacred texts. The explanation of this is that all the early literature was produced orally and handed down orally. This had been an established custom for centuries from the earliest times. Thus the memories of learned priests were, instead of libraries, the repositories of literature. Even in the last centuries B.C. works on grammar and phonetics make no reference to written letters, but only to spoken sounds, and the whole grammatical terminology is concerned with the spoken word only, never with written texts. On the other hand, a few centuries after the beginning of our era the copying and presenting of books are often praised. Hence it is probable that written books really did not exist in the centuries before our era. Yet it seems strange at first sight that writing should have been known for centuries without having been applied to literary purposes. The oral tradition of sacred texts was, however, so well established a habit, that the substitution of any other method would not suggest itself as necessary. It was, in fact, in the interest of the priests who were the custodians of the sacred texts to withhold them from unauthorized persons by not writing them down. We are, moreover, continually told in the early literature that whoever wished to learn any branch of knowledge had to betake himself to a teacher and to acquire it by listening to him and not to do so in any other way. Indeed oral tradition offered a better guarantee for the preservation of the original text than the repeated copying of manuscripts. Thus the hymns of the oldest sacred text, the *Ṛigveda*, have been preserved entirely unchanged for 3,000 years, whereas later works,

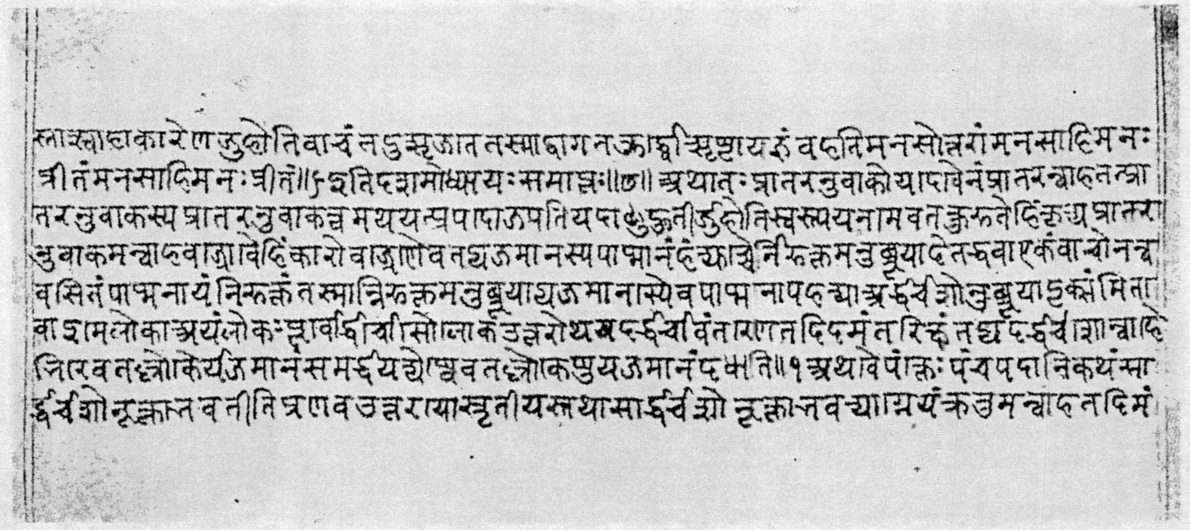

4. VEDIC PAPER MS. FROM THE BODLEIAN LIBRARY

In Devanāgarī script

dating from a period when writing was widely used for literary purposes, have been so much changed that it has in many cases been critically impossible to restore such texts to their original form.

The evidence of manuscripts themselves as to the age of writing in India does not carry us very far back, owing to the unsuitableness of the Indian climate for their preservation. Manuscripts of the thirteenth century A. D. are very rare; extremely few have been discovered in India dating from the twelfth; and only one from the eleventh century. Outside India older specimens have been found: in Nepal, some going back to the tenth century; in Japan, others to the sixth; and in Central Asia a few have turned up belonging to the fifth century. In Chinese Turkistan wooden tablets with Sanskrit writing, which must be as old as 300 A. D., have been dug out of the sands of the desert. The earliest material used for writing in India was palm-leaves; and although paper, which is much more convenient, was introduced with the Muhammadan conquest from about 1000 A. D., manuscripts continued to be written on birch-bark till about 200 years ago, and palm-leaves are still often employed for writing on in different parts of the country, and their use for this purpose can be traced as far back as the first century A. D. in India.

Besides these, wood, leather, metal, and stone were sometimes, though rarely, employed as writing material in early times. Copper-plates were occasionally used for this purpose, perhaps from about 100 A. D. Sanskrit dramas have been found engraved even on rocks. But Sanskrit texts have mostly been written on paper since the Muhammadan conquest. The oldest known paper manuscript found in India dates from soon after 1200 A. D.

Some centuries after the beginning of our era, libraries as

the depositories of Sanskrit manuscripts came into existence in temples, monasteries, the palaces of kings, and the houses of the wealthy. The evidence of his works shows that a Sanskrit poet who lived at the beginning of the seventh century must have possessed a large library. In the eleventh century a famous library was owned by a king named Bhoja of Dhār in the west of India. In the course of centuries large libraries were formed, so that each of the collections at Tanjore, Madras, Poona, Benares, and Calcutta consists at the present time of more than 12,000 manuscripts. In the Bodleian Library at Oxford, Sanskrit manuscripts have in the course of the last hundred years accumulated to the number of nearly 10,000. There are also several other smaller, though considerable collections of Sanskrit manuscripts in the libraries of European capitals. Practically the whole of this vast mass of manuscripts representing Sanskrit literature has been made accessible through catalogues compiled by the directions of librarians in Europe or by the order of the Indian Government, which since 1868 has made a considerable annual grant towards the search for, and the purchase of, Sanskrit manuscripts.

Indian literature is for the most part written in Sanskrit, but in its widest sense it comprises also writings in many Indo-Aryan and some Dravidian languages. It may as a whole be divided into three periods: (1) Ancient Indian, composed or written in an early form of Sanskrit; (2) Medieval Indian, written in Classical Sanskrit and in daughter languages derived from Sanskrit and called Prākrit; (3) Modern Indian, written in the languages spoken in India at the present day.

At the end of the later Vedic period a new era in the history of Indian civilization was about to appear in the rise of new forms of literature, language, and religion.

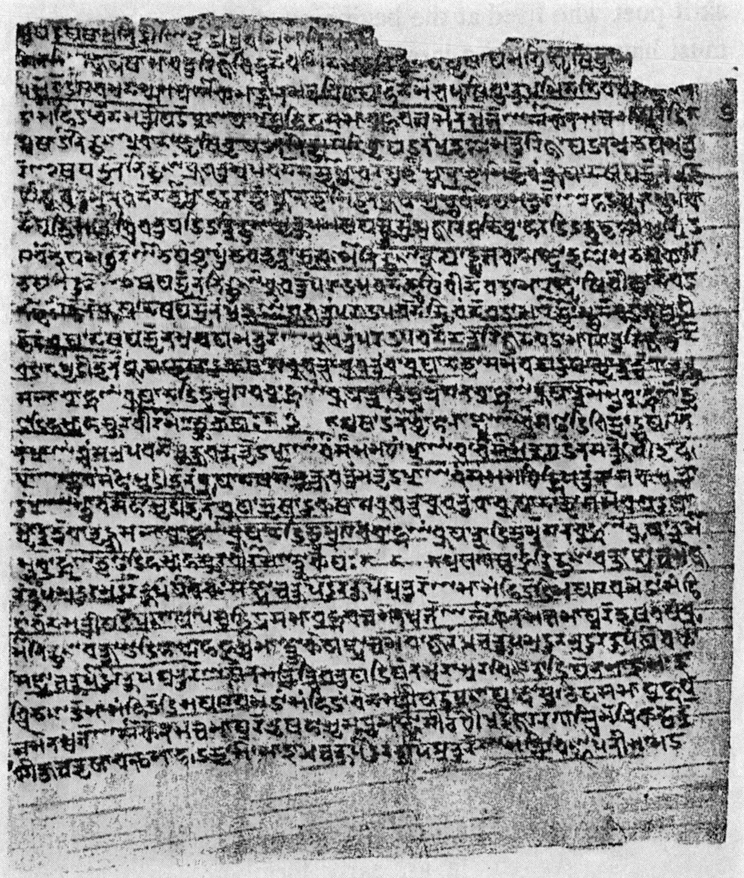

5. VEDIC BIRCHBARK MS. FROM KASHMĪR

In Śārada script

Macdonell, *History of Sanskrit Literature*, pp. 442–3, supplies full bibliography down to 1899. Winternitz, *Geschichte*, i. 163–228; iii. 613–18. Keith, *The Aitareya and Kauṣītaki Brāhmaṇas of the Ṛigveda*, H.O.S., xxv, 1920; Eggeling, ŚB., in SBE. Keith, *The Aitareya Āraṇyaka*, ed. and tr., Oxford, 1909. Deussen, *Sechzig Upanishads*, tr., Leipzig, 1897; *Die Philosophie der Upanishads*, Leipzig, 1899. Hume, *The thirteen principal Upanishads*, tr., Oxford, 1921. Jacob, *Concordance of the principal Upanishads*, Bombay, 1891. Keith, *The Religion and Philosophy of the Veda and Upanishads*, 2 vols., Oxford, 1925.

IV

EARLY POST-VEDIC PERIOD: *c.* 500 B.C. TO 1 A.D.

New linguistic and religious period — Classical Sanskrit the literary vehicle of the Hindus — Three classes of Sūtras — Six kinds of subsidiary Vedic treatises (vedāṅgas) — Yāska's Nirukta — Pāṇini's grammar: dominates Classical Sanskrit literature — Ritual manuals — Sanskrit vehicle of orthodoxy (Hinduism), Prākrit of heterodoxy (Buddhism and Jainism) — Pāli vehicle of Buddhist canon — Contents of Tipiṭaka — The Dhammapada — The Jātakas — The Hīnayāna doctrine — Sanskrit Hīnayāna works — Mahāyāna doctrine — Nāgārjuna — Buddhist religious art: stūpas or burial mounds, caityas or churches, vihāras or monasteries — Conventional figure of Buddha — Jainism — Mahāvīra, its founder — Two sects — Jain Prākrit — Jainism emphasizes asceticism and non-injury to life — Its five vows — Jain sacred canon — Non-canonical literature — Hemachandra — The Pārśvābhyudaya, a biographical poem — Use of Sanskrit in later Jainism — Jain architecture — Selected bibliography.

THE new literary period of India which now opens out has a dual character, both in its linguistic and its religious aspect. It was now that the ancient Indo-Aryan language reached its final stage, assuming, by the elaboration of grammarians, the form known as Sanskrit, which has remained for more than 2,000 years the unchanging literary vehicle of the religion of the Hindus. In this earliest period of Sanskrit were composed the Sūtras, concise treatises in which the religion of the Brāhmaṇas, on its ritual side, was systematically condensed with a view to preserving the ancient sacerdotal literature. They were never regarded as sacred, but were felt to be treatises compiled with the help of oral priestly tradition from the contents of the Brāhmaṇas solely to meet practical needs. The oldest of the Sūtras seem to go back to about the time when Buddhism arose. It is, in fact, not improbable that the rise of the new religion gave the first impulse to the composition of systematic manuals of Brahmanic worship. This literature has a style of its own, consisting of brief rules strung together (*sūtra* 'thread'). The Sūtras may be divided into three classes. The first of these comprises the Śrauta Sūtras, which are concerned with the sacrificial aspect of a particular school attached to any one of the Vedas. They are, in fact, technical guides to the Vedic sacrifice. There are about twelve of these ritual treatises.

Another class is the Gṛihya Sūtras or domestic rules for the many ceremonies applicable to the life of the Hindu from birth to death. These are of unequalled importance for the history and ethnology of the age, forming a useful supplement to the contents of the *Atharvaveda*. More than a dozen of this type of Sūtra are extant. One of the most important is the *Kauśika Sūtra* which, besides treating of the domestic ritual, deals with the magical and medicinal practices belonging specially to the sphere of the *Atharvaveda*. An interesting rite handled by these works is that of initiation (*upanayana*), called the second birth, of boys when they are invested with the sacred cord admitting them to Vedic study. It is a modification of the very ancient and primitive ceremony of initiation on the attainment of manhood. Other ceremonies of much interest are the wedding and the funeral rites, many elements of which survive in India down to the present day.

The third and last class of Sūtras are the Dharma-Sūtras, which are concerned with the customs of everyday life, and constitute the earliest Indian legal works. They deal fully with the religious, but only briefly and partially with the secular side of law. Only some half-dozen of them have survived. Among other subjects they deal with the duties of kings, criminal justice, the laws of inheritance, and of marriage. The oldest, the law-book of Gautama, is composed entirely in prose aphorisms. Among these legal treatises must have been included a *Mānava dharma-sūtra*, forming the basis of the famous later and still extant metrical law-book, the *Code of Manu*.

According to the Indian traditional view the whole body of auxiliary works bearing on the Veda and composed in the Sūtra style form six classes called *vedāṅgas*, or 'limbs of the Veda', comprising the subjects of religious practice, phonetics, grammar, etymology, metre, and astronomy. They all aim at explaining, preserving, or practically applying the sacred texts. Of the greatest interest in these groups are the linguistic works which deal with phonetics, derivation, and grammar; for in these subjects the Indians arrived at more important results than any other nation of antiquity. One of the most important books produced in this period is the *Nirukta* of Yāska, which besides being of great value from the point of view of exegesis and grammar, is highly interesting as the earliest specimen of Sanskrit prose of the classical type, which is somewhat anterior to the date of Pāṇini himself. It should undoubtedly be attributed to the beginning of the Sūtra period. The great grammar of Pāṇini comes later in this period, not earlier than the fifth century B.C.; but it must be regarded as the virtual starting-point of the post-Vedic age, for it almost entirely dominates the whole of the subsequent Sanskrit literature. Regarded as an infallible authority, Pāṇini superseded his predecessors, all of whom except Yāska have disappeared.

To the Sūtras is attached a very large supplementary literature consisting chiefly of manuals, called Prayogas or

Paddhatis, which deal with the sacrificial ceremonial. There is here also a group of Vedic Indexes called Anukramaṇīs, which give lists of the hymns quoted by their initial words, and of their authors, metres, and deities, in the order in which these hymns occur in the various Saṃhitās. One of these indexes supplies the number of stanzas, words, and syllables contained in the *Ṛigveda.*

By the beginning of this period (500 B.C.) the Sanskrit language reached its final development. This was of a negative character, consisting not of growth, but of decay by loss of grammatical forms. Any indications of the nature of growth were limited to the extended employment of periphrastic forms, of compound and adverbial, in place of primary prepositions, and, in syntax, of the use of past participles for finite tenses, and of long compounds. But a fixed grammatical standard was not attained till the appearance of Pāṇini's work, which completely arrested the development of the language. Henceforward it remained the unchanging vehicle of the Brahmin religion.

During the whole of this period, however, there existed a vernacular, descended from a Vedic dialect and remaining parallel with Sanskrit, as the vehicle of Buddhism and bearing the designation of Prākrit. While Sanskrit remained the language of orthodoxy, Prākrit became that of heterodoxy in the two new religions of Jainism and Buddhism, which arose much about the same time and at the beginning of this period (*c.* 500 B.C.). The relation of this language to Sanskrit resembles that of old Italian to Classical Latin, being characterized by the avoidance of conjunct consonants (which are assimilated) and of final consonants, as in *sutta*, compared with Sanskrit *sūtra*, 'thread', and *vijju*, with *vidyut*, 'lightning'. The oldest literary form of Prākrit is Pāli. In this language the sacred canon of Buddhism, in its oldest form, has been handed down.

This Pāli canon, though composed in the north of India, has been preserved only in Ceylon, Burma, and Siam. It contains the doctrine of the older school, called *Hīnayāna*, 'the lesser vehicle', the chief aim of which is to obtain *Nirvāṇa* ('extinction') or release of the individual from suffering. No work of Buddhist literature goes back to Buddha's time, but much contained in the canon, such as the famous sermon of Benares, may preserve the actual words spoken by Buddha. Almost the whole of the earliest Buddhist literature consists of short collections in the form of speeches, poems, tales, rules of conduct, gathered together in larger collections called *piṭakas* or 'baskets', three of which combined form the Pāli canon (*tipiṭaka*). This canon, first constituted in the third century B.C. during the reign of the Buddhist king Aśoka in India, was fixed in the first century B.C. in Ceylon. The *Tipiṭaka* has, on the whole, since then been handed down with great care; but it must have undergone some modifications, for several contradictions which it contains could not otherwise be accounted for. The main contents of the three 'baskets' are the following.

1. The first is concerned with the discipline and the daily life of the Buddhist order.

2. The second, consisting of five collections of lectures, describes the religion of Buddha and his earliest disciples. One of its topics deals with a large number of Brahmin occupations from which the Buddhist monk should refrain. It also treats of the relations of Brahmanism and Buddhism, contrasting the cult of the followers of the three Vedas with Buddhist ideals. It, moreover, describes the 'complete nirvāṇa' (*parinibbāṇa*), which is a continuous

account of the last days of Buddha. There are further sermons which throw light not only on the life of Buddhist monks, but on Brahmin sacrifices, on forms of asceticism, and on the relations of Buddha to the Jains. The fifth section in this *Piṭaka*, 'the collection of small pieces', is later than the rest. Being composed chiefly in verse, it contains all the most important works of Indian Buddhist poetry. One of the works in it is the *Metta-sutta*, in which kindness towards all creatures is praised as the true Buddhist cult. Another work in this *Piṭaka*, the *Dhamma-pada*, or 'Words of religion', being an anthology of Buddhist ethical maxims, is the most famous product of Buddhist literature. The *Itivuttaka* (the book of 'Thus he hath spoken'), which is composed in prose and verse, is a collection of the sayings of Buddha. The *Thera-gāthā* and the *Therī-gāthā*, or 'Songs of monks and nuns', are fine poems exalting mental calm as the religious ideal of Buddhism.

One of the most interesting books here is the *Jātaka*, a collection of about 550 stories of former existences of Buddha in the character of a future saviour.

3. The third *Piṭaka* is concerned with *abhidhamma* or 'higher religion', dealing with the same matter as the second *Piṭaka*, but in a more scholastic manner. As it is composed mostly in the form of question and answer, it resembles a catechism.

The Pāli canon, apart from additions, was entirely composed in India. But the non-canonical literature was produced by Buddhist monks in Ceylon; the only important exception here being the *Milinda-panha*, or 'Questions of Menander'. This work was evidently written in north-western India. It is a dialogue represented as taking place between a Buddhist teacher and the Greek king Menander who in the first century B.C. ruled over the

Indus territory, Gujarāt, and the valley of the Ganges. The original part of this work was probably written about the beginning of the Christian era.

Pāli Buddhism represents the doctrine called the *Hīnayāna*, or 'Little Vehicle'. There was also a Sanskrit canon which followed this doctrine, but only fragmentary parts of three books, one of which is the *Dharma-pada*, have as yet been discovered. A work representing this doctrine is the *Mahāvastu* or 'Book of Great Events'. Its chief content is a miraculous biography of Buddha written in 'mixed Sanskrit'. It is of great importance as containing many old versions of texts that also occur in the Pāli canon, such as the 'Sermon of Benares' and a section of the *Dhamma-pada*. Many of the Jātakas are also found in it. Some traces appear in this work of its having been influenced by the *Mahāyāna* doctrines. The nucleus of the book probably dates from the second century B.C., though it contains some much later additions. There are several other Buddhist Hīnayāna works in Sanskrit, which, though not coming within the limits of this period, may most conveniently be mentioned here.

The *Lalita-vistara*, a biography of Buddha, is a continuous narrative in Sanskrit prose interspersed with long metrical pieces in what is called 'mixed Sanskrit'. As its original part was extended in a *Mahāyāna* sense, it contains both old and new elements. It is thus of interest as presenting the development of the Buddha legend from its earliest beginnings to the deification of Buddha as a god above all gods.

The *Buddha-carita*, or 'Life of Buddha', is an epic in pure Sanskrit, which must have been composed about 100 A.D. It does not contain any pronounced Mahāyāna doctrine.

Another work, dating probably from the fourth century A. D., is the *Jātaka-mālā*. It contains thirty-four stories nearly all of which are found in the Pāli *Jātaka* book. Written in a mixture of verse and prose, it conforms in language and style to the standard of Classical Sanskrit.

Cognate with these works are several collections called *Avadānas*, 'stories of great deeds', which are practically Jātakas. One of these is the *Avadāna-śataka*, or 'Century of great deeds' which probably dates from the second century A. D. and contains pieces from the Sanskrit canon. Another is the *Divyāvadāna*, or 'Heavenly stories of great deeds'. This work often mentions the Sanskrit canon, besides having several legends in common with the Pāli canon.

The great majority of the Sanskrit Buddhists belonged to the new school of the *Mahāyāna* or 'Great Vehicle', the chief aim of which was to attain the condition of a Bodhisattva, or future Buddha, who brings *Nirvāṇa* within the reach of the entire human race. This school, though possessing no canon, has nine religious texts called *dharmas*. Its most important work is the *Saddharma-puṇḍarīka*, 'the Lotus of good Religion'. It is written in Sanskrit prose interspersed with *gāthās* in 'mixed Sanskrit'. In its earliest form it dates from about 200 A. D. Buddha is here no longer a man, who in the Pāli *suttas* was a mendicant, but a god above all gods, who has lived for countless ages and will live for ever in the future as well. His doctrine is that every man can become a Buddha by performing meritorious works and leading a moral life.

Later is the *Karaṇḍa-vyūha*, which is akin to the Hindu Purāṇas, exalting Avalokiteśvara, 'the Bodhisattva who looks down' with infinite pity on all beings, refusing Buddhahood till all are saved. The yearning for salvation has probably never been more powerfully expressed than in this compassionate figure of Buddhism. His cult is known to have existed before 400 A. D.

The Mahāyāna doctrine was systematized by Nāgārjuna, once a Brahmin, who flourished about 200 A. D. Mahāyāna texts were translated into Chinese in the third century A. D., and the Gandhāra type of Buddhist art, which illustrates the Mahāyāna doctrine, came into being about the beginning of our era. Asaṅga, the son of a Brahmin from Peshāwar, who flourished about 300 to 350 A. D., introduced the practice of Yoga into the Mahāyāna doctrine.

From about 600 A. D. Buddhism began to decay in India, as is shown by the approximation of its later literature to that of the Hindu Purāṇas. Not only are Hindu deities such as Vishṇu and Śiva, Sarasvatī and Mahādevī introduced, but also magical spells, which at first containing Buddhist doctrine, finally degenerated into pure gibberish.

The last stage in the degradation of Indian Buddhism is to be found in the Buddhist Tantras, treatises composed in barbarous Sanskrit. Most of them are connected with Yoga, which aims at the highest knowledge of 'nothingness'. The teaching and practice of this *yoga* are a mixture of mysticism, sorcery, and erotics, accompanied by disgusting orgies. These Tantras have no longer any connexion with Buddhism beyond being described as 'promulgated by Buddha'. They do not differ from the Śaivite Tantras, for they inculcate the worship of the *liṅga* and of Śaivite gods, besides introducing many female deities into their cult.

Without the evidence of the religious art of Buddhism, neither the history of that faith nor even of Indian religion in general could be fully understood. In the first period of Buddhism, when the *Hīnayāna* doctrine prevailed, the earliest architectural and plastic religious art of India arose.

6. GREAT STŪPA AT SĀNCHĪ FROM NORTH-EAST

The reign of Aśoka (272–231 B.C.), whose rule extended practically over the whole of India, except the extreme south, is the starting-point of the history of Indian art. Stone then first began to be used in structural monuments.

The earliest of these were *stūpas* or hemispherical burial-mounds, commemorative of Buddha, and enclosing relics of the founder of the faith. The best preserved and one of the oldest surviving *stūpas* is at Sānchī in central India. The hemisphere is built of brick, but the surrounding rail and the four gateways in it consist of stone, though clearly imitations of wooden structures (see frontispiece). On the top of the dome was a box-like structure surmounted by an umbrella, the Indian emblem of sovereignty and symbolical of Buddha's princely descent. This crowning feature, usually called a 'tee', has disappeared from all the structural Indian *stūpas*, but its form can be seen in the sculptural representations of it in the interior or on the façade of rock-cut temples or on the surrounding rail of structural *stūpas*. The *stūpa* has had an interesting development in later Indian and Chinese architecture; and its gateway (*toraṇa*) was introduced with Buddhism into other Asiatic countries from India.

Another class of Buddhist architecture was the *chaitya* or assembly hall, the exact counterpart of the Christian Church, not only in form, but in use. Till recent times only rock-cut examples were known in India. The typical *chaitya* consists of a nave and of side aisles terminating in an apse or semi-dome. The pillars separating the nave from the aisles are continued round the apse. Under the latter and in front of its pillars is a rock-cut *stūpa* serving as an object of adoration by circumambulation. It occupies nearly the same position as the altar does in a Christian church. The tee was doubtless usually surmounted by a wooden umbrella, but it has everywhere disappeared except at Kārli, the finest *chaitya* cave in India. The excavation of these rock-cut assembly halls extended from about 250 B.C. to 600 A.D.

A third architectural class arose in the form of *vihāras* or monasteries as residences for Buddhist monks. Nearly 1,000 rock-cut specimens are to be found in India, almost all situated in the west, chiefly at Ajantā, Nāsik, and Ellora. They generally consist of a hall, surrounding which are a number of excavated sleeping cubicles. The latter in the oldest *vihāras* usually contain a stone bed. About forty of the western monasteries were probably excavated before the Christian era.

Down to the middle of the first century of our era the Buddhist cult followed the doctrine of the *Hīnayāna*, in which there was no worship of Buddha, and no figure of him appeared in sculptural art. Reverence at that time was paid to relics, *stūpas*, bo-trees,[1] footprints of Buddha, and sacred symbols such as the trident (*triśūl*) and the wheel of the law (*cakra*). These are constantly represented as adored by men and even animals in the sculptures of the period at Bhārhut, Sānchī, Bodh Gayā, and in the assembly halls and monasteries of the West. But no figure of Buddha sculptured in India can be dated earlier than about 100 A.D. It was, then, in the beginning of the second period of Buddhist religious art, the epoch of the *Mahāyāna* school, that statues of Buddha appeared in the ancient province of Gandhāra, the modern Yusufzai country and the neighbouring valleys of the Kābul and the Swāt. Here was created the conventional type of Buddha, a seated cross-legged figure adorned with a halo. From this centre it spread to other

[1] Under which Buddha attained enlightenment (*bodhi*).

7. TOP OF NORTH GATEWAY, GREAT STUPA AT SĀNCHĪ

8. TOP OF WEST GATEWAY, GREAT STŪPA AT SÁNCHĪ

parts of India, and was finally diffused all over the Buddhist world.

In the same century (the sixth) as Buddhism, but somewhat earlier, was established the religious system of Jainism. Equally an offshoot of Brahmanism, it was, as denying the authority of the Veda, similarly regarded by the Brahmins as heretical. It is, like Buddhism, a monastic and pessimistic religion. It looks upon life in the world, perpetuated by the transmigration of the soul, as an evil; and it aims at gaining liberation that puts an end to the cycle of births, by the attainment of right knowledge. Like Buddhism and the Hindu Sāṅkhya system, Jainism is atheistic, denying the existence of an absolute supreme god. As both Jainism and Buddhism are monastic systems outside the pale of Brahmanism, and have several external resemblances, it was at one time held by scholars that the former was an offshoot of the latter. But the erroneousness of this theory has since been proved; for the canonical Buddhist books often mention the Jains as a rival sect, besides agreeing with Jain tradition in naming the same place as the locality where Mahāvīra, the founder of Jainism, died. It has been shown that Mahāvīra was a slightly older contemporary of Buddha. He may have been only the reformer of a sect originated by a predecessor named Pārśva. But there is no documentary evidence proving that the latter was an historical person.

The account of Mahāvīra's life in the canonical books of the Jains may be regarded as having an historical foundation. It is this. Belonging to the military clan called Jñāta, he was born near the town of Vaiśālī, 27 miles north of Patna. His parents having died when he was thirty, he became a monk, and entered upon a course of self-mortification lasting twelve years, when he reached the state of omniscience (*kaivalya*, which is equivalent to the Buddhist *bodhi* or 'enlightenment'). At the age of seventy-two he died (*c.* 480 B.C.) at Pāvā.

Both Mahāvīra and the preceding twenty-three mythical patriarchs (*tīrtha-karas*) of Jainism came to be adored as gods (*devas*) and to have erected to them temples in which their idols were-worshipped. Mention is already made in some of the canonical books of this worship, which was fully developed in the first centuries of our era.

Jainism in the first century A.D., split into two sects called the Śvetāmbaras ('white-robed'), and the Digambaras ('sky-clad') who went about stark naked till the Muhammadans compelled them to wear a minimum of clothing. The texts of the Jain religion are composed in a dry didactic style. As they contain little of general human interest, they need only be briefly described here. The Jains designate their complete sacred books by the terms *Siddhānta* or *Āgama*. They call the first and most important part of their canon the twelve Aṅgas ('members' of their religion). The whole canon was edited by Devarddhigaṇi in 454 A.D., having till then been handed down by oral tradition

The language in which it is composed the Jains call *Ardha-māgadhī* ('half-māgadhī') and is that in which Mahāvīra is said to have preached. But as the texts show signs of having been modernized in the process of oral transmission, it is best to call the language of the sacred texts Jain Prākrit Quite different from this language is that of the non-canonical Jain texts, which had best be called Jain Māhārāṣṭrī. The texts of the canon are undoubtedly of different ages, the oldest going back to near the time of Mahāvīra, while its later components, probably come down to near the time of Devarddhi.

According to Jain philosophy, matter, which consists of

9. ROCK-CUT BUDDHIST TEMPLE AT KĀRLI

10. EARLY ROCK-CUT BUDDHIST MONASTERY AT AJANTĀ

atoms, is eternal, but may assume any form, such as earth, wind, and so on. All material things are ultimately produced by combinations of atoms. Souls are of two kinds: those which are subject to mundane transmigration (*saṃsārin*) and those which are liberated (*mukta*). The latter will be embodied no more; they dwell in a state of perfection at the summit of the universe; being no more concerned with wordly affairs, they have reached *nirvāṇa.*

The souls (*jīva*) with which the whole world is filled are different from matter; but being substances they are also eternal. Subtle matter coming into contact with a soul causes its embodiment: being then transformed into eight kinds of *karma* and thus forming as it were a subtle body, it clings to the soul in all its migrations. The theory of *karma* is the keystone of the Jain system. The highest goal consists in getting rid of all *karma* derived from past existences, and acquiring no new *karma.* One of the chief means to this end is the performance of asceticism (*tapas*). The Jain system differs from Buddhism in emphasizing asceticism to a much greater extent, even to the point of religious suicide; and in the total avoidance of taking life of any kind, such avoidance being described as the highest duty.

It is necessary for a Jain, in order to realize *nirvāṇa*, to possess right faith, right knowledge, and right conduct. He is also required to observe the five vows, the first four of which are also acknowledged by the Brahmins and the Buddhists. These five consist of abstention from (1) killing, (2) lying, (3) stealing, (4) sexual intercourse, and (5) all attachment to worldly things, especially the owning of any possessions. Laymen were also to observe these vows, but only to the extent permitted by the conditions of their lives. Thus they were only obliged to refrain from intentionally killing animate beings, for otherwise they could not have gone about their business. Laymen were, in fact, more closely connected with the monastic order in Jainism than in early Buddhism. Jainism thus avoided fundamental changes, and has remained essentially unaltered for more than 2,000 years, while Buddhism underwent great transformations and disappeared from the land of its origin, its last remnants being expelled by Moslem attacks by about 1200 A.D.

Asceticism (*tapas*) is a very important institution in Jainism, for it not only prevents the formation of new *karma*, but extinguishes the old. Its austerities are of two kinds: external and internal. Fasting is the most conspicuous of the former. It has been developed by the Jains to a remarkable degree of elaboration. One of its forms is starving oneself to death. A form of external asceticism which Jainism has in common with Buddhism and Brahmanism is the practice of Yoga, or secluded meditation in certain recognized postures. Of all spiritual exercises the most important is contemplation (*dhyāna*), or the concentration of the mind on a single object. Here there are four stages, in the last of which *karma* is annihilated. The soul then leaves the body and becomes liberated for ever. *Nirvāṇa*, however, cannot be attained unless it is preceded by twelve years of self-mortification.

At the present day (1926) the Jain population of India amounts to 1,178,000. The smallness of this number is to be accounted for by the fact that Jainism is a religion of the upper classes, being no doubt too rigorous for the illiterate masses. But it is important in India owing to the wealth and education of its adherents. Their distinctive peculiarity of abstention from hurting any living thing excludes them from some professions, such as agriculture, and has forced them into commerce, especially money-

II. VOTIVE STŪPAS FROM BODH-GAYĀ

(see p. 66)

lending. This explains both their wealth and their unpopularity.

The aggregate of their sacred books, or their canon, the Jains call their *Siddhānta* or their *Āgama*; but only the Siddhānta of the Śvetāmbara sect is as yet known to us. Besides the most important part of their canon, the twelve Aṅgas, there are in the canon about thirty-six subordinate works, a dozen of which are called *Sūtras.* The parts of the canon composed in verse are more archaic than the prose portions.

In the middle of the fifth century (454 A.D.) there was held a council at Vallabhi in Gujarāt for the purpose of collecting and writing down the sacred texts. Though the age of these according to the tradition of the Śvetāmbaras themselves is comparatively late, there are indications, in inscriptions and bas-reliefs of the first and second century A.D., of their authenticity going back to a much earlier date, especially as this probability is corroborated by the agreement with it, in many remarkable details, of the Buddhist tradition. The oldest elements of the canon may very well go back to the time of the first disciples of Mahāvīra, or at any rate to the council of Pāṭaliputra, which was held according to tradition under the Maurya king Chandragupta at the end of the fourth century B.C., while the latest elements may be nearly as recent as the Council of Vallabhi.

In style we find that the canonical books show a mixture of prose and verse similar to that in the Pāli Buddhist scriptures, but in doctrine much greater stress is laid on the principle of *ahiṃsā* and on rigorous asceticism, in the practice of which even religious suicide is recommended.

One of the Sūtras, called the *Kalpa-sūtra,* is the chief work supplying rules for the guidance of monks and nuns.

The first of four canonical texts called *Mūla-sūtras* is the *Uttarajjhayana* (in Sanskrit *Uttarādhyāyana*) *sūtra*, a religious poem, which is one of the most valuable constituents of the canon. Its oldest parts consist of a series of maxims, parables, dialogues, and ballads of an ascetic type, which have parallels in Buddhist literature. It contains some fine epic dialogues and ballads, in which the ascetic ideal of the Jains is contrasted with that of the two highest castes (the Brahmin and the warrior) of Hinduism.

The non-canonical religious literature of the Jains consists partly of an immense number of commentaries, and partly of independent works on dogma, ethics, and monastic discipline, besides a very extensive body of poetical narrative. Between these two groups are didactic poems, legends of saints, and works on ecclesiastical history. The language in which this literature is written is partly the Prākrit called Jain Māhārāṣṭrī, and partly Sanskrit.

The chief value of the commentaries is that they preserve many old historical or semi-historical traditions, besides a large quantity of popular stories which the Jains, like the Buddhists, employed for illustrating their sermons. This Jain narrative literature has much in common with the Buddhist *Jātakas* and contains many elements which, reappearing in other forms of Indian and non-Indian literatures, are in fact the common property of world literature. Particularly rich in stories is the oldest commentary, consisting of nearly 600 verses, attributed to Bhadrabāhu. The most important, however, of the commentaries are those of Śāntisūri and Devendragaṇi, the former of whom died in 1040 A.D. The Jains adopted a good deal of legendary matter from the Brahmin literature, such as the Kṛishṇa legend, and the epic story of the descent of the Ganges and the destruction of the 60,000 sons of Sagara.

12. BUDDHA IN TEACHING ATTITUDE, PESHAWAR

(*see p. 66*)

In later times the Jains made collections of stories, in which the tales were inserted one within the other and set in a general narrative framework, after the favourite Indian fashion. A rich fund of tales is the *Kathā-kośa*, or 'Treasury of Stories', written in bad Sanskrit, with verses in Prākrit. The well-known *Mahābhārata* episode of *Nala and Damayantī* is one of the tales here introduced in a modified form.

A special type of poems meant for edification are the *caritras* and *prabandhas*. The former are biographies of ancient rulers and saints, while the latter are tales of monks and laymen of historical times. The monk Hemachandra was one of the most many-sided and prolific authors among the Jains, noted both as scholar and poet. He also composed works on such secular subjects as grammar, lexicography, poetics, and prosody. Born in 1089, he made Gujarāt the chief seat of Jainism. His largest work was entitled *Triṣaṣṭi-śalākā-puruṣa-carita*, 'Life of the sixty-three best men'. Much more important from the point of view of literary history is an appendix to this work entitled *Pariśiṣṭa-parvan*, or 'Supplementary Section', the stories in which are evidently derived from a popular source. Hemachandra translated them from Prākrit into Sanskrit.

A work of considerable importance for the textual criticism of one of the most famous poems of Sanskrit literature is the *Pārśvābhyudaya*, a poetical biography of Pārśvanātha, by Jinasena, composed about 800 A.D. In this poem the author incorporates the whole of the *Meghadūta*, a lyric of about 112 stanzas, by India's greatest poet in such a way as to borrow one or two lines in each stanza, which he completes in his own words.

The Jains also competed with the poets of other sects in the composition of religious lyrics. There are many such, called *stotras*, or 'hymns of praise', written in either Sanskrit or Prākrit and not altogether devoid of poetic merit. The oldest known poem of this kind is the *Uvasagga-harastotra*, a hymn of five stanzas addressed to Pārśva and attributed to Bhadrabāhu. A very old didactic poem in 540 Prākrit stanzas, intended to supply moral instruction for monks and laymen, is the *Uvaesa-mālā* by Dharmadāsa. The number of commentaries written on it, two of them dating from as early as the ninth century, attests its popularity.

One of the most important of the didactic poems of the Jainas is the *Yoga-śāstra* of Hemachandra. It consists of a text in simple ślokas and a commentary written in the artificial style of the Kāvyas. The text contains a short sketch of the Jaina doctrine, while the commentary furnishes perhaps the clearest exposition that has ever been written of the whole system. The doctrine of *ahiṃsā* is strongly emphasized. Women, as is usual in this monkish poetry, are very pessimistically characterized. They are, for example, described as 'the torch on the road to the gate of hell, the root of all miseries, and the prime cause of discord'. Many of the verses in this poem on the transitoriness and vanity of human existence are up to the level of the best of the aphorisms of the Sanskrit poet Bhartṛihari (p. 93), as for instance: 'Fortune is fluctuating like the waves of the sea; the meeting of friends is like a dream; youth is like a blade of grass, whirled up by every gust of wind.'

The number of purely learned books on the Jaina religion is very great. One of the most prominent of the writers on philosophy is the voluminous Haribhadra, also known as an important commentator who flourished in the second half of the ninth century. He wrote the *Ṣaḍdarśana-*

samuccaya, 'Compendium of the Six philosophical Systems'. Among these he includes Buddhism and Jainism. He also adds a short appendix on the materialist doctrine of Chārvāka (p. 158).

At a later period of Jainism the Digambara first, and afterwards the Śvetāmbara sect, began to make use of Sanskrit not only for the purpose of writing on their own sectarian subjects. They also applied it in dealing with the secular scientific subjects of the Brahmins. They thus produced valuable works in Sanskrit on grammar and astronomy, and even in some departments of pure literature, which gained the approbation of their religious opponents. They also exercised an influence on the development of the languages of the south, in the literary cultivation of Kanarese, Tamil, and Telugu. The Jains thus occupy an important position in the history of the literature and civilization of India.

The Jain religion, like Buddhism, developed an art of its own, which was, however, evolved from the latter as its main source. Though Jainism as a religion was somewhat older than Buddhism, its art as a whole was much later. A few earlier examples of it have, indeed, survived, but it does not emerge in its main features till about 900 A.D. Its two leading types are simply modifications of the Dravidian and the Indo-Aryan styles of Hindu temple architecture. It is therefore only necessary here to point out its most distinctive features. One of these, especially developed in the south, consisted in free-standing pillars almost invariably erected near the temples. They are the lineal descendants of the Buddhist detached columns bearing emblems or animal figures. These Jain pillars are nowhere so frequent or so elaborately carved as in the south. A variation of the free-standing columns are the commemorative towers (called *kīrti-* or *jaya-stambha*) to be found in the north. One of these is a 'tower of fame' at Chitor in Rājputāna, dating from about 900 A.D. Another tower of this kind at the same place was finished in the year 1468 A.D. It is 122 feet high and consists of nine stories, the whole being covered with ornamental sculpture. Like the column of Trajan at Rome it is a 'pillar of victory', but in the words of Fergusson, the leading authority on Indian architecture, 'it is of infinitely better taste as an architectural object'.

The most distinctive feature of the Jain temple of the north is the porch erected in front of the cell containing the image of the Jain saint sitting cross-legged like the figure of Buddha. This porch consists of a circular dome resting on a group of eight pillars, every adjacent pair of which forms an arch by means of a connecting strut rising from a lower capital constructed some way below the top of the pillar. The strut thus gives additional support to the architrave resting on the summit of the column. The dome is constructed by means of horizontal courses gradually approaching nearer by overlapping till the highest is closed with a slab at the top. The successive courses were doubtless originally octagonal, straight slabs being laid across at the angles. But the slabs came to be cut as segments of a circle, so as to form gradually narrowing rings of masonry till the highest closed the aperture at the top. The great advantage of the horizontally constructed arch is the absence of a lateral thrust from which classical and Gothic buildings using the radiating arch suffer. Hence more slender and elegant pillars are possible in Indian architecture. Another result was the introduction of pendants in the centre of domes to a much greater extent than is found in any other style of building. The ornaments of the dome

13. JAIN TOWER OF VICTORY AT CHITOR, RĀJPUTĀNA

14. WHITE MARBLE CEILING OF JAIN TEMPLE, MOUNT ABU

could here be introduced in concentric rings one above the other instead of on vertical ribs as in Roman and Gothic vaults. This allows far more variety without any lack of good taste, and has rendered some of the Jain domes more beautiful specimens of elaborate roofing than can be seen anywhere else.

The appearance of the Jain arch can be seen in the illustration of the dome on the opposite page.

The next illustration (facing p. 78) shows a free-standing archway at Vadnagar constructed in this style. It is to be noted that the horizontal method of building domes and arches is not peculiar to Jainism, but is a feature common to all indigenous Indian architecture.

SELECTED BIBLIOGRAPHY

Macdonell, *History*, ch. ix (Sūtras), pp. 244–76 and 443–5 (bibliography down to 1899). Winternitz, *Geschichte*, i. 229–46; iii. 618–22 (bibliography down to 1922).

Winternitz, ibid., *Die Buddhistische Litteratur*: ii. 1–228; iii. 635–9. Burgess, *Buddhist Art in India* (tr. of Grünwedel, *Handbuch*), London, 1901.

Bühler, *Über die indische Secte der Jainas*, tr. by J. Burgess, London, 1903. Jacobi, *Jainism*, in Hastings's *Encyclopaedia*, 1914. Margaret Stevenson, *The Heart of Jainism*, Oxford, 1915. Winternitz, *Die heiligen Texte der Jainas*, in his *Geschichte*, ii. 289–356. Translations of some of the principal Jain texts, Jacobi in *SBE.*, xxii and xlv. Cp. Vincent Smith, *A History of Fine Art in India and Ceylon* (Index, s. v. *Jain*), Oxford, 1911; 2nd ed., 1926.

V

THE LATER SANSKRIT PERIOD: EPIC AND CLASSICAL LITERATURE

FIRST TO ELEVENTH CENTURY A.D.

Caste system and transmigration theory now stereotyped — Widow-burning and child-marriage — Sanskrit still the literary language — Rise of religious art — Two types of architecture: Dravidian and Indo-Aryan — Their origin — The innovation in sculpture of many-armed images of gods — Explanation of this abnormity — Epic poetry — Two types: Itihāsa and Kāvya — Mahābhārata and Rāmāyaṇa — Kālidāsa's two court epics — Bhāravi — Māgha — Lyrical poetry — The Meghadūta — The Drama: its origin and characteristics — Probably an established institution by 200 A.D. — The lost plays of Bhāsa — Thirteen plays recently published in Malabar attributed to him — The evidence for this insufficient — Kālidāsa's three dramas — Relation of Śūdraka's Mṛcchakaṭikā to the Cārudatta — Śrīharṣa's three plays — Bhavabhūti's plays — Bhaṭṭa-nārāyaṇa's Venīsaṃhāra — Viśākhadatta's Mudrā-rākṣasa — Rājaśekhara's mastery of both Sanskrit and Prākrit — Hanuman-nāṭaka — The allegorical play Prabodha-candrodaya — Modern dramas — Selected bibliography.

In the period of about a thousand years beginning with the Christian era the civilization of India, in its two main characteristics of the caste system and the belief in the transmigration of souls, was only a continuation of its preceding phase, but in the more widespread and intensified form that has held the Hindus in its grip down to the present day. There are also two other social institutions which developed during this period in India. The first, a custom dating from prehistoric times, which having hardly survived in the Vedic Age except in a symbolic funeral rite,

15. HINDU GATEWAY AT VADNAGAR, GUJARĀT

revived, for some reason that is not quite clear, to such an extent that by about 600 A.D. it seems to have become universal, and would still be prevailing in India had it not been suppressed by the British Government in 1829. This was the practice of the self-immolation of widows, on the death of their husbands, called *satī* ('virtuous woman') in Sanskrit. It may have been one of the economic effects of the caste system. The other, child-marriage, the growth of which was undoubtedly due to the increasing difficulty of securing suitable husbands belonging to the same caste as the daughter, is down to this day a characteristic of Hindu civilization. In 1921 the average age of marriage in Bengal was about twelve and a half for girls and rather under twenty for men.

The literary language of this period, Sanskrit, remained the same as in the preceding phase, for it had been stereotyped by the grammar of Pāṇini, as we have seen, at least as early as the fourth century B.C. But though the growth of grammatical forms was thus arrested, the vocabulary of the language could not in a similar way be prevented from being modified. The same remark applies to style. Compared with the relatively advanced prose of the Brāhmaṇas, Sanskrit literature, in which prose is rare, shows no progress in this later period, for it is still crude and clumsy. Its style, however, betrays some change. For it is much more artificial in consequence of the frequent use of long compounds and of the elaborate rules of poetics to which it is subjected. The bulk of Sanskrit literature, which is now poetry, especially the epics, is written in the Śloka metre, consisting of iambically-ending couplets of two lines of sixteen syllables. The other metres used, though mostly based on Vedic prototypes, are much more rigid in their construction.

The most striking difference between Vedic and Sanskrit literature is that the former is essentially religious, the latter, with few exceptions, profane.

Though the literature of this period is almost entirely secular, it reflects the religion of the period so fully that its character can be judged clearly enough. We can see that it has become very different from that of the Vedic Age. The three gods Brahmā, Vishṇu, and Śiva are the leading deities of the pantheon, while the great gods of the Veda have sunk to a lower level, though Indra is still prominent as the chief deity of the warrior caste. New gods of a lesser order have come into being: such as Kubera, god of riches; Gaṇeśa and Kārttikeya, sons of Śiva, respectively god of learning and of war; Lakshmī, goddess of beauty and of fortune; Durgā, the terrible spouse of Śiva; besides various serpent deities. While the outlook of the Vedas is joyous and optimistic, that of Sanskrit literature is tinged with melancholy and pessimism, which no doubt resulted from the now universally accepted doctrine of transmigration and *karma*. To this is most probably due the elaboration of Vishṇu's Avatārs, which in several cases appear in an animal form to save mankind from calamity.

This main phase of Indian religion, usually called Hinduism, did not begin to express itself in the form of architecture and sculpture till Buddhism was already showing signs of decay. I have already indicated that the Buddhists were the first Indian builders and carvers in stone, though their religion was an offshoot of the much older Brahmin faith. It is only on Buddhist monuments that we find the earliest representations of Hindu deities, such as Indra and Lakshmī, from the second century B.C. onwards. The most ancient remains of independent Hindu religious art, architectural or sculptural, date only from several centuries after

16. MONOLITH VIHĀRA AT MĀMALLAPURAṂ ('SEVEN PAGODAS'), MADRAS PRESIDENCY

17. 'SEVEN PAGODAS' MONOLITH TEMPLES, MADRAS PRESIDENCY

the beginning of our era. These considerations justify the presumption that Hindu religious art is derived from that of the Buddhists. Such a presumption is borne out by the fact that the earliest extant Hindu temples are practically identical in form with the latest Buddhist specimens, differing from them only in having the image of a Hindu deity, instead of one of Buddha, placed in the shrine. Again, some of the sculptures in the earliest Hindu cave temples at Ellora are hardly distinguishable from those of the latest Buddhist specimens at that place. Though the whole surface of India is covered with Hindu temples, the vast majority are modern or comparatively modern. The oldest examples of Hindu architecture date from the sixth century A.D., and the best of them belong to the period between then and the thirteenth A.D. An historical study of these monuments enables us to distinguish clearly between two styles, each of which exhibits a definite type from the beginning. The geographical distribution of these two types is interesting, for the southern or Dravidian style is found only within the tropics, or south of the twenty-third degree of northern latitude. The northern or Indo-Aryan style, on the other hand, appears practically only north of that line. Historical study, moreover, shows that the Hindu temples of both styles are developments of Buddhist prototypes. But the remarkable thing is that they are respectively the descendants of two entirely distinct classes of Buddhist building.

For it can be shown that the Hindu Dravidian temple has been evolved from the Buddhist monastery (*vihāra*), while the Indo-Aryan type has been derived from the Buddhist *stūpa*.

a. *The Dravidian Style*

The earliest representative of this type is a monolith temple at Mahābalipur, one of the seven Pagodas situated near the seashore, 35 miles south of Madras.

It is hewn out of a single block of granite, dating from about 600 A.D. It is clearly Brahmanic in origin, as is shown by its sculptures as well as its inscriptions. It is also a model of a Buddhist monastery of four stories. The plan is square, the pyramidal tower representing the upper stories that contained the cells of the monks. A short way off is a structural shrine on the very brink of the sea.

The design of the regular Dravidian temple is a square base ornamented externally with pilasters and containing the cell that holds the image. Over the shrine rises the *śikhara*, a pyramidal tower always divided into stories, a division that never disappears in Dravidian temples. The tower is crowned with a small dome, either circular or octagonal in shape.

An early rock-cut temple of this kind on a grand scale is the Kailāsa at Ellora, dedicated to Śiva and dating from the eighth century A.D. A monolith on an enormous scale, it constitutes one of the wonders of the world. It is the culmination of the art of rock-cutting in India.

The later Dravidian temples from about 1000 A.D. stand in a large court surrounded by an enclosing wall. A special feature of this later type is the *gopuram*, or great gateway in the enclosing wall opposite the shrine. It has a storied tower resembling that of the shrine itself; but it is oblong, not square in shape, being twice as wide as it is deep. The best specimen of this later style is the temple at Tanjore, erected in 1025 A.D. The body consists of two

18. RAFT TANK, MADURA

19. DRAVIDIAN HINDU TEMPLE AT TANJORE

stories about 80 feet high, while the pyramidal tower rises in eleven stories to a total height of 190 feet.

To each of the great Dravidian temples is attached a large tank for the religious ablutions of the worshippers. Such sacred tanks not within the temple area are frequent in southern India. These are called *teppa kulam* or raft tanks, across which at certain festivals the image of the god is taken on a raft to the shrine in the middle.

The Dravidian temple at Halebīd, left unfinished in 1270 A. D., is one of the most remarkable monuments in India, being unmatched for the variety of detail and the exuberance of fancy in its ornamentation. There is perhaps no other temple in the world on the external carving of which such a marvellous amount of labour has been spent. Thus the lowest band of the frieze surrounding it contains a procession of about 2,000 elephants, no two of which exactly resemble one another.

b. The Indo-Aryan Style

The essential parts of the Indo-Aryan temple are the rectangular cell containing the image or symbol of the god, and a curvilinear steeple with vertical ribs by which it is surmounted. A porch is generally added in front of the doorway to the cell, but this is not essential.

The temple represented opposite page 84 is well adapted to throw light on the origin of the Indo-Aryan style. Among the earliest of the northern type are some of the temples in the large group at Bhuvaneśvara in Orissa, about 250 miles south of Calcutta. The older specimens seem to date from about 800 A. D., the series coming down to about 1300 A. D. The early form of this type is best represented by the Mukteśvara shrine, which is called by Fergusson 'the gem of Orissan art'.

The origin of the Indo-Aryan spire has always been a puzzle to Eastern archaeologists. Thus Fergusson remarks: 'Neither the pyramid nor the tumulus affords any suggestion as to the origin of the form, nor the tower, either square or circular; nor does any form of civil or domestic architecture. It does not seem to be derived from any of these.' My own view that this spire has been evolved from the *stūpa* cannot be elaborated here, because too many illustrations would be required to substantiate this theory. A comparison of the few illustrations here given must suffice in corroboration.

A somewhat analogous evolution of the Buddhist *stūpa* can be followed outside the bounds of India.

In the sculptural representation of the Hindu gods a remarkable innovation took place by the end of the first Christian century. Before that time they appeared in ordinary human form with two arms and one head in Buddhist sculpture. Literary and numismatic evidence further combine to indicate that down to the first century A.D. the gods were regarded as normally human in appearance.

Now the epic and classical Sanskrit literature after the beginning of our era describe the most important gods as having four arms and one of them four heads also. The same abnormality appears in early Hindu sculpture and remains a divine characteristic ever afterwards. This feature is most conspicuous in the three leading gods Brahmā, Vishṇu, and Śiva. All three are represented with four arms, which hold the symbols distinctive of each. It is characteristic of Brahmā to have four heads as well, for in Sanskrit literature he regularly bears the epithet 'four-faced'. It is of Śiva, however, that we have the earliest concrete representation with four arms. The evidence of coins is here able to show, within the narrow limits of half a century,

20. INDO-ARYAN HINDU TEMPLE, BANKURA DISTRICT

21. INDO-ARYAN TEMPLES AT BHUVANESVAR, ORISSA

when this innovation arose. On a coin of the Gracco-Indian king Kadphises II, dating from about 50 A. D., Śiva still appears as a two-armed deity ; but in the reigns of his successors Kaniṣka, Huviṣka, and Vāsudeva, four-armed gods become common beside two-armed examples, though the latter still continue to appear on coins till about 200 A. D. We are thus justified in asserting that four-armed gods appear on coins from about 100 A. D. onwards, and that they had become an established type by 200 A. D. The first step in this innovation was the addition of two extra arms rising from the back of the shoulders. The four-armed type having once been established as a divine characteristic, the number of arms was gradually increased in Indian iconography. Thus eight-armed figures occur at least as early as 600 A. D. From the eighth century onwards Vishṇu occasionally has eight arms, and some of his Avatārs more than four. Śiva also has eight and, as a dancing figure, sixteen arms. Though Hindu deities appear in the Buddhist sculptures of Gandhāra in normal human form only, the influence of the many-headed Hindu type made itself felt in the latest centuries of Mahāyāna Buddhist sculpture in India. The figures of the Bodhisattva Avalokiteśvara are found with four or six arms, and even eleven heads. This feature followed Mahāyānist Buddhism from India to other countries. Thus in Chinese Buddhist temples there appears a goddess with sixteen arms. This abnormality, however, does not seem ever to have extended to the figure of Buddha himself anywhere, probably because his image had early acquired a stereotyped character.

As the Indian gods originally lacked individuality, the early artist employed two means of differentiating them in sculpture. One was the addition of the *vāhana*, or animal conveying the deity, as the elephant on which Indra rides.

It is noteworthy that in all such cases the deity has only one head and only two arms; for the *vāhana* serves to indicate both the divine nature and the identity of the deity. The second means of identification was the possession of many arms and heads, besides the holding of characteristic symbols. When the Indian artist found it necessary to omit the *vāhana*, how was he to meet the difficulty when the two hands of the deity, being engaged in some kind of action or gesture, could not hold any symbol of identity? The addition of two extra arms might easily occur to him as an expedient, for this is obviously their purpose in Indian iconography. The addition would, moreover, be no new idea, but merely the concrete expression of a Vedic figure of speech. Though the gods are normally regarded in the *Ṛigveda* as one-headed and two-armed, they are yet occasionally referred to figuratively as having an abnormal number of heads and arms. Thus Agni is said to be three-headed, obviously because the sacrificial fire burns on three altars; and Viśvakarmā is four-armed (*viśvato-bāhu* 'with an arm on every side'). The further divine characteristic of having four heads was added in the case of Brahmā because his Vedic prototype Viśvakarmā is in the *Ṛigveda* described as 'facing in all directions' (*viśvato-mukha*), and in post-Vedic literature as 'four-faced' (*catur-mukha*). Hence Brahmā always appears in sculpture with four heads as well as four arms. The above considerations show that what is usually thought a monstrous feature of Hindu iconography is the natural outcome of an inherent necessity requiring the expression in sculpture of the divine character in general and the individuality in particular when the gods were represented in concrete form.[1]

[1] Cp. Macdonell, *History of Hindu Iconography*, in Gangoli's *Rūpam* (Calcutta), October, 1920.

22. INDO-ARYAN VIŚVANĀTH TEMPLE AT KHAJURAHO
Chattarpur State, Central India

23. Group of Indo-Aryan Hindu temples at Bhuvanesvar, Orissa

24. Indo-Aryan Hindu temple at Khajuraho, Chattarpur State, Central India

The products of Sanskrit literature, which are many-sided, may be divided into six groups: epic, lyric, dramatic, sententious or didactic, narrative, and scientific. The beginnings of all of them may be traced back to the preceding era of Sanskrit, but the earliest extant forms of at least the first five groups do not appear till after the commencement of our era. We have seen that as an actual fact the rich Pāli literature of Buddhism arose in earlier centuries. The most ancient type of Sanskrit poetry in the shape of epic tales must have grown up in the preceding age also. Even in the *Ṛigveda* there are some hymns of a narrative character. Later, in the Brāhmaṇas, several short legends appear, some of them partly metrical, as the story of Śunaḥśepa in the *Aitareya Brāhmaṇa*. The etymological work of Yāska, the *Nirukta*, written in Classical Sanskrit about 500 B. C., contains many prose tales; and the earliest extant collection of Vedic legends, the metrical *Bṛhaddevatā*, must be nearly as old.

a. *Epic Poetry*

But the epics, in the form in which they have come down to us, date from after the beginning of the Christian era. Two classes of Sanskrit epic poetry must be distinguished. The first type, the language of which is simpler and conforms less to the strict rules of grammar, and the character of which is freer and of more spontaneous growth, is called *itihāsa*, 'story', or *purāṇa*, 'ancient legend'. The second, more regular in language and style, is termed *kāvya*, 'poetical composition', representing a more artificial class, strictly subject to the rules of grammar and poetics, and the work of an individual poet. By far the most important as well as the oldest representative of the former class is the vast epic called *Mahābhārata*, 'the great Bhārata story'.

The group of eighteen Purāṇas, or 'ancient legendary poems', are similar in style, but much later in date. The earliest representative of the artificial class is the other great Sanskrit epic, the *Rāmāyaṇa*, 'the adventures of Rāma'. This type of epic reached its culmination under Kālidāsa, about the beginning of the fifth century A. D.

The *Mahābhārata* is a vast poem containing about 100,000 couplets, equivalent to about eight times the length of the Homeric poems. There is inscriptional evidence that it had attained that aggregate bulk by about 400 A. D. Its epic kernel, amounting to about one-fifth of the whole work, became so much overgrown with didactic matter that it could hardly be regarded as an epic at all, and has rather taken the place of a moral encyclopaedia in Indian literature.

It consists of eighteen books called *parvan*, to which is added as a supplement a nineteenth named the *Harivaṃśa*. For this immense congeries of epic and didactic matter tradition invented as the name of its author the designation Vyāsa ('arranger').

Though three main editions of this great epic have been printed in India, at Calcutta, Bombay, and Madras respectively, no critical edition has yet appeared. Much uncertainty prevails as to the authenticity of the text because research has proved that it has undergone numerous changes, additions, and omissions. The readings of the Northern and the Southern manuscripts are widely divergent, and even within these two groups many differences appear. In the former group, again, at least five varying recensions have been distinguished, and in the southern group the divergences may prove to be still greater. The need of a critical edition is therefore evidently a pressing one. A considerable amount of preliminary work on the manuscript material has already been done, but whether a single text representing

25. OLD INDO-ARYAN TEMPLE, GUJARĀT

26. BRAHMANYA (KARTTIKEYA), GOD OF WAR (*see p. 86*)

Perur, Coimbatore, Madras

what the epic was about 400 A. D. can be produced is very doubtful. Inscriptions of the fifth century A. D. prove that the epic had the same length and character (i. e. was regarded as a *dharma-śāstra* or 'compendium of ethics') in that century as it has now.

The epic nucleus of the *Mahābhārata*, comprising about 20,000 couplets, relates how the dynasty of the Kurus was overthrown by the Pāṇḍus. The king of the Kurus in a gambling match cheats the Pāṇḍus, robs them of their kingdom, and banishes them for nineteen years. Finally a great battle lasting eighteen days takes place, when the Kurus are annihilated.

The main story is constantly interrupted by lengthy disquisitions, philosophical, religious, and moral, one of them extending to no fewer than 20,000 couplets. There are also several narrative episodes. One of the oldest and most beautiful of these is the story of Nala and Damayantī, two lovers who after enjoying several years of happy married life become separated by misfortune, but after many trying adventures are reunited in the end. The story contains numerous fine and pathetic passages. The emaciation and grief-stricken plight of Damayantī, as she wanders alone in the forest, is described as follows.. She appears

Like the young moon's slender crescent
Obscured by black clouds in the sky;
Like the lotus-flower uprooted,
All parched and withered by the sun;
Like the pallid night when Rāhu[1]
Has swallowed up the darkened moon.[2]

The most famous of the philosophical episodes of the *Mahābhārata* is the *Bhagavad-gītā*, the 'Song of the

[1] The demon of eclipse.

[2] As translated by the author in *The History of Sanskrit Literature*, London, 1900.

Adorable One'. It is one of the most important works of Sanskrit literature. It is introduced at the point where the rival armies confront each other, ready to begin the great battle. Arjuna, the leader of the Pāṇḍus, hesitates to fight against his kinsmen. Kṛishṇa, who, being an incarnation of Vishṇu, acts as his charioteer, puts an end to his scruples by showing that action, as the performance of one's duty in the world, is necessary, though in the end concentration on the supreme spirit is the only way to secure salvation. There is no evidence showing when this episode was incorporated in the epic, and who was its author.

The stages by which the epic developed from its original germ till it reached its final encyclopaedic form are matter of conjecture. It is, however, not improbable that it had assumed the character of a didactic compendium before the beginning of our era.

Essentially related to the *Mahābhārata* is a group of legendary works called Purāṇas, of which there are eighteen. Deriving their subject-matter from the epics, the earliest of them cannot be older than the sixth century A.D. They are didactic religious sectarian manuals inculcating the worship chiefly of Vishṇu, though some of them are associated with Śiva. They deal mostly with cosmogony, the genealogy of the gods and patriarchs, and the history of royal dynasties. In that part of their matter which is peculiar to them they agree so closely that they must go back to some older work as a common source. The *Bhāgavata Purāṇa*, which contains about 18,000 ślokas and derives its name from being a glorification of Bhāgavata or Vishṇu, has exercised a more powerful influence in India than any other poetical work of this type.

Beside the *Mahābhārata* arose a second epic cycle, the *Rāmāyaṇa*, which is not popular in character, but artificial, both in the style of its descriptions and in the use of poetical figures. It is the forerunner of the later Court epics which are called Kāvyas as a class. The *Rāmāyaṇa* relates the adventures of Rāma, son of Daśaratha, king of Ayodhyā (now Oudh). It consists of about 24,000 couplets and is divided into seven books. It has been shown to have originally consisted of five books (ii–vi), in which some interpolated passages occur as well. Apart from interpolations this epic is the work of a single poet named Vālmīki. The plot consists of two distinct elements, the first of which has every appearance of being based on historical tradition. The foundation of the second is mythological; for it is full of marvellous and fantastic incidents, and the main figures are traceable in Vedic literature. The original epic, as composed by the poet Vālmīki, was transformed, by the addition of the first and last books, into a poem glorifying Vishṇu, of whom Rāma is represented as an incarnation. This identification has turned the hero of the epic into an object of lasting worship among the Hindus, and has secured to the *Rāmāyaṇa* a greater popularity in India than probably any other product of Sanskrit literature. Its story has furnished the subject of many other Sanskrit poems as well as plays. It has also been translated into many Indian vernaculars. The most important adaptation is the Hindī version of Tulasī Dās (1532–1623), the greatest poet of medieval Hindustān; for it is a kind of bible to nearly 100,000,000 of the people of northern India.

As the *Mahābhārata* was the chief source of the Purāṇas, so the *Rāmāyaṇa* became the model of a number of Court epics almost all of which belong to the period between 400 and 1100 A.D. From the direct evidence of a dated inscription and of the poet Bāṇa, who lived under King

Harshavardhana, the ruler of the whole of northern India from 606 to 648 A.D., we know that Kālidāsa and other famous classical poets flourished before 600 A.D. There is, moreover, some valuable literary and epigraphical evidence that this type of poetry originated not later than about 200 B.C. and continued to be cultivated during the succeeding centuries. The earliest preserved of the post-Christian Kāvyas is the *Buddha-carita*, 'Life of Buddha', by Aśvaghosha, one of the oldest Buddhist works in Sanskrit, belonging to the end of the second century A.D.

As to Kālidāsa, the most famous poet of India, we have good reason to believe that he flourished in the first half of the fifth century. His knowledge of Greek astronomy in any case indicates that he cannot have lived earlier than 300 A.D. His two Court epics are the *Raghu-vaṃśa*, 'the Race of Raghu', and the *Kumāra-sambhava*, 'the Birth of the War-god'. The former describes the life of Rāma, besides giving an account of his forefathers and successors. It contains much genuine poetry. The style, though still comparatively simple, is in many passages too artificial for the western taste. As nearly one-half of the *Kumāra-sambhava* is concerned with the courtship and wedding of the god Śiva and the goddess Pārvatī, the parents of the youthful divinity, description is its prevailing characteristic. Both in originality of treatment and beauty of style and thought, these two epics are superior to later works of this type.

The subjects of these later poems are derived from the two great epics. Intermingled with lyric, erotic, and didactic elements, they become more artificial the further they are removed from Kālidāsa's time.

The *Kirātārjunīya* by Bhāravi, who lived not later than the sixth century A.D., is a poem describing a combat between Śiva, disguised as a *Kirāta* or mountaineer, and Arjuna.

One of its cantos includes a number of stanzas illustrating various kinds of verbal tricks. One stanza, for instance, contains no consonant but *n*, except a single *t* at the end.

Another artificial epic, the *Bhaṭṭi-kāvya*, ascribed to the poet and grammarian Bhartṛihari, who died in 651 A.D., relates the story of Rāma, with the sole object of illustrating the forms of Sanskrit grammar.

The *Śiśupāla-vadha*, or 'Death of Śiśupāla', by the poet Māgha, dates from the second half of the seventh century. One of its cantos teems with metrical puzzles, some of a highly complex character. Thus one stanza read backwards is identical with the preceding one read in the ordinary way. This work, nevertheless, does not lack poetical beauties and striking thoughts.

The *Nalodaya*, or 'Rise of Nala', dealing with a well-known episode (p. 89) of the *Mahābhārata*, describes the restoration to power of King Nala. The chief aim of the author is to display his skill in manipulating artificial metres and elaborate tricks of style. The exiguous narrative running through the poem is interrupted by long descriptions and lyrical effusions. The most noteworthy feature of this work is the introduction of rime, which is employed not only at the end, but in the middle of metrical lines. This is an innovation in Sanskrit poetry shared by the *Gīta-govinda* and the *Moha-mudgara* mentioned below (p. 96). This novel feature is probably due to Prākrit influence; for rime was an essential element of versification in Prākrit, as it is of modern Indian vernaculars.

The culmination of artificial ingenuity is the *Rāghava-pāṇḍavīya*, an epic composed about 800 A.D. by a poet named Kavirāja. By the use of ambiguous words and phrases the story of the *Rāmāyaṇa* and that of the *Mahābhārata* are here related at one and the same time.

b. *Lyrical Poetry*

This branch of Sanskrit literature must have arisen in the early centuries of our era, for a specimen of its fully developed form has been preserved from the early fifth century in Kālidāsa's *Meghadūta*, or 'Cloud Messenger'. It consists of some 112 stanzas of four lines and is composed in a metre of seventeen syllables to the line called *mandākrāntā* ('advancing slowly'). The theme is a message which an exile in central India sends by a cloud to his wife in the Himālayas. The sight of a dark cloud moving northward at the approach of the rainy season fills him with yearning and suggests the thought of entrusting to this aerial envoy a message of hope to his wife in his mountain home. In the first half of the poem the exile delineates with much power and charm the various scenes to be traversed by the cloud on its northward course. In the second half he describes the beauties of his home on mount Kailāsa, and then the loveliness, the occupations, and the grief of his wife. The following is a stanza of his message:

In creepers I discern thy form; in eyes of startled hinds thy glances;
And in the moon thy lovely face; in peacock's plumes thy shining tresses;
The sportive frown upon thy brow in flowing waters' tiny ripples:
But never in one place combined can I, alas! behold thy likeness.

But looking forward to their reunion he adds:

And then we will our heart's desire, grown more intense by separation,
Enjoy in nights all glorious and bright with full-orbed autumn moonlight.[1]

[1] Quoted in Macdonell, *History of Sanskrit Literature*, p. 335.

There is another beautiful lyrical poem entitled *Ṛtu-saṃhāra*, or 'Cycle of the Seasons', consisting of 153 stanzas divided into six cantos and composed in various metres. It is a highly poetical description of the six seasons into which the Indian year is divided by Sanskrit poets. By introducing love-scenes the author skilfully combines the expression of human emotions with glowing accounts of the beauties of nature. Perhaps no other Sanskrit poem manifests such strikingly deep sympathy with the physical world, keen powers of observation, and skill in depicting an Indian landscape in vivid colours. This poem is attributed to Kālidāsa, and, judged by its merits, such an ascription might very well be correct. The poem also seems to belong to the age of Kālidāsa. But the fact that the *Ṛtusaṃhāra* is never quoted in the Sanskrit works on poetics weighs heavily against its attribution to Kālidāsa.

There are two other lyrics, the *Caura-pañcāśikā* and the *Ghaṭa-karpara*, comprising respectively fifty and twenty-two stanzas, but otherwise much of this type of literature is found in the dramas. The greater part of Sanskrit lyrical poetry appears in the form of single stanzas in which an amatory situation or sentiment is drawn with a few strokes and often by a master hand. Several poets composed collections of these miniature lyrics, which frequently display great wealth of illustration and depth of feeling. The most distinguished poet of this type is Bhartṛihari, who lived in the first half of the seventh century A.D. (p. 96). His *Śṛṅgāra-śataka*, or 'Hundred Stanzas of Love', shows him, in graceful and meditative verse, to be fully susceptible to the charms of women and well acquainted with the arts by which they captivate the hearts of men. The most important collection of love-lyrics is the *Amaru-śataka*, or 'Hundred Stanzas of Amaru'. The author is a master in the art of painting lovers in all their moods—bliss and dejection, anger and devotion. His main strength perhaps lies in depicting the various stages of estrangement and reconciliation. The love that Amaru, like other Indian lyrists, delineates is undoubtedly of the sensual type, not the romantic and ideal. Delicacy of feeling and refinement of thought are, however, not lacking in this poetry. The plant and animal world, which here plays an important part, is treated with much charm.

The following stanza from Bhartṛihari may serve as an example of Indian lyric poetry.

> Beside the lamp, the flaming hearth,
> In light of sun or moon and stars,
> Without my loved one's lustrous eyes
> This world is wholly dark to me.[1]

The transition from pure lyric to pure drama is represented in form, though not chronologically (for it dates from the twelfth century A.D.), by the *Gīta-govinda*, or 'Cowherd in Song'. It is the earliest literary specimen of a primitive type of play that still survives in Bengal, and must have preceded the developed drama. There is no dialogue in the proper sense, for each of the three characters merely engages in a kind of lyrical monologue, to which one of the other two is generally supposed to listen. The subject is the love of Kṛishṇa for the beautiful Rādhā, their estrangement, and final reconciliation. It is a highly artificial poem in which its author Jayadeva shows great perfection of form by combining grace of diction with ease in handling the most intricate metres. He makes much use of alliteration and very complex rimes, adapting, with unsurpassable skill, the most varied and melodious measures

[1] Quoted in Macdonell, *History of Sanskrit Literature*, p. 341.

to the expression of exuberant erotic emotions. This poem brings us to the regular Sanskrit drama, which is a combination of lyric stanzas and prose dialogue.

c. *The Drama*

The origin of the acted drama of India is wrapped in obscurity. Even as early as the *Ṛigveda*, dialogue is the form of some of its hymns. But between these and the actual Sanskrit plays that have come to us, to none of which can an earlier date than 200 A.D. be assigned, the gap is enormous. Nor is there any direct evidence of any connexion between the two. The indirect testimony of language, however, furnishes a clue as to the source of the Sanskrit drama. The Sanskrit words for 'actor' and 'play' are *naṭa* and *nāṭaka* respectively. These are Prākrit derivatives of the root *naṭ*, the vernacular form of the Sanskrit *nṛt*, 'to dance', and familiar to English ears in the guise of 'nautch', as the performance of professional female dancers in India. These names, as vernacular words and because of their meanings, suggest that the Indian drama was popular in origin, and that some rude form of pantomime was its starting-point. Pāṇini, in the fourth century B.C., speaks of *naṭas*, or 'dancers', and mentions *naṭa-sūtras*, or 'handbooks for dancers'. The contents were later utilized by Bharata in a larger treatise entitled *Nāṭya-śāstra*, or 'Principles of the Dramatic art', the age of which cannot be fixed with certainty, but which may possibly date from as early as 200 B.C. It deals with all that concerns the drama: singing, music, dancing, metre, the use of different dialects, and so on. All later works on the drama are based on Bharata's treatise. The most important of these is the *Daśa-rūpa*, or 'the Ten kinds (of drama)', which deals with drama in the narrow sense and was composed by Dhanaṃjaya in the tenth century A.D.

As regards the ultimate source of the Indian drama, various scholars are inclined to find it in several hymns of the *Ṛigveda*, which, being unconnected with the ritual, are of a narrative character and sometimes appear in the form of a dialogue. This inference is *a priori* possible, but there is no evidence to prove that such a development actually took place. Other scholars trace the origin of the Indian drama to the influence of the Greeks. They argue that at the time of Alexander the Great's invasion of India (326 B.C.) numerous Greek artists accompanied his expedition, and that subsequently the frontier countries of India were ruled by Greek kings, who must have supported Greek theatres. But there are no ascertained facts to substantiate this theory; nor is it necessary to explain the existence of the Indian drama in this way. For its whole development can be satisfactorily accounted for by Indian antecedents. Indian plays are throughout not very dramatic in style. The delineation of character is weak, being concerned rather with types than with human beings of real flesh and blood. The development of the story often depends on an external accident such as a curse, and the plot itself is often nothing more than a loosely connected series of pictures or epic scenes. The Greek theory is chiefly based on the *Mṛcchakaṭikā*; but the earliest Indian plays that have survived are of quite a different kind, and have no resemblance to the Greek drama. It is true that one of the names of the curtain (*yavanikā*, i.e. 'Ionian') is the 'Greek (appliance)'; but it is more likely that the whole stage or the drama itself should have been designated by 'Greek', if the latter had been introduced from a foreign country. Not only does the Greek theory err in overlooking the earliest Indian dramatic productions, but the chief class of the Indian drama, called *nāṭaka*, bears no similarity to the Greek mime. The most likely explanation is that the Indian drama derives its origin from scenes of an histrionic and a popular character which are imitated in the Vedic ritual; as when a Brahmin buys Soma from a Śūdra, who is then driven out with sticks. Such scenes of horseplay would be accompanied by dance, song, and music, which are designated as the most important elements of the dramatic art (*nāṭya*). It is also noteworthy that the ordinary words for 'actor', 'play', and 'dramatic art' are, as has already been said, derived from the vernacular root *naṭ* 'to dance'. The mimic dance becomes drama as soon as words are added. We know from the ritual Vedic texts that dance, music, and song were employed at sacrifices and religious festivals. We are informed that on such occasions the *naṭas* celebrated the performance in song; that they occasionally composed the accompanying words and sometimes produced much laughter. This points to the existence of actual mimes. The use in this way of popular artists naturally led to their art being systematically treated in handbooks. Some light is further shed on the development of the drama by a number of modern plays and by the so-called *yātrās*, which represent a mythological subject and especially the Kṛishṇa legend. Several features of the regular plays indicate that a popular pantomime was a preliminary aspect of the Indian drama: the dialogue between the stage-manager and actress at the beginning of the play; the employment of different dialects; the mixture of prose and lyrics; the combination of dance and music; the simplicity of the stage; and the retention of the jester (*vidūṣaka*). The great antiquity of these Indian phenomena excludes a Greek origin. It was at one time believed by Sanskrit scholars that Patañjali (second century B.C.) in his *Mahābhāṣya*, a commentary on Pāṇini's grammar, mentions the existence of an actual Indian drama, but as the passage in which this was supposed to be stated has been proved to be mistranslated, it has no chronological value in this question.

The rise of the Indian drama is thus most probably due to the coalescence of recited epic legend with ancient pantomimic art. But we know nothing of the history of the actual drama till we come across it fully developed about 200 A.D. It probably arose in the land of the Śūrasenas at Mathurā, their capital. We have no reason to suppose that it came into being more than a century before the time of Aśvaghosha.

The main characteristics of the Sanskrit drama are these. Lyrical stanzas, composed in various metres, interchange with prose dialogue. In *Śakuntalā* the former comprise about one-half of the whole play. The prose of the dialogue is often very commonplace, serving only to introduce the lofty sentiment of the following lyric. Sanskrit plays consequently appear deficient in action when compared with European dramas. A further peculiarity is that they employ different dialects according to the social position of the speakers. Sanskrit is used by heroes, kings, Brahmins, and men of rank. Prākrit (*Śaurasenī*, *Māhārāṣṭrī*, *Māgadhī*) is spoken not only by women, but by men of the lower orders. Tragedy is unknown on the Indian stage. No deeply tragical incident, such as death, may take place on it, nor is there ever a sad ending. Hence terror, pity, and grief are always assuaged by the happy conclusion of the story. The plot is commonly derived from history or epic legend. The main theme of most Indian plays is love. The hero, who is usually a king and already married to one or more wives, falls in love at first sight with some beautiful girl. The heroine reciprocates his love, but conceals her passion. The ensuing doubts and delays plunge both into a state of melancholy and despair. The depressing effect produced by their doleful plight is counteracted by the lively activity of the heroine's confidantes and especially of the jester (*vidūṣaka*), who usually plays a prominent part as the constant companion of the hero. Finally all ends happily.

The structure of a Sanskrit play is this. It is divided into acts which vary in number according to its character. The act is divided into scenes, which are marked off by the entrance of one character and the exit of another. The stage is never left vacant, and the locality remains the same till the end of the act. The play usually opens with a prologue on the stage, where the manager and one or two of the actors converse about the piece that is to follow. Goethe adopted this feature from Kālidāsa's *Śakuntalā* in his *Faust*.

A necessary part of the stage arrangement was a curtain, divided in the middle, which did not separate the audience from the stage, but formed its background. Behind the curtain was the tiring room, whence the actors entered the stage. The scenery and decorations being very simple, much was left to the imagination of the spectator, as in the Shakespearian drama. Owing to intercourse between heaven and earth being frequently represented, there was, however, probably some kind of contrivance suggesting an aerial car, in which the impression of motion and speed would be produced by the gestures of the actors.

We do not know when the first actual play was written in India. But the earliest dramatic author of whose work anything has survived is Aśvaghosha, the famous Buddhist teacher of the Mahāyāna school. He wrote at least one drama, the *Sāriputra-prakaraṇa.* It is divided into nine acts, its subject being the conversion of the two chief pupils of Buddha, Sāriputra and Maudgalyāyana. Manuscript fragments of this drama, which go back to Kuṣaṇa times (*c.* 100 A. D.), have been found at Turfan in Central Asia, and have been edited. Certain features, such as the figure of the *vidūṣaka* or jester, indicate that the author had predecessors. It does not, however, seem likely that the drama had a long history before Aśvaghosha. As he was, according to tradition, a teacher of King Kaṇishka (125), Aśvaghosha has been assigned to the second century A. D. Fragments of two other Buddhist dramas have been found in the same region of Chinese Turkistān and appear on palaeographic grounds to belong to the same period; but there is no evidence showing who wrote them. A Sanskrit Buddhist work, the *Avadānā-śataka* (p. 63), which was translated into Chinese in the third century A. D., mentions a Buddhist drama acted by South Indian players before the king of Sobhāvatī. There thus seems good reason to believe that by 200 A. D. the Sanskrit drama was an established institution.

The best surviving specimens of the Sanskrit drama produced between *c.* 200 and 800 A.D. number nearly a dozen. The greatest playwright was Kālidāsa, who cannot have lived earlier than about 400 A. D. He had a famous predecessor named Bhāsa, whose works were, however, till recently regarded as lost long ago. The evidence for the existence of this ancient poet is the following. Kālidāsa (*c.* 400 A. D.) in his drama *Mālavikāgnimitra* mentions Bhāsa as a poet whose fame he cannot rival. Bāṇa, in the introduction to his historical romance *Harṣa-carita* (*c.* 620 A. D.), states that Bhāsa obtained fame by plays (*nāṭaka*) in the beginning of which the *sūtradhāra*, or stage manager, appeared. A verse of Rājaśekhara (*c.* 1000 A.D.) mentions a *svapna-vāsavadatta*, or 'Dream-Vāsavadattā', as Bhāsa's work, which, being thrown into the fire as a test of its merit, stood the test successfully. In the *Gaüḍavaho*, or 'Death of Garuḍa', by the Prākrit poet Vākpatirāja (*c.* 750 A.D.), Bhāsa receives the designation *jalaṇa-mitta*, or 'friend of conflagration', perhaps in allusion to the same incident. We have thus four references in Sanskrit and Prākrit literature up to 1000 A.D. proving the existence of Bhāsa as an eminent dramatic poet. There also occur in his commentary, on a rhetorical work entitled *Dhvanyāloka*, by Abhinavagupta (*c.* 1000 A.D.) and in the Sanskrit anthologies of later centuries about a dozen quotations there attributed to Bhāsa.

Some fourteen years ago (1912) there were published in southern Malabar, at Trivandrum, thirteen Sanskrit plays that were by the editor, followed by most Sanskrit scholars, identified with the long lost works of Bhāsa. The sole basis of this far-reaching identification is that, although all these plays are anonymous, the title of a single one of them, *svapna-nāṭaka* (in one manuscript entitled *svapna-vāsavadatta*), may be the same as that of the only play, *svapna-vāsavadatta*, twice mentioned by ancient authorities as the work of Bhāsa. The uncertainty as to the same play being meant by the divergent titles is increased by the fact that a verse quoted by Abhinavagupta on the *Dhvanyāloka* as occurring in the *svapna-vāsavadatta* is not to be found in the *svapna-nāṭaka*. The supposed identity of these two titles is the only clue available as to the authorship of the *svapna-nāṭaka*. For, contrary to the general practice of Sanskrit dramas, the *svupna-nāṭaka* does not name its author. Thus even this support for the identification of the recently edited Trivandrum play with the ancient *svapna-vāsavadatta* of the real Bhāsa is wanting.

The very dubious identification of the Trivandrum *svapna-nāṭaka* with the *svapna-vāsavadatta* of the ancient poet Bhāsa, on the strength of the possible identity of their titles, but without the support of any corroborative evidence, is made the basis of the much more far-reaching and uncertain conclusion that the other twelve recently published plays are, owing to their great similarity of style and the possession of many passages in common, not only the production of one and the same poet, but that that poet is Bhāsa. Not only are all these plays anonymous, but we do not even know any of the titles of the plays of the ancient Bhāsa except only *svapna-vāsavadatta*. Now the similarity in style of these thirteen plays may very well be due to the peculiarities and exigencies of the stage in Malabar, where alone these plays are known and acted. No attempt at investigation in this direction has yet been made, at least by any of the western supporters of this hypothesis. Again, many of the views expressed as to the relative merits of these plays are purely subjective, and can have no decisive cogency in regard to facts.

No confirmation of the Bhāsa hypothesis is to be derived from the quotations attributed to Bhāsa in rhetorical works and anthologies. For none of the fourteen quotations there ascribed to Bhāsa occur either in the *svapna-nāṭaka* or in any of the other twelve plays; nor have any of the verses occurring in the Trivandrum plays been found in rhetorical works and anthologies even ascribed to some other author than Bhāsa.

The diction of these plays shows familiarity with the style of the Purāṇas, and contains far more grammatical irregularities than the classical Sanskrit dramas do.

On the definite assumption, which, however, has no sound basis, that these thirteen Trivandrum plays are the work of the one author Bhāsa, attempts have been made to fix their approximate date, chiefly on the evidence of the Prākrit appearing in the prose passages. By a comparison of this Prākrit with that of Aśvaghosha and Kālidāsa, one of the conclusions arrived at is that Bhāsa comes chronologically midway between these two, and therefore belongs to the third century A.D. Though this, of course, cannot prove anything as to the individual authorship of the plays, it could show that they were composed at the time when Bhāsa probably lived, and that consequently he might have been the author of some of them. But here it seems necessary to investigate the position of Prākrit in Malabar very carefully before it can be made the basis of decisive chronological conclusions. For here it was an exotic, the natural development of which, on its transplantation to the entirely alien linguistic area of a Dravidian country, at once became arrested, while in its home in northern India it would be liable to regular change as the literary form of a spoken vernacular. Estimates of the age of these plays on the evidence of their Prākrit should thus be undertaken with great caution. As it is, the calculation of their age, whether based on the character of their Prākrit or on other considerations, varies very greatly: that of Western scholars between the second and seventh century A.D., that of Indian scholars between the fifth century B.C. and the tenth A.D.

The above summary criticisms probably suffice to show that the attribution of these thirteen plays, or even of one of them, to Bhāsa is subject to much doubt at every point. Far more cogent evidence than is yet available is necessary to prove that any one of the lost plays of Bhāsa has survived to the present day. The verdict, in my view, cannot as yet be any other than 'not proven'. A certain conclusion based on data no one of which is more than a possibility is inadmissible. The difficulties of this problem may perhaps be successfully grappled with by minutely investigating the history of the Sanskrit drama in Malabar.

The two greatest Sanskrit playwrights were Kālidāsa and Bhavabhūti. The former of these is the more eminent, famous as an epic and a lyric poet as well. He wrote three dramas, *Śakuntalā*, *Vikramorvaśī*, and *Mālavikāgnimitra*. The first two are the best specimens of the romantic drama of India. They represent the love adventures of two famous kings of ancient days, dealing with matters heroic and divine, far removed from the realities of everyday life. The third is a palace and harem drama of contemporary love and intrigue.

In *Śakuntalā* the poet presents the romance of King Dushyanta and the daughter of a celestial nymph. Engaged in the chase, the king sees Śakuntalā, whom he falls in love with and marries. After his return home, Śakuntalā is sent by her guardian, the hermit Kaṇva, to her husband, who, however, in consequence of the curse of an angry sage, fails to recognize her. A long separation ensues, till finally the two are reunited through the agency of a ring which, having been formerly given by the king to his wife and having later been swallowed by a fish, has been recovered by fishermen. Its lack of action renders *Śakuntalā*, like almost all Sanskrit dramas, defective as a stage play. But it has many beauties. The richness of his creative fancy, and his skill in expressing tender sentiment and sympathy with nature, gives Kālidāsa a high place among the world's dramatic poets. The following few lines may serve as a specimen. They are uttered by the old sage

Kaṇva when his ward Śakuntalā is about to leave her home, the forest hermitage, to rejoin her husband:

My heart is touched with sadness when I think
'Śakuntalā must leave to-day'; my throat
Is choked with flow of tears repressed; mine eyes
Grow dim with pensiveness; but if the grief
Of this old forest hermit is so great,
How keen must be the pang a father feels
When freshly parted from a cherished child!

Then, turning to the trees of the grove to give Śakuntalā a sign of farewell, he adds:

The trees, the kinsmen of her forest home,
Now to Śakuntalā give leave to go:
They with the Kokila's[1] melodious cry
Their answer make.

Then voices in the air utter the following good wishes as she departs:

Thy journey be auspicious; may the breeze,
Gentle and soothing, fan thy cheek; may lakes
All bright with lily cups delight thine eye;
The sunbeams' heat be cooled by shady trees;
The dust beneath thy feet the pollen be
Of lotuses.[2]

Kālidāsa also shows moderation and sense of proportion, somewhat rare qualities in Indian literature. The perfections of *Śakuntalā* earned the highest praise from so eminent a critic as Goethe. To its widespread popularity in India is probably due the fact that this drama exists in four recensions, none of which can be said to represent the original text more closely than any of the others. *Vikra-*

[1] The Indian cuckoo.

[2] These passages are, with slight modifications, taken from my *History of Sanskrit Literature*, pp. 356–7.

morvaśī, or 'Urvaśī (won) by Valour', deals with the romance of King Purūravas and the nymph Urvaśī, the earliest form of which occurs in the *Ṛigveda*, far more than a thousand years before. Urvaśī is parted from her lover as the result of his being summoned before the throne of the god Indra; but, after undergoing many trials caused by separation, the lovers are re-united in consequence of Indra's favour, which Purūravas gains by his services against the demons.

Mālavikāgnimitra, though inferior to the other two dramas in poetic merit, has many beauties of its own. Based on the ordinary palace life of Indian princes, it affords a good picture of the social conditions of the time. Its theme is the loves of King Agnimitra, who reigned at Vidiśa (Bhīlsa) in the second century B. C., and of Mālavikā, one of the attendants of the queen. As the heroine finally turns out to be a princess by birth and there is therefore no longer any impediment to her union with the king, all ends happily.

A drama entitled *Mṛcchakaṭikā*, or 'The Little Clay Cart', is attributed to a king named Śūdraka, whose date it seems impossible to determine, but is probably not far removed from that of Kālidāsa. An incomplete form of it, consisting of its first four acts, but without introductory and concluding verses, has been preserved under the title of *Cārudatta*, as one of the thirteen plays published in the Trivandrum Sanskrit Series, and regarded by the adherents of the Bhāsa hypothesis as the work of Bhāsa. It looks like another recension of the *Mṛcchakaṭikā* adapted for performance on the Malabar stage. The *Mṛcchakaṭikā* is pre-eminent among Indian plays for the distinctively dramatic qualities of vigour, life, and action, as well as skill in the delineation of character. The scene is laid in the city of Ujjain, and is crowded with characters. The hero is Chārudatta, a Brahmin merchant reduced to poverty by excessive liberality, and the heroine Vasantasenā, a rich courtezan, who loves and ultimately marries Chārudatta. The play abounds with comic situations diversified with many serious scenes.

Two plays are attributed to King Śrīharsha, whom we have already come across as Harshavardhana of Kanauj (606–48 A.D.). One of these is *Ratnāvalī*, or 'The Pearl Necklace', which reflects the court life of the age, and somewhat resembles the *Mālavikāgnimitra* of Kālidāsa. It represents the love-story of Udayana, king of Vatsa, and of Sāgarikā, an attendant of his queen Vāsavadattā. The heroine ultimately turns out to be Ratnāvalī, princess of Ceylon, who has found her way to Udayana's court after suffering shipwreck. Forming a sequel to the popular love-story of Vāsavadattā, this drama is an agreeable work with well-drawn characters and many poetical beauties. Of the latter, the following passage on the approach of night may serve as an illustration:

> Our minds intent upon the festival,
> We saw not that the twilight passed away:
> Behold, the east proclaims the lord of night
> Still hidden by the hill where he will rise,
> Even as a maiden by her pallid face
> Reveals that in her heart a lover dwells.[1]

Similar is the plot of another play by Śrīharsha, entitled *Priyadarśikā*, after a princess who was the daughter of the king of Aṅga, and was destined for king Udayana. By the vicissitudes of war she becomes an attendant, under the name of Āraṇyikā, in the harem of the king, who sees

[1] Quoted, with some variations, in my *History of Sanskrit Literature*, p. 312.

and falls in love with her. Queen Vāsavadattā, becoming suspicious, has her locked up. But on finding out that she is a princess of Aṅga she recognizes her as Priyadarśikā, releases her, and arranges to have her married to Udayana. Śrīharsha's third play is the *Nāgānanda*, the plot of which is derived from the legendary store of the *Bṛhatkathā* (p. 125). It is a sensational piece of considerable merit, with a Buddhist colouring.

The second greatest Indian dramatist, the authenticity of whose plays is undoubted, Bhavabhūti, lived in the first half of the eighth century. He was a Brahmin of Vidarbha, now Berār, a territory to the north of the Hyderābād state. He was well acquainted with the city of Ujjain, but spent part of his life under the patronage of King Yaśovarman of Kanauj. Three of his plays, all abounding in poetical beauties, have come down to us. They differ from the works of the earlier dramatists in various points. Owing to Bhavabhūti's deeply serious temperament, the comic element is almost entirely lacking, and the jester does not appear in his plays. He prefers to depict the grand and sublime rather than the delicate and mild aspects of nature. He also displays skill in expressing depth and force of passion, as well as tender and noble sentiment. The most popular of his plays is the *Mālatī-mādhava*. Ujjain is the scene, and the plot is concerned with the love-story of Mālatī, daughter of a minister of the country, and Mādhava, a young scholar studying in the city. They fall in love, and in spite of the king's determination that the heroine shall marry his favourite, whom she detests, the lovers succeed in being finally united.

The other two plays deal with the fortunes of Rāma, but, owing to lack of action, they have the character of dramatic poems rather than of dramas. The earlier part of Rāma's career is presented in the *Mahāvīra-carita*, or 'Adventures of the Great Hero'. The *Uttara-rāmacarita*, or 'Later Adventures of Rāma', contains some passages of more genuine pathos than perhaps any other Indian drama.

Though his date cannot be fixed with certainty, the dramatist Bhaṭṭa-Nārāyaṇa must have lived before 800 A.D., as he is quoted by Vāmana, the writer on poetics, in the eighth century. A well-known play by him is the *Veṇī-saṃhāra*, or 'Binding of the Braid of Hair', the main incident of which is derived from the *Mahābhārata*. Its popularity in India is chiefly due to its partiality for the cult of Kṛishṇa. Probably not later than 800 A.D. was composed a play of a unique type, Viśākhadatta's *Mudrā-rākṣasa*, or 'Rākshasa and the Seal'. Love does not enter into the plot, for it is entirely a political piece, full of life, action, and sustained interest. The plot is concerned with the endeavour of the Brahmin Chāṇakya, the minister of Chandragupta, to win over to his master's cause the noble Rākshasa, formerly minister of a king deposed by Chandragupta in 315 B.C.

About 900 A.D. lived, during the reigns of the rulers of Kanauj, Mahendrapāla and his successor Mahīpāla, the dramatist Rājaśekhara, noted for his command of Sanskrit and Prākrit, as well as his knowledge of the spoken vernaculars. He uses many rare words and provincialisms. He also shows great skill in the employment of artificial metres. Now and then he avails himself of rime, which he borrowed from popular poetry. He is particularly fond of using proverbial phrases.

Two of his dramas deal with epic subjects. One is the *Bālarāmāyaṇa*, or 'Rāmāyaṇa for Boys', which treats at excessive length the story of the whole *Rāmāyaṇa* in ten acts. The *Bālabhārata*, or 'Mahābhārata for Boys', has been left uncompleted or, with the exception of the first two acts, has been lost. These deal with the marriage of Draupadī and with the gambling scene of the epic in which she is dragged by her hair before the assembly by one of the Kauravas.

Another of Rājaśekhara's plays, the *Viddhaśālabhañjikā*, or 'the Statue', is not lacking in comic situations, for which the fact that the heroine is a girl disguised as a boy affords abundant opportunities.

His *Karpūra-mañjarī* is one of the best comedies in Indian literature. It is the only extant well-known drama entirely composed in Prākrit. Rājaśekhara apparently wanted to show that, after making his name as a Sanskrit poet, he was able to deal with the most difficult metres in Prākrit quite as well as in Sanskrit. Rājaśekhara's plays deserve to be studied for the correctness of their diction and the smoothness of their verses both in Sanskrit and Prākrit, as well as for the proverbial sayings with which they abound and the allusions which they contain to the customs prevailing in his day. He is, however, not a great poet, for he lacks taste and originality.

The *Hanuman-nāṭaka*, or 'Play of Hanumat', a rambling piece of little merit, represents the adventures of Rāma in so far as they are connected with his ally, the monkey king. It is also known by the title *Mahānāṭaka*, 'the Great Drama'. It must have been written before 850 A.D., as it is quoted by Ānandavardhana, the writer on poetics, in his *Dhvanyāloka* (*c.* 850 A.D.). It is known in two rather widely divergent recensions, one of which, the western, ascribed to Dāmodara-miśra, contains 581 stanzas in fourteen acts, while the other, that of Bengal, attributed to Madhusūdana, contains 730 stanzas in nine acts. The text abounds in interpolations. It can hardly be regarded as a drama, but rather comes half-way between an epic and a dramatic poem. It has no *vidūṣaka*, nor does it contain any Prākrit speeches.

One of the most remarkable products of Indian literature, which dates from *c.* 1100 A.D., is the *Prabodha-candrodaya*, or 'Rise of the Moon of Knowledge', by Kṛishṇamiśra. It is an allegorical play in which practically all the characters are abstract notions and symbolical figures. Its main strength lies in the effectiveness of its moral and philosophical stanzas, but the action of its allegorical figures cannot be said to show any dramatic power. The dialogue is sometimes not without humour, and the author handles his favourite metres with skill; he also uses rimed verses in Prākrit. The whole play is a glorification of the cult of Vishṇu as a form of orthodox Brahmanism, much as the allegorical plays of the Spanish poet Calderon exalt the Catholic faith.

Kṛishṇamiśra had many imitators of this type of play in later centuries; but nearly all of them are without merit.

Other kinds of drama, which belong to modern times and have been preserved in great numbers, may be passed over here. But two types, which have been very popular in India, though they have little literary value, may be mentioned. One of these, the Bhāṇas, all of which seem to come from southern India, deal with low life presented in the form of monologue. The Prahasanas, or farces, represent everyday life, in which rogues and various kinds of worthless characters indulge in altercations and fraudulent proceedings.

Macdonell, *History*, x–xii, pp. 277–345, 445–8 (down to 1899). Winternitz, *Geschichte*, i, pp. 257–483; iii. 1–160, 623–35, 641–4.

Sylvain Lévi, *Le Théâtre Indien*, Paris, 1890. Wilson, *Select Specimens of the Theatre of the Hindus*, 2 vols., London, 1871. Sten Konow, *Das indische Drama*, Berlin and Leipzig, 1920. Keith, *The Sanskrit Drama*, Oxford, 1924. Macdonell, *History*, ch. 13. Winternitz, *Geschichte*, iii. 160–263, Leipzig, 1922. Pischel, *Die Kultur der Gegenwart*, 210–17.

The literature on the authorship of the thirteen plays attributed to Bhāsa and published in the Trivandrum Sanskrit series is already considerable: V. S. Sukthankar's *Studies in Bhāsa*, 1923 (reprinted from the Journal of the Bombay branch of the Royal Asiatic Society, xxvi, no. 75), contains a full bibliography of 111 articles on the subject, ranging from 1912 to 1923. Later appeared C. Kunhan Raja, *Bhāsa, another side*, in *Zeitschrift für Indien und Iran*, ii, 1924; J. Ghatak, *The Dramas of Bhāsa*, Calcutta, 1925; A. K. Pisharoti, *Bhāsa's Works*, Trivandrum, 1925; L. Sarūp, *The Vision of Vāsavadattā*, Lahore, 1925; *Festgabe Jacobi*, pp. 114–134, Bonn, 1926; Hīrānanda Śāstrī, *Bhāsa and the authorship of the Thirteen Trivandrum Plays*, No. 28. Calcutta, 1926.

VI

STORIES, FAIRY TALES, AND FABLES

This the most original branch of Indian literature — Has had more external influence than any other — Its general literary characteristic is intercalation of one story within another — The Pañcatantra — Its recensions — Its migrations throughout the world — No other secular book ever translated into so many languages — Sir Thomas North's rendering from an Italian version in 1570 — Pañcatantra's influence on European story-books — Some of its stories in European oral tradition — Indian or Greek origin of some of its fables conjectural — The Bṛhatkathā collection of stories — Somadeva's Kathāsaritsāgara — Other story-books — Tale of Sindbad derived from India — The Śukasaptati — Its Persian and Turkish translations — Indian influence on 'Arabian Nights' — Prose romances: Daśakumāra-carita, Vāsavadattā, Kādambarī, Harṣa-carita — The campū type of story-book — Selected bibliography.

The narrative matter which we find treated in the court epics and the dramas based on ancient legends brings us to the most valuable product of Indian literature, its folklore, which in India was earlier and to a wider extent raised to the rank of actual literature than among other nations of antiquity. Such matter takes a prominent place, not only among the sacred books of the Buddhists and the Jains, but also among the works of Sanskrit literature. For us it is in many respects more valuable than all the other branches of Indian literary production. When we find how in the court epics and in the dramas the same old legendary material is, with few exceptions, treated over and over again, and similar plots recur with trifling changes, we are almost inclined to believe that the Indians show a complete lack of inventive power. But the folklore literature introduces us to a world of infinite originality, in which the characters are no longer stereotyped, as in the epics and the drama, but are human beings with individual traits, not only heroic warriors, virtuous kings, and beautiful princesses, but people of the most varied kind—peasants, merchants, artisans, and all sorts of doubtful characters, thieves, vagabonds, selfish Brahmins, hypocritical monks, courtezans, and procuresses. It is an imaginary world, full of marvellous and complicated fairy tales, of wit in the invention of serious and comic scenes, of wealth of fancy in the creation of ever new material in story and romance. This is in fact the most original department of Indian literature. It is also the one that has exercised a greater influence on foreign literatures than any other branch of Indian writing. The history of how Indian fairy tales and fables migrated from one country to another, to nearly all the peoples of Europe and Asia, and even to African tribes, from their original home in India, borders on the marvellous. It is not a case of single stories finding their way by word of mouth through the agency of merchants and travellers from India to other countries, but of whole Indian books becoming through the medium of translations the common property of the world. After this had been demonstrated, it was at one time even believed that India was the source of all fairy tales, but the progressive study of folklore has irrefutably disproved such an assumption. It is, however, true that many fairy tales current among the most various peoples can be traced to their original home in India. Long before there were extensive collections of this character in Indian literature, all kinds of separate stories and fairy tales circulated among the people simply as a means of amusement, and also single fables invented by religious and secular teachers for the purpose of edification. Fairy tales, stories, and anecdotes long in general circulation, and fables introduced in various parts of already existing literary works, became the sources or the models of the stories contained in folklore collections. Fairy tales have at all times, in India and elsewhere, supplied the place of what in our times is entertaining literature. This is what distinguishes the fairy tale from the myth, which endeavours to explain some physical problem or satisfy some religious doubt, while the fable is always intended to instruct and to point a moral. Fairy tales thus lived long among the people before they were introduced into literature in Prākrit books. The fable arose in literature itself, probably in Sanskrit from the beginning. The beast-fable, however, most likely originated in the beast fairy tale, a didactic maxim being combined with the story. For edification is always an essential element in the fable literature.

The earliest form of the literary narrative is a mixture of prose and verse. Certain stories are already found in Vedic literature, like that of Purūravas and Urvaśī, but these belong to the sphere of myth and legend rather than to that of fairy tale in the strict sense. It was only in the later days of the post-Vedic period that works of literary narrative were composed entirely in verse. Works written entirely in prose are rare; in the historical romances verses are to a limited extent introduced.

The oldest actual fables in Indian literature are to be found in the *Mahābhārata*. That fables existed in India as early as the third century B.C. is proved by the reliefs on the *stūpa* of Bhārhut, which dates from that time and on which the titles of many stories are engraved. Again, the Sanskrit grammarian Patañjali, in explaining the formation of certain compound words such as *kāka-tālīya-vat*, 'like (the story of) the crow and the palm-tree', proves the same fact for the second century B.C.

The works comprising the narrative literature that have come down to us may be grouped in two main classes, each of which includes two subdivisions. The first class is didactic in character. It consists (*a*) of collections of stories compiled for the purpose of religious edification: such were the Jātakas and other story-books of the Buddhists (p. 61) and the Jains (p. 72) written in Prākrit; (*b*) story-books written in Sanskrit for the express purpose of inculcating political doctrine and worldly wisdom: such was the *Pañcatantra*. The second class embraces works written for the purpose of amusing. These were either (*a*) story-books, which were first composed in Prākrit, like the *Bṛhatkathā*, but later in Sanskrit, like the *Śukasaptati* (p. 128); or (*b*) novels and romances written in classical Sanskrit prose, like the *Daśakumāra-carita* and the *Vāsavadattā* (p. 131).

All but the first of these four groups were the works of individual authors, who themselves invented them and in part derived their material from current stories or from other collections.

The general construction of these story-books was intercalation, that is to say, the insertion of a group of stories within the framework of a single narrative. Within a subordinate story another could be similarly introduced and the process further repeated. This style of narration was borrowed from India by the Arabs, who employed it in composing works of their own. The most notable example is the *Arabian Nights*, into which several stories originally Indian have found their way.

The main book belonging to this department is the *Pañcatantra*, which has had a longer and more eventful history than any other work of Indian literature. Two

German scholars have been concerned with the elucidation of that history. Theodor Benfey was the first both to translate it from Sanskrit and to trace its migrations, by translation, into the literatures of almost innumerable countries. The second is Professor Johannes Hertel, who has, by means of critical editions of its most important recensions and by numerous researches, laid bare its fortunes in India itself. It is only natural that the original form of a text of this kind, consisting of a number of stories and maxims, should have undergone frequent alterations in the course of many centuries. But its original character was never quite effaced. It always remained a work intended to teach political science and worldly wisdom in the form of fables, stories, and maxims. In its earliest form it was a work for the instruction of princes, but later it became more a book for the education of youth generally. Purely moral stories were to a certain extent introduced only in later recensions. Although the original form of the *Pañcatantra* has not been preserved, we are able to draw well-founded conclusions regarding it from its earliest surviving recensions. There are five such.

The *Tantrākhyāyika*, or 'Treatise of Instructive Stories', is the form that best represents the original text. Two recensions of it have been preserved in Kashmīr. Another is the text that was translated into Pehlevi in 570 A.D. Though both this text and the Pehlevi translation have been lost, the Syriac and Arabic versions from the Pehlevi and the European translations from the Arabic enable us to infer what the original Sanskrit text was like. Thirdly, there was an abstract of the *Pañcatantra* contained in the lost Kashmīrian work called the *Bṛhatkathā*, of which two metrical recensions have been preserved in Kshemendra's *Bṛhatkathā-mañjarī* and in Somadeva's *Kathāsaritsāgara*;

the latter of these throws the more valuable light on the old text of the *Pañcatantra*. There is further a greatly curtailed abstract generally called the South Indian *Pañcatantra*, which is closely related to the *Tantrākhyāyika* and has been shown to go back to an abstract made in north-west India after the seventh century A.D. Finally, there is a Nepālese abstract of the stanzas contained in the *Pañcatantra*, preserved in a single manuscript, nearly related to the Southern *Pañcatantra* and going back to a north-western text. This, too, is of considerable critical importance. All these five are derived from a common original text of the *Pañcatantra*, to which, however, the *Tantrākhyāyika* appears to come nearest. Though the latter is a product of the artificial Sanskrit style of composition, its artificiality is moderate and falls far short of that of romances like those of Bāṇa. The author was evidently a writer of ability and originality.

As to the age of the *Pañcatantra*, we know that by the middle of the sixth century A.D. it was so famous that by order of the Sassanian king Chosru Anushirvan (531–79 A.D.) it was translated into Pehlevi and from Pehlevi into Syriac as early as 570. But research has hitherto been unable to prove when the original first came into being. Nothing more definite can be said than that it most probably arose between 300 and 500 A.D. There can be no doubt that in the form of the *Tantrākhyāyika* it is one of the earliest products of the artificial literature of India. But as that recension contains undoubted interpolations, the date of the original *Pañcatantra* must be still earlier. No chronological conclusions can be drawn from the religious and social conditions that it reflects. The general atmosphere is that of Brahmanism, while no relation to Buddhism can be found in the book. The view once rather widely held that the *Pañcatantra* was of Buddhist origin must therefore be rejected.

The most popular and most widespread in India of the old texts of the *Pañcatantra* is designated the 'textus simplicior', which has also been the longest and best known in Europe. Before the discovery of the *Tantrākhyāyika* it was regarded as the standard *Pañcatantra*. It is, however, a completely new revision of the old work, in fact almost a new book; for many new stories and stanzas have been added in it, while many old stanzas are lacking. The style in this text is clear and simple, and the stories are told better and at greater length than in the *Tantrākhyāyika*. The 'textus simplicior' ultimately goes back to the north-western text that was the basis both of the Pehlevi translation and of the abridgement forming the southern *Pañcatantra*.

On the 'textus simplicior' is chiefly based the 'textus ornatior', which was produced in 1199 by a Jain monk named Pūrṇabhadra. It is the best preserved of the later revisions of the *Pañcatantra*. As compared with the older texts it contains many new stories and maxims.

The most important of all the modern adaptations of the *Pañcatantra* is the *Hitopadeśa*, or 'Salutary Advice', which is widely diffused in Bengal and is best known in India and Europe. Though in fact a totally new work, its chief source is the *Pañcatantra* in its north-western recension, which is also the source of the southern *Pañcatantra*. About its date nothing more certain can be said than that it was composed between 1000 and 1300 A.D. Its place of origin was probably Bengal. The author is very independent in the way in which he has altered and rearranged the subject-matter. The *Hitopadeśa* contains seventeen stories which are not found in any of the recensions of the *Pañcatantra*. The character of a work on political science is more apparent in the *Hitopadeśa* than in any other adaptation of the *Pañcatantra.* It adds a large number of maxims of this type. The *Hitopadeśa* is one of the works of Indian literature that has been known longest and best in Europe. Besides being extensively studied in the original, it has been translated into many Indian vernaculars, including Bengali, as well as repeatedly into European languages.

The *Pañcatantra* itself has of course also been frequently translated into the Indian vernaculars. A Hindī version of it was known to the Arabic scholar Albērūnī about 1030 A.D. It was also translated into Gujarātī, Marāṭhī, and the Dravidian languages of the south. The diffusion of translations outside India was much wider still. During many centuries the *Pañcatantra* enriched in this way the literatures of three continents, and exercised an extraordinary influence on the narrative works of the whole Middle Ages. This was shown by Theodor Benfey in the introduction to his translation of the *Pañcatantra.* He traced with extraordinary acuteness the migration of Indian stories in the most various languages of the East and West throughout the world. He thus became the founder of the comparative history of literature.

India presents a soil particularly favourable to the invention of fables, animal stories, and fairy tales. For here we find the belief in transmigration, which effaces the difference between the human and the animal worlds, and which thus renders it quite natural for animals to be the heroes of stories. Consequently no other country has produced so extensive a literature of stories as India. Thus not only single Indian tales but whole story-books are to be found in foreign literatures. We can very often even trace the actual routes by which fables and fairy tales have made their way from India throughout the world. By far the most important work of this type was the *Pañcatantra.* The translation into Pehlevi, the literary language of medieval Persia, has indeed been lost, but the Syriac version made from that in 570 A.D. under the title of *Kalilag and Damnag*, though somewhat imperfectly preserved, is still extant. Another was the complete translation into Arabic (750 A.D.) entitled *Kalīla and Dimna.* Both titles are distortions of the names of the two jackals, Karaṭaka and Damanaka, that appear in the first book of the *Pañcatantra.* This Arabic translation is the source to which the numerous versions, direct or indirect, found in European and Asiatic languages are to be traced. To be more precise, translations of the *Kalīla and Dimna* have been made into forty languages, besides those from Sanskrit into fifteen Indian vernacular tongues. Probably no book except the Bible has been translated into so many languages, certainly no secular book. It has truly been said regarding this narrative literature that 'the story of the migration of Indian fairy tales from East to West is more wonderful and instructive than many of those fairy tales themselves'. The best and most famous of the versions of the *Pañcatantra* in the Middle Ages was the German one of Anton von Pforr entitled 'Das Buch der Beispiele der alten Weisen', which first appeared in 1483, soon after the invention of printing, and was reprinted afterwards. For a long time it contributed most to a knowledge of the original in the whole of Europe. It not only influenced German literature in many ways, but was also itself translated into Danish, Icelandic, and Dutch. This German version was four times removed from the Arabic one which started the *Pañcatantra* on its westward wanderings.

On the Latin translation of John of Capua (1263) was based a Spanish one (1493), from which was derived an

Italian one in two parts (1552). The first of these parts was rendered into English by Sir Thomas North in 1570. This appeared exactly 1,000 years after the Syriac translation made from Pehlevi in 570 A.D. No fewer than six renderings intervened between it and the original Sanskrit text of the *Pañcatantra.* The geographical separation between the starting-point and this goal was also one of the greatest. It appeared under the title of 'The Morall Philosophie of Doni'.

It is thus no wonder that the most popular European story-books contain traces of Indian fables and fairy tales, such as the *Gesta Romanorum,* the works of Boccaccio, Chaucer, and Lafontaine, and even, in the nineteenth century, Grimm's *Tales.* Some such stories have passed from literature into oral tradition in Europe, and have acquired a local colouring in their new home. An instance of this is the Welsh story of Llewellyn's dog Gelert, who, with his mouth besmeared with blood, joyfully fawns on his master as he returns from the chase. Llewellyn rushes into the house to find his child's cradle overturned and traces of blood scattered about. But on examining the cradle he finds the child sleeping peacefully and a dead wolf lying by his side. This is the Welsh transformation of the *Pañcatantra* story about the Brahmin who, having left a mongoose to guard his child in a cradle during his absence, returns and is greeted by the mongoose who rolls at his feet. But the Brahmin, seeing his mouth covered with blood, assumes he has bitten the child and kills him on the spot. Afterwards, finding the child uninjured and a dead serpent near him, he is overwhelmed with remorse.

When, however, stories are identical in East and West, while there is no evidence, from translations passing westward, of their Indian origin, we can only conjecture which side is the recipient. The same is the case when a fable is identical in Greece and India. There are several such, as that of the ass in the lion's skin. On this question there is great difference of opinion among scholars: some holding Greece, others India, to be the source of all; others again favour India, but admit that some fables must have come from Greece. The criteria seem here too subjective to justify definite conclusions. A weighty consideration is the fact that the Greek fable flourished as early as 500 B.C. in the time of Aesop, whom Herodotus (484–425 B.C.) knew as a writer of fables. The oldest Indian fables go back only conjecturally to the fourth and fifth century B.C., and only a few with certainty to the third century B.C. But it by no means necessarily follows that those fables which the Indians have in common with the Greeks are certainly derived from the oldest period (sixth and fifth centuries B.C.) of Greek fables. The great majority both of the Aesopian and Indian fables may date from the time when there was an active intellectual interchange between Greece and India. Greek fables might then have easily come to India and Indian fables to Greece. This was the time, the third century A.D., when Babrius (*c.* 200 A.D.) wrote his collection of Aesopian fables. The truth probably is that the fable as a type did not arise exclusively either in India or in Greece, but that it came into being independently in each country, and that an interchange of individual fables between Greece and India took place when communication between the two countries arose.

According to the evidence of the romance writers, Daṇḍin, Subandhu, and Bāṇa, there existed in the sixth century A.D. a work of entertaining literature, which consisted of a collection of stories, the *Bṛhatkathā* by Guṇāḍhya, written not in Sanskrit, but in Paiśāchī, a dialect probably of the north-west, and not otherwise used in literature. Though this work has not been preserved, two Sanskrit translations, made from it probably centuries later, have come down to us. These have been preserved in two recensions, the Kāśmīrian and the Nepālese. The former is known to us in two metrical forms, both of which date from the eleventh century. The earlier, Kshemendra's *Bṛhatkathā-mañjarī*, composed about 1037 A.D., is meant to be an abridgement of the *Bṛhatkathā.*

The later form of the Kāśmīrian recension, the *Kathā-sarit-sāgara*, or 'Ocean of Narrative Streams', was composed between 1063 and 1081 A.D. Though Somadeva writes in the Kāvya style, he does not make an exaggerated use of poetic ornament or of metre, for he adapts the form to the matter. There can be no doubt that he is one of the most pleasing and skilful poets of India. It is likely that the defects of this work are due to the original *Bṛhatkathā.* The chief one is the faulty arrangement of the matter. Very often stories appear that do not suit the context, and the same story is found in two, occasionally even three, different forms. The main story is, moreover, much less interesting than those of which it is the framework. Somadeva evidently thought less of the latter than of the interwoven tales. He incorporated in it whole books, like the *Pañcatantra*, as well as long, independent novels in which other shorter stories are inserted.

The *Kathāsarit-sāgara* throws much light on the contemporary social and religious conditions prevailing in India. It is also important in its relation to world-literature, for several of its stories reappear in the West.

The Nepālese recension of the *Bṛhatkathā* by Buddhasvāmin, which is entitled *Bṛhatkathā-śloka-saṃgraha*, and is incomplete, seems more original than the Kāśmīrian recension. The arrangement and subject-matter differ so much from the latter, that in some places it seems quite another work.

The *Vetāla-pañcaviṃśatikā*, or 'Twenty-five (tales) of the Vetāla', is a collection of stories which was contained in the Kāśmīrian recension of the *Bṛhatkathā*, for it appears both in Kshemendra's and Somadeva's poems. Its oldest form was lost, but Kshemendra and Somadeva preserve it in probably an older shape than that in which it has survived as a separate work. As such it exists in the two recensions of Śivadāsa and Jambhaladatta. The former, who probably wrote in the twelfth century, seems to have handed down the more original form of the narrative, a mixture of prose and verse. The framework of this collection of stories is associated with a Vetāla, or ghost infesting cemeteries, and magic plays an important part in these tales. This work, like the *Pañcatantra*, has contributed many stories to world-literature.

A later, but also well-known and popular story-book is the *Siṃhāsana-dvātriṃśikā*, 'Thirty-two Tales of the Throne', which is also entitled *Vikrama-carita*, or 'Career of Vikrama'. It is found in three recensions, one in prose, another in verse, and a third in a mixture of both. Of these, the South Indian prose recension probably comes nearest to the original form of the work. These thirty-two tales are very fantastic and fall far below the intellectual level of the *Vetāla-pañcaviṃśatikā*. As King Bhoja of Dhārā is mentioned in the main story forming the framework in every recension, the book cannot be earlier than 1000 A.D. It may, however, possibly have been composed in the reign of that ruler. It was translated into Persian in 1574 A.D., and there are many versions in Indian vernaculars, as well as in Siamese and Mongolian.

One of the most famous and popular Indian story-books is the *Śuka-saptati*, 'Seventy Tales of a Parrot'. As is so often the case with such works, the original form of it must be regarded as irretrievably lost, though there are in existence many widely divergent recensions, translations into Indian vernaculars, and versions in foreign languages. The form in which it is composed is simple prose alternating with sententious verse, the latter being partly in Sanskrit, partly in Prākrit. Many of the maxims are to be found in other story-books, especially the *Pañcatantra*, and several of the tales, particularly the fables, are taken from that work. Nothing is known about the author or the time when it was composed. A fact of great importance in connexion with world-literature is that the *Śuka-saptati* was translated into Persian early in the fourteenth century under the title of *Tutināmeh*. The rough and uncouth quality of this rendering induced Nachshabi, a contemporary of Hafiz and Sadi, to mould its matter into an artistic poem. Based on the latter was another Persian version made in the seventeenth century, as well as a Turkish one dating from about a century after Nachshabi. Through the *Tutināmeh* many Indian stories migrated to Western Asia and Europe. The best known of these was the tale of the fraudulent ordeal, rendered famous in Gottfried von Strassburg's 'Tristan und Isolde'. There were many later imitations of the *Śuka-saptati* both in Sanskrit and the vernaculars.

Nearly related in matter to the *Śuka-saptati* is the story of Sindbad, a famous tale of world-literature. It was probably based on an Indian original; for the Arabian writer Masūdi (who died in 956 A.D.) said of the *Kitāb el Sindbād*, 'Book of Sindbad', that it was derived from India. This work is essentially identical with the Persian

Sindibād-nāmeh, the Syriac *Sindban*, an Arabic version contained in the 'Arabian Nights', the Hebrew *Sandabar*, the Greek *Syntipas*, and a number of other books in European languages. The introduction is Indian, quite similar to that of the *Pañcatantra*, as well as the idea that the stories are told to save somebody's life. Most of the tales recur in some Indian story-book, as that of the death of the innocent mongoose in the *Pañcatantra*. There can be no doubt that the 'Arabian Nights' are the result of Indian influence. All the main elements of its framework are derived from Indian ideas, and a large number of its stories are of Indian origin. The evidence, however, is not sufficient to prove that the Pehlevi original was a translation from Sanskrit. We cannot as yet reach a more definite conclusion than that a Persian poet composed the framework as well as a number of the tales, imitating Indian originals, of the 'Arabian Nights'.

Contemporary with the artificial epics, and composed not long before or after 600 A.D., were a few prose romances that are classed as Kāvyas by the Sanskrit writers on poetics because, though not written in verse, they have all the characteristics of that style: descriptions filled with similes and figures of speech, immensely long compounds, puns, and other ornaments. Narrative here occupies a very subordinate place, being chiefly employed as the thread connecting a series of lengthy descriptions full of long strings of comparisons and often teeming with puns. Owing to the frequent use of immense compounds, their style makes them difficult reading. Their matter, however, is not derived from mythology or heroic legends, but mostly from the literature of fairy tales.

The earliest of these, the *Daśakumāra-carita*, or 'Adventures of the Ten Princes', was written by Daṇḍin and dates from the sixth century. It differs from Guṇāḍhya's *Bṛhatkathā* by its elaborate Kāvya style rather than by its matter. For it consists of stories and fairy tales enclosed in a framework. The narrative is so complicated that its thread can only be followed with difficulty. It is often dependent on arbitrary occurrences, such as a curse or dream, and not on inner necessity. The caprice of the fairy tale everywhere prevails. The erotic element is always prominent, the author being fond of dwelling on descriptions of female beauty or of love-scenes. Daṇḍin shows himself to be a master of the most ornate Kāvya style, which, however, he varies with simple unadorned narrative. The whole of the seventh chapter represents a trick of style, which excludes every labial sound from its diction. It is difficult to judge of the extent of Daṇḍin's inventive power, because we do not know how much he borrowed from predecessors. His work is particularly interesting owing to the light it sheds on social life, especially the activity of the dishonest classes, such as vagabonds, thieves, gamblers, and courtezans. The daily life of a king is related with much detail in the story of Vīrabhadra in chapter viii. The work has been preserved in a somewhat incomplete form.

Subandhu, as the author of the romance *Vāsavadattā* (the story of which has nothing to do with the plot of the play attributed to Bhāsa), was famous as one of the best of poets. Of his life nothing is known, nor is any other work of his mentioned anywhere. The plan of the tale, which was probably not invented by him, contains features commonly occurring in fairy tales, such as love originating in a dream, speaking birds, magical horses, transformation into a pillar of stone, and so forth. His chief aim is not to invent stories of adventure, but to display his masterly skill in the Kāvya style (cp. p. 129). His *Vāsavadattā*, which recounts the popular story of a princess of Ujjayinī bearing that name, was composed by Subandhu about 600 A.D. The author of two celebrated romances was Bāṇa, the first Indian poet about whose date we have certain knowledge. He lived at the court of King Harshavardhana (606–48 A.D.) of Thānesar (in Sanskrit Sthāneśvara). He wrote his *Kādambarī*, which relates the fortunes of a princess so named, early in the seventh century.

The story is borrowed from a fairly tale in the *Bṛhatkathā* of Guṇāḍhya. The narrative consists of a series of stories one within another. The style is similar to that of the *Harṣacarita*, but the story is less interesting. Though the patience of the reader is generally tried by the almost unendurable complexity of the diction, it is occasionally relieved by short sentences of natural, unstrained prose, as is the case in Subandhu's *Vāsavadattā*. Though not to the same extent as the *Harṣacarita*, the *Kādambarī* throws much light on the manners and customs of the times, especially on the religious life of the adherents of the Śivaite sects.

The *Kādambarī* remained uncompleted owing to the death of the author, but it was continued and finished by the poet's son in his father's style.

Bāṇa's chief work is the *Harṣacarita*, 'the Life and Doings of Harsha', a prose historical romance, in which a few verses are intermingled. Here Bāṇa gives some account of the career of his patron Harṣavardhana of Kanauj. This work contains many data that are of importance for literary and political chronology. Thus Bāṇa mentions a number of his predecessors, including Subandhu, Śātavāhana (Hāla), Bhāsa, Kālidāsa, Guṇāḍhya, and some others. Though he scarcely equals Subandhu in the matter of puns and other literary devices, he is far superior to him in true poetical endowment. His work is a mixture of truth and fiction, the former of which is of some chronological value, being of especial importance as illustrating the social and still more the religious conditions of the time. Himself a Brahmin, he mentions many sects, towards all of whom he is tolerant. But he does not refrain from criticizing the failings of religious men. Thus he remarks: 'A Brahmin who is not avaricious, a wandering ascetic who is not voracious, are hard to find.'

The first two chapters of the *Harṣacarita* contain an autobiography supplying valuable information regarding the poet's life. But though the narrative is often of interest, it is much impeded by the great space given up to the description of persons, localities, and natural phenomena, teeming with similes and puns. Thus the panegyric of Harsha, when seen for the first time by Bāṇa, occupies ten printed pages. The end of the work seems to have been lost.

Some idea of the style of these romances may be gained from the following quotation from the *Harṣacarita* describing a disconsolate princess lying prostrate in a wood: 'lost in the forest and in thought, bent upon death and the root of a tree, fallen upon calamity and her nurse's bosom, parted from her husband and happiness, burnt with the fierce sunshine and the woes of widowhood, her mouth closed with silence as well as by her hand, she was held fast by her companions as well as by grief. I saw her kindred and her graces all gone, her ears and her soul left bare, her ornaments and her aims abandoned, her bracelets and her hopes broken, her companions and needle-like grass-spears clinging round her feet, her eye and her beloved fixed within her bosom, her sighs and her hair long, her limbs

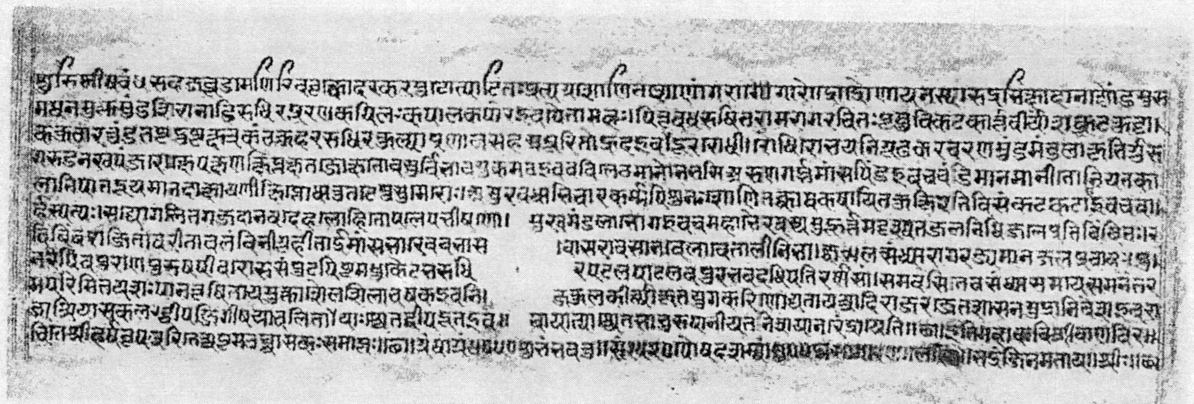

27. DEVANĀGARĪ SANSKRIT MS. OF BĀṆA'S HARSHACHARITA, A.D. 1463

and her merits exhausted, her aged attendants and her streaming tears falling at her feet', and so forth.

There is no probability that the least influence was exercised on these romances by the Greek novel, or vice versa, as a literary type. But individual short stories or fairy tales may very well have been incorporated from the other on each side, especially as the result of oral interchange rather than of immediate literary borrowing.

There is a special kind of story-book called *campū*, in which verse in elaborate metres alternates with artificial prose, but without either predominating. The verse serves the same purpose as the prose: it is not here used, as, for instance, in the *Pañcatantra*, to introduce sententious matter, or to summarize the story, or to emphasize important points. The best known of these works is the *Nala-campū* or *Damayantī-kathā*, by Trivikrama-bhaṭṭa, whose date is known by an inscription of 915 A.D. Here the famous story of Nala and Damayantī is treated over again in this form.

SELECTED BIBLIOGRAPHY

Benfey, *Pañcatantra*, German tr., Leipzig, 1859. Hertel, *Tantrākhyāyika*, German tr., Leipzig, 1909. Pūrṇabhadra's *Pañcatantra*, Harvard Oriental Series, xi (1906) and xiii (1912). Johnson, *Hitopadeśa*, 1848. Pincott, *Hitopadeśa*, tr. 1880. Keith-Falconer, *Kalila and Dimnah*, tr., Cambridge, 1885. Tawney, *Kathāsaritsāgara*, tr., 2 vols., Calcutta, 1880–4. *Śukasaptati*, German tr., Stuttgart, 1899. Meyer, *Daśakumāra-carita*, tr., Leipzig, 1902. Gray, *Vāsavadatta*, tr., New York, 1913. Cowell and Thomas, *Harshacarita*, tr., London, 1897. Ridding, *Kādambarī*, tr., London, 1896. Winternitz, *Geschichte*, iii. 265–376, 647–9.

VII

TECHNICAL LITERATURE

Theological origin — earliest works composed in sūtra style — a. Grammar: Sanskrit, Prākrit, Pāli — b. Lexicography: Amarakośa; Hemachandra's dictionaries; Pāli lexicon — c. Philosophy: six orthodox systems —. Vedānta: The Commentator Śaṅkara — the Vedānta-sāra — Rāmānuja's doctrine of bhakti — Madhva's dualistic Vedānta — Sāṅkhya system: Sāṅkhya-kārikā and Sāṅkhya-sūtra — Yoga system: Yoga-sūtra — haṭha-yoga and rāja-yoga — Nyāya system of logic: the Kusumāñjali — Dignāga — the Tarka-saṃgraha — the Vaiśeṣika or atomic school: the Bhāṣā-pariccheda — Materialistic school of Chārvāka — Possible connexion between Greek and Indian philosophy — d. Legal literature: metrical law-books — the code of Manu — its age — relation to the Mahābhārata — its commentaries — Yājñavalkya — Nārada — the dharma-nibandhas — e. Artha-śāstra or practical arts: Kauṭilya — Nīti-sāra 'essence of conduct' — f. Kāma-śāstra 'art of love' — g. Medicine: Charaka, Suśruta, Vāgbhaṭa — later medical works — h. Astronomy: two periods — Greek influence — Varāhamihira, Āryabhaṭa, Brahmagupta, Bhāskarāchārya — i. Astrology: Bṛhatsaṃhitā, Horā-śāstra — later astrological literature — Muhūrtas — j. Mathematics: arithmetic — algebra — geometry — Śulva-sūtras — trigonometry — Selected bibliography.

ALL technical literature in India had its rise in theology. The study of the Vedic hymns early led to phonetic, grammatical, and metrical investigations as well as the beginnings of lexicography. Philosophy, developed in the Upanishads, was never completely dissociated from theology. Vedic ritual, requiring observation of the heavenly bodies, gave rise to the beginnings of astronomy. The construction of the sacrificial altar entailed measurements and led to geometry. Many of the spells of the *Atharvaveda* contain the germs of medical science. The regulation de sacrificial worship ended in religious science, which of course necessarily remained a branch of theology. With this who connected the science of *dharma*, concerned with religious and secular custom, which, gradually leaving the area of re ligion, developed into an extensive legal literature. These were forms of technical knowledge which in their earls stage were first studied in Vedic schools, but the develop ment of departmental schools finally relegated the Vedie schools to the background.

Only a few branches of secular science developed independently of theology: poetics (*alaṃkāra*), the arts of practical life, especially that of government (*artha-śāstra*), and the art of love (*kāma-śāstra*). The earliest form in which all science appeared in writing was the aphoristic prose style called *sūtra*. The leading characteristic of the *sūtra* and technical literature in general was a syntax in which substantives were almost exclusively used, and verbs practically disappeared. Another was fondness for abstract nouns and compounds. In connexion with the sūtras was developed an expository style, first probably in grammar and philosophy, of learned prose. Being based on the disputations, at assemblies of scholars, for the purpose of establishing a particular doctrine, the technical literature of India has a scholastic and dialectical character almost throughout. This style is often enlivened by illustrative analogies (*nyāya*). Thus an argument serving two purposes is stated to be used 'on the analogy of the lamp on the threshold', which shines in both directions, inwards and outwards. The oldest works in the department of technical science have seldom been preserved, because they were generally superseded by later commentaries or compendia.

a. Grammar

Grammar, called in Sanskrit *vyākaraṇa*, or 'analysis', is by the Indians regarded as the first and most important of the sciences because it is the foundation of all of them. The greatest achievement of Indian science, it has rendered eminent services to Western philology. The Sanskrit grammarians of India were the first to analyse word-forms, to recognize the difference between root and suffix, to determine the functions of suffixes, and on the whole to elaborate a grammatical system so accurate and complete as to be unparalleled in any other country. Grammatical study began with the linguistic investigation of the Vedic hymns. Śākalya's Pada text of the *Rigveda*, in which not only the words of the sentence but the parts of compounds and even of certain inflected word-forms are separated, presupposes grammatical analysis. The following line of the *Ṛigveda* as it appears in the Saṃhitā text, *gómātaro yác chubhάyante añjíbhis*, becomes *gó-mātaraḥ*, *yát*, *śubhάyante*, *añjí-bhiḥ*, in the Pada text.

The phonetic works called Prātiśākhyas and Śikshās may be regarded as grammatical treatises. Technical grammatical terms occur in the Brāhmaṇas, the Āraṇyakas, and the Upanishads, and Yāska's *Nirukta* shows that a considerable grammatical development had taken place by his time; but no actual grammar has come down to us from the Vedic period. The oldest grammatical work in Sanskrit is the celebrated grammar (*śabdānuśāsana*, or 'doctrine of words') of Pāṇini in eight sections. It deals with Vedic grammar in the form of exceptions to Classical Sanskrit. The basis of his grammar is the usage of the Brāhmaṇas, Upanishads, and Sūtras rather than that of Classical Sanskrit. The date of Pāṇini is usually assumed to be about

350 B.C., but the evidence for this is very doubtful: it is perhaps safer to say that he lived after, probably soon after, 500 B.C. His birthplace was Śalātura in the north-west of India, near the present Attock. Pāṇini mentions ten predecessors by name, but his work was of such pre-eminent merit that it superseded all of them. His grammar has always been highly esteemed by the Indians, and has filled all Western scholars who have studied it with admiration. His rules are expressed with algebraic brevity. For instance, his last rule is: '*ă ă*'. This means that 'short *ă* is in this grammar treated as if it were the short form of long *ā*, though it is really pronounced like a close short *ă*' (as the *u* in English *bŭt*). A characteristic feature of Pāṇini's system is that he derives all words from verbal roots. It was formerly held by various Western scholars that Pāṇini's system treated many roots and forms as existent that did not actually occur in the language, and that he had an inadequate knowledge of the Veda; but this view has been refuted.

The language that Pāṇini's successors, Kātyāyana and Patañjali, had in view was essentially Classical Sanskṛit. Patañjali is the author of the *Mahābhāṣya*, 'the Great Commentary', which does not discuss Pāṇini's rules, but Kātyāyana's *vārttikas*, which are short criticisms on about one-third of Pāṇini's sūtras. In these *vārttikas* Kātyāyana criticizes the rules of Pāṇini, not by any means in a hostile spirit, as was once thought, but with a view to correct or supplement them quite impartially, and he seldom rejects them. Patañjali is mainly concerned with explaining and criticizing the *vārttikas*; but he also continues Kātyāyana's work in examining Pāṇini's sūtras in his *Mahābhāṣya*. The latter is the oldest extant work in the expository or Bhāshya style, which here takes the form of an actual conversation, like a direct and often very lively dialogue. The language is simple and clear, and the sentences are short. The date of Patañjali has been much debated, but the view is now generally accepted that he lived in the second century B.C. It is certain that a considerable interval must have elapsed between Kātyāyana and Patañjali, and a still greater one between Pāṇini and Kātyāyana. It is therefore a good working theory to assign Pāṇini to 450 B.C., Kātyāyana to 250 B.C., and Patañjali to 150 B.C.

These three names bring the development of the science of Sanskrit grammar to a conclusion. We have no knowledge of their predecessors, while the later Indian grammarians have added nothing new. For they did not write about Sanskrit grammar directly, but only about the grammatical rules of Pāṇini.

The best commentary on the complete sūtras of Pāṇini is the *Kāśikā Vṛtti*, 'the Commentary of Benares', by Jayāditya and Vāmana, the former of whom died not later than 662 A.D. This work is distinguished by both brevity and clearness.

In 1625 A.D. Bhaṭṭoji Dīkshita wrote the *Siddhānta-kaumudī*, or 'Moonlight of Settled Conclusions', in which the sūtras of Pāṇini are arranged according to subjects, such as phonetics and declension, and commented on concisely and clearly. It is easy to understand and well adapted as an introduction to the Indian system of grammar.

An abridgement of this work is the *Laghu-kaumudī* of Varadarāja.

A philosophic grammarian was Bhartṛihari, who died in 651 A.D. He wrote the *Vākyapadīya*, which deals with grammar from the point of view of the science of language. A good many treatises and commentaries deal with grammatical works supplementary to Pāṇini. Such is Nāgojibhaṭṭa's *Paribhāṣenduśekhara*, which is concerned with the *paribhāṣās* or interpretative key-rules to Pāṇini's grammar. The versified *Gaṇaratna-mahodadhi*, 'the Ocean of Gems of Word-groups', treats the *gaṇas* or lists of words to which grammatical sūtras apply. It was written about 1140 A.D. by Vardhamāna. One of the supplements to Pāṇini is the *Uṇ-ādi-sūtras*, which give rules for the derivation of certain nouns from verbal roots by particular suffixes enumerated in a list beginning with *uṇ*, that is, *u*. The best commentary on this is by Ujjvaladatta, who flourished about 1250 A.D. The *Phiṭ-sūtras* give rules for the accents of the Vedic language as well as of Sanskrit. These rules are by Śāntanava, who lived after Pāṇini and was probably unknown to Patañjali.

The earliest of grammatical works which, though unable to emancipate themselves from Pāṇini, aimed at forming new systems, is the *Kātantra* of Śarvavarman. It is an elementary work, well suited for beginners, dating probably from about 300 A.D. A commentary written on it is mentioned by Albērūnī. The *Cāndra-vyākaraṇa*, the grammar of Chandragomin, is the Sanskrit grammar best known in the Buddhist countries of Kashmīr, Nepāl, Tibet, and Ceylon. The author utilized both the sūtras of Pāṇini and the commentary of Patañjali. His grammar was composed about 600 A.D.

Śākaṭāyana's grammar, the *Śākaṭāyana-vyākaraṇa*, which makes use of Pāṇini and the *Mahābhāṣya* as well as the grammar of Chandragomin, and employs the technical terms partly of Pāṇini and partly of Chandragomin, was composed by the grammarian Śākaṭāyana, a namesake of one of Pāṇini's predecessors, in the ninth century A.D.

The grammar of Hemachandra, which is really an improved edition of Śākaṭāyana, is more practical in arrangement and terminology than the works of Pāṇini, Chandragomin, and Śākaṭāyana. Being meant for Jains it does not of course deal with the Vedic language and the rules of accent.

There are various other grammars that have only a local popularity. The most widely known one in Bengal is the *Mugdhabodha* of Vopadeva, which differs from Pāṇini both in arrangement and in technical terminology. The author lived in the second half of the thirteenth century.

The system of Pāṇini was transferred to Prākrit, which was regarded simply as a literary language derived from Sanskrit. The oldest Prākrit grammar extant is the *Prākṛta-prakāśa* of Vararuchi. That it was a comparatively old work appears from the fact that Bhāmaha (*c.* 650 A.D.), the earliest writer of a treatise on poetics (*alaṃkāra*), composed a commentary on it. Vararuchi treats of only four Prākrit dialects, Māhārāshṭrī, Paiśāchī, Māgadhī, and Śaurasenī. He and all later grammarians start from the assumption that Māhārāshṭrī is the real and best Prākrit because it is nearest to Sanskrit. One of the older works is the *Prākṛta-lakṣaṇa* of Chaṇḍa, a treatise which is of uncertain date, and the text of which has been very badly preserved.

Hemachandra also wrote a Prākrit grammar which, though largely based on the work of predecessors, is the most important because of its comprehensiveness and the abundance of its linguistic material. He deals with three other dialects in addition to the four of Vararuchi, besides including the Jain form of Māhārāshṭrī. It is interesting to note that for Paiśāchī he quotes passages from the no longer existing *Bṛhatkathā* of Guṇāḍhya.

The value of the Prākrit grammars has been very

seriously questioned, but not always with justice. At least the earlier ones are indispensable to our knowledge of the Prākrit dialects, for the purpose of understanding both Prākrit poetry and the Prākrit portions of the dramas.

The Pāli grammarians of Ceylon and Burma, similarly deriving their material exclusively from the literature, have slavishly followed the model of Sanskrit grammar. The oldest Pāli grammar is that of Kātyāyana, the *Kaccāyana-ppakaraṇa.* He differs from others in treating Pāli as an independent language, not as derived from Sanskrit; yet he uses the terminology of Sanskrit grammar, and frames his sūtras on that model. He has utilized Pāṇini and his successors (including the *Kāśikā Vṛtti*) as well as the *Kātantra.* His work seems to date from between 500 and 1000 A.D. After 1000 A.D., when it began to be studied in Burma, Pāli became the vehicle, in that country, of grammatical works on the language.

b. Lexicography

The origin of Sanskrit lexicography is to be traced to the Vedic Nighaṇṭus; but the real dictionaries, called by the name of *kośa* ('treasury' of words), are separated from these by a long interval. The transition is formed by the *Dhātu-pāṭhas*, or 'Lists of Roots', and the *Gaṇa-pāṭhas*, or 'Lists of Word-groups'. The Nighaṇṭus contain verbs as well as nouns, but the Kośas only nouns and indeclinables. The Nighaṇṭus, again, relate to individual Vedic texts only, while the Kośas have no specific reference. The dictionaries are collections of rare and important words and meanings for the use of poets. Themselves written in verse (chiefly in the *śloka* metre), they are, like the treatises on poetics (*alaṃkāra*), indispensable aids to poetical composition.

They are of a general character, for they contain the technical terms of other literary departments, such as astronomy. There are two kinds of dictionaries: the synonymous and the homonymous. The synonymous class embraces groups of words systematically arranged according to subjects that have the same meaning; for instance, all words expressive of 'earth'. The homonymous class comprises words with more than one meaning, which, as well as the gender, is often indicated by the locative case; for instance, *dine* = 'in (the sense of) day'; *trișu*, 'in three (genders)' = 'adjective'. The fact that the arrangement is not generally alphabetical is due to the dictionaries being intended to be learnt by heart and not to be looked up. The older dictionaries, which are known to us only in a fragmentary way, are quite unsystematic and prolix in their definitions, the explanation often occupying a whole couplet (*śloka*). Many are known from quotations in commentaries only. The *nāma-liṅgānuśāsana* of Amara-siṃha, generally called the 'Dictionary of Amara', or *Amara-kośa*, superseded nearly all the predecessors of Amara. The author was a Buddhist, though he does not specially favour the Buddhist vocabulary. Nothing certain is known of his date, but the probability is that he lived between 550 and 750 A.D. His work is a dictionary of synonyms in three sections. Of the fifty commentaries on this lexicon, few are known, the best being that of Bhaṭṭa Kshīra-svāmin, who probably lived *c.* 1050 A.D.

A supplement to the *Amarakośa* is the *Trikāṇḍa-śeṣa* of Purushottama-deva. It is one of the most important and interesting extant Indian lexicons, containing as it does many words peculiar to Buddhistic Sanskrit, as well as inscriptional and even Prākrit words. Its author also compiled a concise lexicon, both synonymous and homonymous, entitled *Hārāvalī*, or 'String of Pearls', which contains more rare words than the former work. Nothing is known of his date, but it cannot well have been far removed from 700 A.D.

Old and important is the *Anekārtha-samuccaya*, a homonymous lexicon by Śāśvata. An indication of its antiquity is its arrangement; for it begins with words the explanation of which requires a whole *śloka*; then follow those that need a half, and lastly those that take up one-fourth couplet; then come supplements and a section on indeclinables.

The earliest old lexicon that is approximately datable is the *Abhidhāna-ratna-mālā* of Halāyudha, who wrote about 950 A.D. It is short, consisting of only 900 couplets. One of the most extensive lexicons is the *Vaijayantī* of Yādava-prakāśa, another South Indian, who lived about a century later. The words are arranged according to the number of their syllables, then by the gender, and in every subdivision according to the initial. It is of great importance because it contains many words not to be found in other dictionaries.

Between 1123 and 1140 A.D. a Digambara Jain named Dhanaṃjaya wrote a lexicon entitled *Nāma-mālā* or 'Garland of Nouns'. The poet Maheśvara compiled the homonymous *Viśvaprakāśa* in the year 1111 A.D. as he himself states. Another poet named Maṅkha composed his *Anekārthakośa*, accompanied by a commentary, about 1150 A.D.

Of the greatest importance are Hemachandra's dictionaries, which, according to his own statement, he compiled as supplements to his grammar. His lexicon of synonyms is the *Abhidhāna-cintāmaṇi*, which consists of an introduction dealing with the different classes of words, and of six sections enumerating the Jain gods, the Brahmin gods, men, animals, denizens of the lower regions, while the last is concerned with abstracts, adjectives, and particles. As a supplement to this lexicon he compiled the *Nighaṇṭu-śeṣa*, which is a botanical glossary in 396 ślokas. He also wrote the *Anekārtha-saṃgraha*, a dictionary of homonyms in seven sections, of which the first six deal with substantives and adjectives according to the number of their syllables, while the seventh treats of indeclinables.

Of later lexicographical works, only two homonymous dictionaries need be mentioned. About 1200 A.D. Keśavasvāmin compiled the *Nānārtha-saṃkalpa*, in which the words are well arranged according to the number of syllables, the alphabet, and the gender. The much-quoted *Nānārthaśabda-kośa* of Medinīkara probably dates from the fourteenth century. It is generally called *Medinī-kośa* or simply *Medinī*. It seems to have been based chiefly on the *Viśvaprakāśa*.

There are also several special glossaries. Some are associated with particular Buddhist Sanskrit works, resembling the Vedic Nighaṇṭus as being intended for individual texts and not having a metrical form. The oldest extant Prākrit dictionary is the *Pāiya-lacchī-*[1]*nāma-mālā* of Dhanapāla written in 279 *āryā* stanzas and dated 972 A.D. The words are here not arranged on any particular system, except that they begin with the names of gods and of sacred objects. This work was used by Hemachandra in his *Deśī-nāma-mālā*, or 'Glossary of Provincial Words', as distinct from *tat-samas* or pure Sanskrit words and from *tad-bhavas*, or words derived from Sanskrit. It is very important for the study of Prākrit, because the dictionaries on which Hemachandra's work is founded have not been preserved.

[1] In Sanskrit *Prākṛta-lakṣmī* 'wealth of the Prākrit language

The only early Pāli dictionary extant is the *Abhidhāna-ppadīpikā*, or 'Lamp of Words', of Moggallāna. Dating from about 1200 A.D., and composed in verse, it follows completely the model of the *Amara-kośa*.

Zachariae, *Die indischen Wörterbücher*, in Bühler's *Encyclopaedia*, i. 3, 1897 (full bibliography down to 1897); Macdonell, *History*, p. 451 f.; Winternitz, *Geschichte*, iii. 408–17.

c. PHILOSOPHY

Philosophy, in Sanskrit termed *Ānvīkṣikī*, or 'science of research', has during a period of more than 2,000 years never succeeded in becoming independent of religion in India. The systems called *darśanas* ('views') are not merely the doctrines of particular philosophical schools, but of particular religious sects. The Indians generally consider these systems to be six in number, consisting of three more closely associated pairs. These are regarded as orthodox because they hold the Veda to be the principal means of knowledge. They are the *Pūrva-* and *Uttara-mīmāṃsā*; the *Sāṅkhya* and *Yoga*; the *Nyāya* and *Vaiśeṣika*. The Jain Haribhadra substituted for the first and fourth Buddhism and Jainism. These eight as well as other systems, altogether sixteen, are critically described in the *Sarva-darśana-saṃgraha*, 'Compendium of all Philosophical Systems', by the great Vedānta scholar Mādhava (fourteenth century), brother of the famous Vedic commentator Sāyaṇa.

Philosophy as a whole is not regarded as a *śāstra* or branch of knowledge, like grammar and others, but each individual system or *darśana* is one in itself. The literature of each of these *śāstras* consists of a *sūtra* work as its foundation, and a succession of commentaries. But the date of none of these fundamental texts can be traced with certainty, nor is anything known about their authors, who are nothing but names, some of which seem to be actually mythical. The basic *sūtras*, which form the starting-point of a system, in reality represent the end of a long and extensive literary development that has been lost. They are all the productions of schools, not of individuals. Even if we could determine the date of the *sūtras*, this would prove nothing regarding the time when the philosophical systems and schools came into being. Thus, though the *Sāṇkhya-sūtra* is the latest of all philosophical *sūtras*, the Sāṇkhya philosophy as reduced to a system is regarded as the oldest.

1. *The Pūrva and the Uttara Mīmāṃsā*

Most closely connected with the Vedic religion are the two systems called the *Pūrva-mīmāṃsā* and the *Uttara-mīmāṃsā*, the latter better known under the name of *Vedānta*. They are the real philosophy of orthodox Brāhmanism, the ultimate appeal of which is the Veda. The former means 'the discussion of the first (practical) part', the latter, 'the discussion of the second (theoretical) part' of the Veda, which is concerned with the doctrine of the world-soul. The *Pūrva-mīmāṃsā* was originally concerned with the rules (*nyāya*) for the correct interpretation of the texts relating to ritual acts. There must have been such rules centuries before Christ; but it by no means follows that the fundamental text, the *Pūrva-mīmāṃsā-sūtra* of Jaimini, goes back to such an early time. Here no other way of salvation is laid down but that of works, that is, of sacrifices and ceremonies, and no higher authority for religious duties (*dharma*) than the Veda. These *sūtras* contain little of what we would consider philosophy. Their importance consists in their representing the method of discussion which has been adopted in the whole of the philosophical and scientific literature of India.

The oldest extant commentary is that of Śabara-svāmin, who quotes a predecessor named Upavarsha, probably belonging to the fifth century A.D. He combats the two philosophical systems of the Buddhists. Two schools of interpretation of Śabara's commentary grew up. The more famous scholar representing one of them was Kumārila, who wrote a very extensive commentary in three parts on Śabara-svāmin's work. It is full of hair-splitting learning and acuteness. His polemics are directed chiefly against the Buddhists, who denied the authority of the Veda. Written about 700 A.D., it is of great importance owing to the many references it contains to contemporary literature and social life. Kumārila was a south Indian, and had a knowledge of the Dravidian languages. A later manual was the *Nyāya-mālā-vistara* of the famous Vedānta scholar Mādhava. There was an original opposition between the *Pūrva-* and the *Uttara-mīmāṃsā*, because the former regarded works, the latter knowledge, as the only means of salvation; but finally their antagonism became merged in their common Brahmanic orthodoxy.

The basic text of the *Uttara-mīmāṃsā* is the *Vedānta-sūtra* ascribed to Bādarāyaṇa. It must have been constituted contemporaneously with that attributed to Jaimini, because these two authors refer to each other's works. The *Vedānta-sūtra* contains only catchwords, unintelligible without a commentary; and as there is no uninterrupted tradition between Bādarāyaṇa and Śaṅkara, whose commentary is the oldest extant, it is not always certain what Bādarāyaṇa's doctrine was. It appears, however, to be undoubted that one of the main doctrines of the later Vedānta, that of *māyā*, which holds the phenomenal world to be an illusion, has not yet been developed in the *Vedānta-sūtra*. It is first met with in the *Kārikās* of Gauḍapāda, which, excepting the *sūtras*, are among the earliest products of Vedānta literature.

Śaṅkara, the chief of the Vedānta philosophers, was the principal exponent of the *a-dvaita* ('non-dualistic') doctrine, or strict monism. He distinguished a lower kind of knowledge suited to the comprehension of the many, and a higher kind which met the requirements of strict philosophic thought. His chief works were commentaries on the Upanishads, the *Bhagavadgītā*, and the *Vedānta-sūtra*. Many other works, of which he was not the author, are attributed to him. We know nothing about his life, but in all probability he flourished from about 800 A.D. onwards. Every word of the Upanishads is irrefutable truth to both Bādarāyaṇa and to Śaṅkara, but they differ in their interpretation. The style of Śaṅkara is no longer that of a living disputation, but rather that of a scientific treatise. His sentences are long and involved. But his exposition is clear and transparent compared with that of the later philosophic commentaries. His *Gītābhāṣya*, or 'Commentary on the *Bhagavadgītā*', is rather an independent religio-philosophic treatise than a commentary in the strict sense. From the *Gītā* he tries to adduce proofs for his own doctrine, especially its exoteric part relating to the performance of social duties. Of his other works may be mentioned the *Ātmabodha*, a compendium of the Vedānta doctrine in sixty-seven stanzas, with an appended commentary. The subsequent literature of Śaṅkara's monistic doctrine is very extensive. One of the most devoted of his followers was Mādhava, who wrote the *Pañcadaśī*, the most popular exposition of the Vedānta in the India of to-day.

The best known and favourite short handbook of the Vedānta, serving as an excellent introduction to the system, is the *Vedānta-sāra*, 'the Quintessence of the Vedānta', by Sadānanda, who must have lived before or soon after 1500 A.D., as commentaries on his work were already written in the sixteenth century. In this treatise Sāṅkhya ideas are found intermingled with the Vedānta framework of the system.

As the followers of Śaṅkara also formed a religious sect, so the other Vedānta schools represent as many religious sects. The next in importance to the adherents of Śaṅkara were those of Rāmānuja, who, in propounding the doctrine of 'qualified monism', sought to combine with belief in one deity the doctrine of the love of God (*bhakti*). Rāmānuja's activity ranges between 1175 and 1250 A.D. He was a south Indian, a native of Conjeeveram. The names of his father, mother, and teachers are known. Originally a monist, he became the founder of the theistic Vaishṇava sect of south India. His chief work is the *Śrībhāṣya*, or 'Glorious Commentary'. Though a convinced believer in the truth of the Upanishads and of the *Vedānta-sūtras*, he combated the views of Śaṅkara on the relation of action and knowledge, on true knowledge, on the mutual connexion between Brahman and the world, on salvation, and so on. His chief aim, the reconciliation of the doctrines of the Upanishads, the *Bhagavadgītā*, the *Mahābhārata*, and the Purāṇas, with his own religion and philosophy, was theological rather than philosophical. To Rāmānuja the legendary Vyāsa was the seer and arranger not only of the Veda and the *Mahābhārata*, but of the *Vedānta-sūtras* as well. He assumes three principles: the individual soul, the inanimate world, and God as the Supreme Soul. His theories of the external world are based on the Sāṅkhya philosophy and the Purāṇas. His doctrine of devotion (*bhakti*) to a personal deity he sought to combine with his conception of nature. In addition to his chief work, Rāmānuja also wrote the *Gītā-bhāṣya*, a commentary on the *Bhagavad-gītā*.

A well-known founder of a religious sect was Madhva (1197–1276), who wandered about the country preaching his doctrine. He wrote commentaries on the seven old Upanishads, the *Vedānta-sūtra*, the *Bhagavadgītā*, and the *Bhāgavata Purāṇa*, as well as a number of independent works. By very forced interpretations of the texts he endeavoured to reconcile his dualistic conception of the world by combining the Vedānta with the Sāṅkhya system and the Bhāgavata religion. He summarized the doctrines of his dualistic Vedānta in his *Tattva-saṅkhyāna*. He wrote as a strenuous opponent of Śaṅkara.

The founder of another sect was Vallabha (1478–1530), who was devoted to the cult of Kṛishṇa. He wrote a commentary on the *Vedānta-sūtra* entitled *Anubhāṣya*.

The Vedānta philosophy allied itself not only with Vishṇuite, but with Śivaite sects. Here, too, we find that the original monistic doctrine branches off in dualistic and Bhakti directions.

2 (*a*). *The Sāṅkhya System*

The earliest philosophical ideas are to be found in the Veda, and later the doctrines regarding Brahman and Ātman in the Upanishads, but the oldest philosophy that was elaborated as a system was the Sāṅkhya, or 'enumerative philosophy', so called because classification of principles is characteristic of the system. It is the philosophy of realism, which arose in opposition to the idealism of the Upanishads.

The doctrine of Kapila, the legendary founder of th. system, was independent of the authority of the Veda. For it was not based, like the Vedānta, on the interpretation of Vedic writings. It was only later that it attached itself to Brāhmanism. For the founder rejects the conception of Brahman and the world-soul. He distinguishes matter, which is real, and an infinite plurality of individual souls, which are not regarded as emanations of a single world-soul. The ultimate cause of the world is primeval matter (*prakṛti*), which in spite of its oneness consists of three constituent elements called *guṇas*. Suffering arises from the non-distinction of soul and matter; but discriminative knowledge causes deliverance from suffering. The Sāṅkhya is thus not only a system explaining the world, but also a method of salvation. But of all these doctrines there is nothing in Vedic literature; they thus form a direct contrast with those of the Veda. The teaching of the Sāṅkhya, however, already exercised some influence on the second chronological stratum of the Upanishads: the *Kaṭha*, the *Śvetāśvatara*, the *Praśna*, and the *Maitrī*.

There is a mixture of Sāṅkhya with Vedānta doctrines in the philosophical sections of the *Mahābhārata*, the Purāṇas, and the *Dharma-śāstra* of Manu. The Sāṅkhya indeed pervades the Purāṇas to such an extent that what is generally called 'Epic philosophy' might more correctly be styled 'Purāṇic philosophy'. It cannot be doubted that Buddha grew up in the atmosphere of Sāṅkhya thought, for it is the essential basis of his world-view. There seems, in fact, good reason to believe that the Sāṅkhya doctrine came into being as a system between 800 and 550 B.C.

That it spread in early times beyond the confines of India is indicated by the Sāṅkhya parable of the co-operation of the blind and the lame man being known in China in the second century B.C.

The oldest and completely preserved work of the Sāṅkhya philosophy is the *Sāṅkhya-kārikā* of Īśvara-kṛishṇa. This work, with a commentary, was translated into Chinese between 557 and 569 A.D. It seems not unlikely that both text and commentary were anterior to the Buddhist teacher Vasubandhu, and came into existence about 300 A.D. It is written in the *āryā* metre, and presents a clear exposition of the Sāṅkhya doctrine. A very competent judge, the late French Sanskritist Auguste Barth, regarded it as the pearl of the whole scholastic literature of India. The account given of the Sāṅkhya doctrine by the Arabic scholar Albērūnī in 1030 A.D. is based on this work.

The most valuable commentary on the *Sāṅkhya-kārikā*, and at the same time the best methodical account of the Sāṅkhya doctrine in general, is the *Sāṅkhya-tattva-kaumudī* of Vāchaspati-miśra.

The *Sāṅkhya-sūtra*, or *Sāṅkhya-pravacana*, probably dates, in the form in which we possess it, from the fifteenth century, but is in all likelihood based on an older *Sāṅkhya-sūtra* that was known many centuries earlier. Its oldest commentary, the *Sāṅkhya-sūtra-vṛtti*, was written about 1500 A.D. by Aniruddha.

About 1550 A.D. was composed the *Sāṅkhya-pravacana-bhāṣya* by Vijñāna-bhikshu, who as a strict Vedānta theist gives a forced interpretation of the *Sāṅkhya-sūtra* in conformity with his own views. He divides the doctrine of salvation into four parts, probably suggested by the four noble truths of Buddhism. This division, however, seems to be ultimately derived from Indian medical science, which separates its subject-matter into the four sections of disease, health, cause of disease, and cure, as Vijñāna-bhikshu himself tells us.

2 (*b*). *The Yoga System*

While the Sāṅkhya arose independently of religious belief, the Yoga was the immediate result of religious needs. Its origin may be traced to pre-Vedic ideas. The primary meaning is the 'yoking' of the mind with a view to concentrate thought on a single point; for these exercises aim at the regulation of breathing, sitting, and restraining the senses for the purpose of exclusive concentration on a single supernatural object, in order to obtain as a result supernatural knowledge and supernatural powers. Such practices are prehistoric, going back to a time when there was no essential difference between a saint and a magician. That they were pre-Buddhistic in India appears from the great part these exercises play in ancient Buddhism. As restraint of the senses forms part of them, they evidently include morality. In this aspect, Yoga could be combined with any philosophical system. In one form or another, Yoga is to be found among all Indian ascetics, including Buddhists and Jains. As a system it became closely associated with the Sāṅkhya, from which it differs only in its ascetic practice and in its adoption of theism. But its connexion with belief in a god is a somewhat loose one. The god (*īśvara*) of the Yoga system does not create, reward, or punish. He is only a separate soul which is eternally combined with the most subtile constituent of matter, thus possessing the attributes of power, goodness, and wisdom. Devotion to God is only one element in Yoga morality (*kriyāyoga*). Its philosophical basis is otherwise entirely the Sāṅkhya system. Hence *Sāṅkhya-pravacana* is the common title of the *Sāṅkhya-sūtra* and the *Yoga-sūtra*.

The *Yoga-sūtra*, the foundation of the Yoga philosophy, is ascribed to Patañjali, who, however, is probably not identical with the grammarian, the author of the *Mahābhāṣya*. It consists of four sections, which deal with the nature of concentration, the means of concentration, the miraculous powers acquired by concentration, and salvation, which consists in the isolation (*kaivalya*) of the soul. The philosophy of the system is contained in the commentaries. The oldest of these is the *Yoga-bhāṣya*, ascribed to the legendary Vyāsa, and probably dating from about 500 A.D. This work was further commented on by Vāchaspati-miśra, Vijñāna-bhikshu, and King Bhoja (eleventh century). To a later period belong the treatises on *haṭha-yoga* or 'strict Yoga', which are practical manuals giving rules on the external aspects of Yoga, such as postures, breathing, diet, and so on, as opposed to the *rāja-yoga*, 'royal Yoga' of Patañjali, which is chiefly concerned with meditation.

3. *The Nyāya and Vaiśeshika Systems*

More closely complementary than the Sāṅkhya and Yoga were the two systems called Nyāya and Vaiśeshika, which finally coalesced to a single principle. Being essentially independent of religious belief, they may be described as strictly scientific systems of logic and the theory of knowledge.

Nyāya properly means 'method', applicable to any kind of argumentation. Disputations and learned contests play such a part in ancient India that a system of dialectics called *nyāya-śāstra*, a body of rules for correct thinking, arguing, and inferring was naturally developed. The founder of the Nyāya system and author of the *Nyāya-sūtra* is by tradition unanimously reputed to have been Akshapāda Gotama. It cannot, however, be doubted that the *Sūtra* attributed to him is the work of a school, not of an individual man. Its original form must also have undergone modifications and interpolations. It consists of five books, of which the first two deal with logic and the theory of knowledge and dialectics; the third with psychology; the fourth with rebirth and salvation; while the fifth is a supplement. It may date from about 300 A.D. in its latest shape, but its original form must be much older. There is a very old commentary, the *Nyāya-sūtra-bhāṣya*, which bears a certain likeness to Patañjali's *Mahābhāṣya*, by Pakshila-svāmin Vātsyāyana, who lived not improbably about 350 A.D.

The whole orthodox Nyāya-śāstra consists of five works: the *Sūtra*, its commentary, and three super-commentaries. The *Nyāyasūtra-bhāṣya* was commented on by Uddyotakara, who is quoted by the poet Subandhu, and who himself quotes the Buddhist logician Dharmakīrti. The latter lived about 635 A. D. and on his part refers to Uddyotakara. Hence it is highly probable that these three writers were contemporaries about 635 to 650 A.D. Udayana, a highly esteemed writer on Nyāya and Vaiśeshika, lived in the tenth century, one of his works being dated 984 A.D. He was the author of the *Kusumāñjali*, or 'Handful of Blossoms' (on the tree of Nyāya). This work aims at proving the existence of God from the Nyāya point of view. The author especially attacks the atheistical doctrine of the Mīmāṃsakas as well as the law of causality in the Vedānta, in the Sāṅkhya, and in Buddhism. He also wrote a special polemical work against the Buddhists.

The five works mentioned above constitute the 'old school' of logic. The great Buddhist logician Dignāga inaugurated the medieval school. This is chiefly represented by Buddhist and Jain scholars. Many of their works are only preserved in Tibetan translations. A pupil of Dharmapāla, who before 635 A.D. had been head of the school at Nālanda, was Dharmakīrti. He wrote the *Nyāya-bindu*, to which Dharmottara, who lived about 800 A.D. in Kashmīr, composed a commentary.

The famous Jain scholar Hemachandra wrote a work on logic entitled *Pramāṇa-mīmāṃsā* in the *sūtra* style. The 'new school' of logic at Navadvīpa in Bengal begins with the *Tattva-cintāmaṇi*, a systematic treatise on the Nyāya, by Gaṅgeśa, written about 1200 A.D. After this the Nyāya system degenerated into a very barren scholasticism.

An extremely useful glossary of Nyāya technical terms is the *Nyāya-kośa*, which was compiled at the instigation of Professors Bühler and Kielhorn in 1874.

The Vaiśeshika system which, independently of religious belief, endeavoured to explain the origin of the world from atoms, seems to have been akin to the *lokāyata* materialistic philosophy. The Nyāya and Vaiśeshika were the philosophy of non-theological scholars and 'heretics'. It is significant that the Buddhists and Jains had a considerable share in their development. There is a close affinity between the Vaiśeshika and the Jain philosophy. The former may have arisen before the Jain and the Buddhist canon, about the second century; but the *Vaiśeṣika-sūtra*, which is the basis of the system, and the authorship of which is attributed to Kāśyapa Kaṇāda, is certainly not so old in its extant shape. In this form it is a Brahmanic work with a religio-ethical tendency. But there can be little doubt that it was originally a purely secular scientific work, which was later turned into an orthodox Brahmanical text in a quite superficial manner. No old commentary of the *Vaiśeṣika-*

sūtra has been preserved. The *bhāṣya* of Praśastapāda entitled *Padārtha-dharma-saṃgraha* probably dates from about 700 A.D., and is really an independent manual in which the subject-matter is systematically arranged. It is at the present day acknowledged as their text-book by adherents of both Nyāya and Vaiśeshika. The commentary with which in 991 A.D. Śrīdhara supplied this work was the first Vaiśeshika text to set forth theism formally. The first commentary, in the strict sense, on the *Vaiśeṣika-sūtra* was the *Upaskāra* of Śaṅkara-miśra. It seems to have little value, for, as it was written as late as about 1600 A.D., the tradition of the original interpretation had long died out.

There is a great mass of commentaries and other works on the Nyāya and Vaiśeshika which, in the later period, are indistinguishable. This literature tends rather to obscure than to explain the two systems. A number of compendia dating from this later time exist. They are well adapted to serve as introductions not only to the Nyāya-Vaiśeshika, but to Indian scientific literature in general. The oldest of these handbooks is the *Sapta-padārthī* of Śivāditya, who cannot have lived later than the twelfth century. A treatise on logic, studied all over India, is the *Bhāṣāpariccheda*, a manual of the Navadvīpa school, whose author also wrote a commentary on the *Nyāya-sūtra* in the year 1634. The best known in Europe of these handbooks is the *Tarka-saṃgraha* by the south Indian Annam Bhaṭṭa. It is a short and clear summary of the most important tenets of logic and dialectic. The date of the author is uncertain, though it cannot be later than the sixteenth century.

Śivaite sects attached themselves closely to the Nyāya and Vaiśeshika, though these systems were, as we have seen, purely secular in origin.

Outside the orthodox systems was the doctrine of materialism called *lokāyata*, 'directed to the world', the founder of which was held to be Chārvāka. That it was an old school is indicated by the fact that in the *Vinaya-piṭaka* the Buddhist monks were forbidden to occupy themselves with this doctrine. Of the literature of the adherents of Chārvāka nothing has survived, and their doctrines are known to us only from the accounts of opponents. We are informed that their philosophy was laid down in a *sūtra* attributed to Bṛihaspati, and in the *Bhāgurī* mentioned by Patañjali in the *Mahābhāṣya.* It is not surprising that these works have perished, because the materialists were detested by all religious sects, not only as repudiating the Veda, but as hostile to religion in general. They regarded the soul as only an attribute of the body consisting in intelligence. They regarded it as coming into being when the body is formed by the combination of elements, just as the power of intoxication arises from the mixture of certain ingredients. When therefore the body is destroyed, the soul necessarily disappears. Thus results cannot be produced by transmigration, but by the true nature of things. Hell, they assert, is nothing but earthly pain produced by earthly causes; and salvation is simply the dissolution of the body. They do not admit the existence of anything supernatural. The Vedas they describe as the incoherent rhapsodies of knaves, and as tainted with the three blemishes of falsehood, self-contradiction, and tautology; Vedic teachers as impostors, whose doctrines are mutually destructive; and the ritual of the Brahmins as of no value except as a means of livelihood. If an animal that is sacrificed reaches heaven, why, they ask, does the sacrificer not rather offer his own father? The only end of man they regard as sensual pleasure to be enjoyed by ignoring as far as possible any pains it may involve. 'While life remains', they say, 'let a man live happily, let him feed on pleasant food, even though he run into debt; when once the body has been reduced to ashes, how can it ever return to life?' It is perhaps not surprising that the literature in which such views are set forth should not have survived in an environment so uncongenial to them as the general trend of Indian thought.

The question whether Greek and Indian philosophy were in any way connected has often engaged the attention of scholars. The characteristic peculiarities of Indian philosophical literature are such that the possibility of the Greeks ever having directly studied Indian philosophical texts is extremely remote. Any influence exercised by Indian on Greek philosophy must have been due to oral intercourse. The similarity between the Eleatic school of Xenophanes and Parmenides and the Vedānta is probably due to parallel development rather than borrowing. The influence of the Sāṅkhya on Greek philosophy is possible and perhaps even probable. In the case of Pythagoras, Indian influence is by some scholars thought to be undoubted. On the other hand, Greek influence on the Nyāya and Vaiśeshika has been suggested though not proved. Thus the Aristotelian doctrine of the syllogism may have influenced the later development of Indian logic, and the atomic theory of Empedocles may have affected the parallel atomic doctrine in India.

Cowell and Gough, *Sarvadarśana-saṃgraha*, 'A Compendium of all Philosophical Systems', tr., 2nd ed., London, 1894. Max Müller, *The Six Systems of Indian Philosophy*, new ed., London, 1903. Macdonell, *History*, ch. xv, pp. 451–2 (bibliography). Winternitz, *Geschichte*, iii. 417–78.

d. Legal Literature

Dharma-śāstra is the designation of legal literature in Sanskrit. Here the word *dharma* has a much wider connotation than 'law', for it includes religion, custom, good conduct, duty, in fact all that comes within the sphere of right. The oldest treatises on this subject are the *dharma-sūtras*, which grew up in close connexion with the works on ritual (*kalpa*). They are not compendia of law, but deal with the religious duties of man. They proceeded from the Vedic schools and were used by Brahmins for the purpose of instruction, not for practical application in law courts. They form part of Vedic literature, giving directions regarding daily religious rites, purifications, penances, duties, and rights of householders, Brahmins, kings, ascetics, forest-hermits, besides discussions on cosmology and eschatology. It is only where the duties of kings are concerned that sections occur on family law, legal procedure, civil and criminal law (*vyavahāra*). They are written in the *sūtra* style, but in all of them, verses, generally in the *śloka*, often in the *triṣṭubh* metre, are interspersed.

The best preserved of these works is the *Āpastaṁbīya-dharma-sūtra*, belonging to the school of Āpastamba of the Black *Yajurveda* in south India. On grounds of language and subject-matter it can hardly be estimated to date from later than about 400 B.C. A little later, and attached to the school of Hiraṇyakeśin, is a *sūtra* which differs but slightly from that of Āpastamba. Somewhat older than Āpastamba's is the *sūtra* of Baudhāyana, also representing a south Indian school of the Black *Yajurveda*. But this work has not been well preserved, for some of its sections are certainly later additions to its original form.

Most probably the oldest of this class of treatises is the *Dharma-śāstra* of Gautama, which belongs to a school of the *Sāmaveda*. Though quoted by some of the earliest Dharma-sūtras, it seems to contain some interpolations. Later than Gautama is the *Vāsiṣṭha-dharma-sūtra*, which probably belonged to a north Indian school of the *Ṛigveda*. This, too, contains a good many interpolations. It quotes a *Dharma-sūtra* of Manu, which was probably the basis of the famous *Mānava-dharma-śāstra*. The latter work once quotes the *Vāsiṣṭha-dharma-sūtra*, which probably dates from some centuries before our era. A more extensive legal work than any of those mentioned is the *Vaiṣṇava-dharma-śāstra*, also called the *Viṣṇu-smṛti*. It is founded on an old Dharma-sūtra of the Kāṭhaka school belonging to the Black *Yajurveda*. The Vishṇuite redaction, in which form it has come down to us, cannot date from earlier than about 200 A.D., as is proved by the occurrence of the names of the seven days of the week, including the term *jaiva*, for Thursday, which is based on the Greek name *Ζεύς*. The passages in which widow-burning is recommended belong to the same time. But the oldest parts of the work must go back to a very early period, for the texts of the Kāṭhaka school, with which the *Viṣṇu-smṛti* is connected, are among the oldest remains of Vedic literature.

A very early and extensive Dharma-sūtra, which belongs to the Maitrāyaṇīya school of the Black *Yajurveda*, is that of Hārīta, quoted by both Āpastamba and Baudhāyana. As is the case both in the *Baudhāyana-sūtra* and in the *Vāsiṣṭha-dharma-śāstra*, the *sūtras* are interspersed with *ślokas* and with *triṣṭubh* stanzas.

Although the chronology of the legal literature is uncertain, it can be assumed with probability that the older Dharma-sūtras belonging to the Vedic schools date from between

800 and 300 B.C. At any rate, they represent the oldest phase of the legal literature, because they characteristically deal with religious duties and rites to a far greater extent than with secular law. Thus the juristic part of the *Āpastamba-dharma-sūtra* amounts to only about one-seventeenth of the whole work.

The teaching of *dharma* in Vedic schools early gave place to general law schools meant for all classes. It was in these legal schools that the metrical Dharma-śāstras and Smṛitis arose. These were no longer handbooks for the narrow circle of a particular Vedic school, but for the teaching of the religious and secular rights and duties of all the three twice-born classes. These manuals naturally became more extensive, and treated law in the strict sense in much greater detail. The *sūtra* style was no longer adequate for the purpose, and the metrical form, especially the *śloka* verse, long familiar as the vehicle of the simple epic, as well as of the didactic poetry so closely akin to the epic, was adopted. This sententious poetry was indeed one of the chief sources of the Dharma-śāstras. The teachers of *dharma* themselves name as its sources, besides *śruti* and *smṛti*, the practice of the cultured (*śiṣṭāḥ*) and customary law (*ācāra*). The rules of the latter two authorities were early expressed in *ślokas,* many of which go back to the time of the Dharma-sūtras or even farther. Much old material is thus preserved in the Dharma-śāstras, which are themselves chronologically later productions. Numerous ethical and legal maxims in metre are found in the epics, especially the *Mahābhārata.* Hence the epic (*itihāsa*) is stated to be a fifth source of *dharma.*

These metrical law-books have been studied as authoritative for centuries all over India down to the present day. Though claiming validity for all castes, they are primarily written in the interests of Brahmins. But they deal to a much larger extent with the rights and duties of the king.

No work has enjoyed so great a reputation and authority throughout India for centuries as the *Mānava-dharma-śāstra*, also called the *Manu-smṛti*, or 'Code of Manu'. Not only in India, but among early European Sanskrit scholars, fantastic views were held regarding the age of this work. Thus Sir William Jones attributed it to the thirteenth century B.C., and A. W. v. Schlegel to not later than 1000 B.C. It has been shown to be based on an antecedent *Dharma-sūtra*, which was later versified. It is in fact probably one of the earlier examples of the transformation of an old Dharma-sūtra into a metrical Dharma-śāstra. Even yet the limits of time within which it must have come into being have not been narrowed down to a shorter period than about four centuries: between 200 B.C. and 200 A.D.

The relation of the *Manu-smṛti* to the *Mahābhārata* is of some importance in investigating its date. In the latest sections of the *Mahābhārata*, especially Book XIII, passages of a *Dharma-śāstra* of Manu are quoted and actually occur in our *Manu-smṛti*. On the other hand, a large number of identical verses occur in both works without being designated as quotations. As the varieties of reading are sometimes better in the one text, sometimes in the other, the conclusion is that such verses have in both texts been derived from the floating sententious poetry which we have seen to be one of the sources of the metrical Dharma-śāstras, and of which it would be vain to attempt to assign the priority in the one text or the other. We seem to be justified in inferring that the oldest parts of the *Mahābhārata* are older than our *Manu-smṛti*; that its latest parts quote a work which was virtually identical with our *Manu-smṛti*;

and that both texts borrowed a considerable amount of identical material from the sententious poetry that was the common property of the educated. No more definite chronological conclusions are justified in the present state of our knowledge.

The contents of the *Manu-smṛti* show that the interval between it and the oldest Dharma-sūtras, which, like Āpastamba's, have remained unmodified by interpolation, must be considerable. The purely legal parts of the *Manu-smṛti* amount to rather more than one-fourth of the whole work. Owing to the sources from which a considerable portion of the book is derived, it produces on the whole the impression of a didactic poem, in which imagery, similes, and elevated diction abound. The author evidently aimed at producing a literary work rather than a dry manual of jurisprudence.

A testimony to the widespread fame of *Manu* is the number of commentaries composed on it in every part of India. Medhātithi, who lived in Kashmīr, probably in the ninth century, was the author of the oldest surviving commentary; he frequently refers to predecessors, some of whom he speaks of as ancient. Another commentator, probably belonging to the twelfth century, is Govindarāja, whose work is distinguished by accuracy, and is valuable for its explanations of difficult passages. The best known, because most frequently printed, commentary is that of Kullūka, written at Benares in the fifteenth century. It is of little independent value, being virtually a plagiarism of the earlier work of Govindarāja.

The reputation of *Manu* extended to Burma, Siam, and the islands of Java and Bali, whose law has been greatly influenced by this code.

Next in age to *Manu* is the *Yājñavalkya-smṛti*, the

Dharma-śāstra of Yājñavalkya. It is probably based on a no longer extant *Dharma-sūtra* belonging to eastern India and attached to the White *Yajurveda* ; for it has been shown to have affinities with the *Gṛhya-sūtra* of that Veda. It is evident that *Yājñavalkya* represents a more advanced stage than *Manu*, for it is more concise, more clearly arranged, and more systematic. While *Manu* confines the sphere of evidence to the statements of witnesses, and in the matter of ordeals treats only of those by fire and water, *Yājña-valkya* deals exhaustively with written documents as evidence, and knows five kinds of ordeals. This law-book also contains far fewer passages resembling didactic poetry than *Manu*. Many indications appear in it that it dates from no earlier than 300 A.D. The most famous of the many commentaries on *Yājñavalkya* is the *Mitākṣara* of Vijñān-eśvara. This is, however, more than a commentary, being really a juristic work based on *Yājñavalkya.* The author was a south Indian who lived between 1050 and 1100 A.D. His work early acquired a great reputation in Benares as well as the Deccan, and as late as the beginning of last century acquired a new importance within the jurisdiction of British India through Colebrooke's translation (1810) of its section on the law of inheritance. Quite a number of commentaries were written on this authoritative work.

The date of the *Nārada-smṛti* seems to be somewhat later still, as would appear from internal evidence. It is much more advanced in its treatment of law than *Manu.* Thus it emphasizes written procedure and documentary evidence. It has much more elaborate subdivisions under various heads. Thus *Manu's* eighteen titles of the law have in *Nārada* 132 subordinate divisions. The occurrence of the word *dīnāra* (the Latin *denarius*), as the name of a gold coin, shows that the *Nārada-smṛti* could not have come into being before the second century B.C., and that it was probably not composed before the fourth century A.D., because though Roman gold coins were already in abundant use in India in the first century A.D., the word *dīnāra* is not met with till 400 A.D. in inscriptions.

The *Bṛhaspati-smṛti*, of which only fragments have been preserved in medieval quotations, is still more closely connected with *Manu* than *Nārada*; for it resembles a commentary, which, always starting from the dicta of *Manu*, supplements and extends them. It deals exhaustively with legal documents, and recommends widow-burning, which is not done in the earlier law-books. Representing, taken in all, a more advanced stage of development than *Nārada*, it probably came into existence a century or two later.

There are numerous other Dharma-śāstras which also are known only in a fragmentary way from quotations. Many other later Smṛitis, preserved in manuscripts or printed in collections, deal not with the whole of *dharma*, but only with parts. One of the more important and comparatively old legal works is the *Parāśara-smṛti*, which was commented on by Mādhava in the fourteenth century. It is uncertain whether this Parāśara is identical with the one mentioned by Medhātithi in the ninth century.

Of greater importance than the later law-books are the *Dharma-nibandhas*, which are systematic and sometimes very extensive works on *dharma*. This type of legal literature began to be produced from about 1100 A.D., and continues to appear even at the present day. Many of these works are important on account of the numerous quotations they contain from older works that have since been lost. One of the earliest books of this class is the *Smṛti-kalpa-taru* by Lakshmīdhara, the minister of a king who is identical with Govindachandra of Kanauj (1105–43 A.D.).

Between 1260 and 1309 A.D. Hemādri wrote a bulky work entitled *Caturvarga-cintāmaṇi*, which in five chapters deals with vows, almsgiving, places of pilgrimage, salvation, funeral rites (*śrāddha*), and the sacrificial calendar. It also teems with quotations from the Purāṇas and the Smṛitis. Other compendia treat of law in the strict sense (*vyavahāra*). One of these is the *Dharma-ratna* of Jīmūta-vāhana, written probably in the fifteenth century. A portion of this work, the *Dāyabhāga*, on the law of inheritance, is the chief authority of the Bengal school of law, and was translated into English by Colebrooke.

In the eighteenth century several *Dharma-nibandhas* were compiled by pandits who were commissioned for the purpose in the interest of the law-courts.

Jolly, *Recht und Sitte*, in Bühler's *Encyclopaedia*, ii, part 8, 1896. Macdonell, *History*, 428–30. Winternitz, *Geschichte*, iii. 479–504 (bibliography down to 1922).

e. Science of Practical Life (*Arthaśāstra*)

In connexion with the doctrine, which we find mentioned before our era, that there are three chief aims in human life (*trivarga*): the good (*dharma*), the useful (*artha*), and the desirable (*kāma*), there was developed a branch of literature called *arthaśāstra*, comprehending practical arts, economics, administration, and especially politics. The latter as an independent branch is also called *nītiśāstra* or 'science of conduct or government'. Since the king was regarded as requiring a knowledge of the other aspects of *arthaśāstra*, the term *nītiśāstra* is sometimes used as a synonym. Because to the Indian mind government meant monarchical rule only, this science is also called *rājanīti*, 'the conduct of kings', that is, the policy of government.

The extant metrical Dharma-śāstras presuppose *artha-śāstra* as a special science, and the twelfth book of the *Mahābhārata* attests its existence. The former teach duties ultimately based on revelation; the latter the measures that conduce to gaining material results apart from considerations of religion or morality. Thus the poet Māgha (p. 93) speaks of self-aggrandizement and the subjugation of the enemy constituting the essence of policy (*nīti*). The Buddhists were entirely opposed to its methods, rejecting the notion that morality should give way to advantage, and regarding *nīti* as systematic mendacity.

By far the most important work of this type of literature is the *Kauṭilīya-arthaśāstra*, a treatise on the art of government and administration attributed to Kauṭilya (otherwise Chāṇakya or Vishṇugupta), the minister of Chandragupta of the Maurya dynasty. No work of Indian literature supplies such full information on the political and economic conditions of ancient India. Though its existence was long known, it was not edited till 1906. It is written in prose consisting in a mixture of *sūtra* and commentary which it is hardly possible to separate. A few verses are interspersed in it, and every chapter ends with one or more stanzas generally well adapted in sense to the preceding prose. As regards its teaching of duty, the *Arthaśāstra* is entirely Brahminical, inculcating the duties of each caste and each stage of life exactly like the *smṛtis*. One of its chapters is concerned with the various means of getting rid of traitors and enemies of the state; and nothing, it is indicated, is too perfidious to accomplish such an end. Besides the unique extent to which this work throws light on the life of ancient India, it would have a special chronological value if it could be shown to be the work of King Chandragupta's famous minister. For then we should have the first and only certainly datable evidence regarding Indian literature and civilization for such an early period as the fourth century B.C. But unfortunately we know nothing of any activity of Kauṭilya either as a teacher or an author. Chandragupta ascended the throne about 322 B.C., and in 302 B.C. the Greek Megasthenes came to his court as the ambassador of Seleukos Nikator. We possess a fragmentary account of India written by him during his long stay in the country. But neither he nor any other ancient author knows anything of the celebrated minister of Chandragupta. A careful comparison of Megasthenes' account with Kauṭilya's *Arthaśāstra* does not confirm the assumption that these two authors were contemporaries. No appreciable agreement is to be found between the conditions prevailing at the time of Aśoka and those described by Kauṭilya. Patañjali in the *Mahābhāṣya* mentions the Mauryas and the court (*sabhā*) of Chandragupta, but not a word about Kauṭilya. All our information about Kauṭilya belongs to the region of legend and poetry; and even here there is nothing about his activity as a teacher and author. In the *Arthaśāstra* itself there is no trace of any reference to the Nandas, the Mauryas, or King Chandragupta and the conditions prevailing in his day. It is true that final verses in the first two chapters and at the conclusion of the whole book state the *Arthaśāstra* to be the work of Kauṭilya, but the probability is that the chapters containing these verses were added at the final redaction of the work. In the book itself the author is never called Chāṇakya or Vishṇugupta, but always only Kauṭilya, and it is highly improbable that the minister of Chandragupta would have called himself by a name signifying 'crookedness', 'perfidy'. The name of Kauṭilya, too, is mentioned in the same way as in Sūtras, to indicate the text of a school, not of an individual author. The conclusion thus appears to be justified that the *Artha-śāstra* is ascribed to Kauṭilya because the legendary minister of Chandragupta was regarded as the typical master of the science of politics, cunning and unscrupulous, but devoted to his prince. In this way all political maxims came to be traced to Chāṇakya. Surveying the work as a whole, we find that, in addition to politics in the narrow sense, it contains a mass of material, requiring expert knowledge, on subjects like architecture, mining, military science, and so on, all of which no individual man, even in ancient India, could have mastered. The works of specialists must therefore have been incorporated without much alteration. A long literary activity both in the theory of politics as well as in various technical sciences must be presupposed before all such matter could be combined in a single work. From a consideration of all the branches of literature which it presupposes or shows agreement with, the conclusion seems justified that it is not older than 200 A.D. at the very earliest. It is valuable to have a work supplying evidence for even so remote a period as this. Some scholars, however, have been inclined to assign this book to so mythical a date as at least 500 years earlier. The designation of Kauṭilya as the Indian Machiavelli is justified in so far as the unscrupulous methods of both apply to a monarchical state only. But Machiavelli bases his methods on the teaching of history, an aspect entirely absent in Kauṭilya, who founds his methods solely on theory, as to what means are best adapted to safeguarding the ruler, though his theory probably often corresponds to actually prevailing conditions.

A later and somewhat different kind of work is the *Nītisāra* of Kāmandaki or Kāmandaka. Entirely written in verse, it has rather the nature of a didactic poem than of a manual of politics. Like a Kāvya it is divided into cantos. In his introductory verses the author eulogizes Vishṇugupta as having by the efficacy of his intrigues secured the earth for Chandragupta. Elsewhere he speaks of Kauṭilya as his *guru*, that is to say, as the master on whom he draws as his chief source. Probably several centuries lie between Kauṭilya and Kāmandaki, the literary evidence regarding whom points to his dating from between 700 and 750 A.D. Though the contents of the *Nītisāra* partially coincide with the *Arthaśāstra*, a considerable portion differs entirely. Hence its author must have used other sources as well.

In the tenth century the Jain author Somadevasūri composed in Kashmīr his *Nītivākyāmṛta*, or 'Nectar of Political Doctrines'. It shows close dependence on the *Arthaśāstra*, with which it often verbally agrees. It frequently paraphrases the text, and may then actually serve as its commentary. It is, however, a work of a totally different kind; for it is not a practical manual of politics and economics, but rather an educational work intended for the guidance of kings. The author includes in *nīti* not only political wisdom, but also moral conduct. Although a Jain, he assumes the outlook of a Brahmin and is a strict adherent of the caste system. It is a prose work written in short, terse sentences, but not at all in the *sūtra* style, the language being clear and simple. The author is fond of introducing sentences of a proverbial type. Such are: 'A man who has not studied science is blind even though possessed of eyes'; 'Better is a world without a king, than having a dunce for a king'. A Jain touch appears in the precept: 'One should not indulge in any sport that involves injury to living beings'.

A short work by the well-known Jaina monk Hemachandra is the *Laghv-arhan-nītiśāstra*, 'Brief Manual on Politics for Jainas'. It is composed in *ślokas* interspersed with occasional explanations in prose. By far the greater part of the work, however, deals not, as its name seems to imply, with politics, but with civil and criminal law in connexion with the Dharma-śāstras, especially the *Manusmṛti*.

There are several other works on *nīti*, some of them attributed by their writers to mythical sages of old. The editor of two of these endeavoured to show that the ancient Indians were acquainted with fire-arms and gunpowder!

Belonging to the sphere of *arthaśāstra* are all kinds of manuals dealing with special branches of practical knowledge, such as the treatment of horses and elephants, the art of war (*dhanurveda*), architecture, the science of gems, and so on. The term *śilpa-śāstra*, though strictly speaking the lore of plastic art, is specially applied to architecture, which is also called *vāstuvidyā*, 'science of building'. One of the chief works on architecture is the *Māna-sāra*, or 'Quintessence of Measurements' as connected with the foundations and building of houses and temples, town-planning, construction of images, and so forth.

There are also works on the art of music (*saṃgīta-śāstra*) both vocal and instrumental. At a later stage were produced special handbooks covering the whole ground of musical art: notation, scales, melodies, singing; musical instruments, dance and mimicry; organization of musical bands and of concerts, besides many other details. An old work of the kind is the *Saṃgīta-ratnākara* by Śārṅgadeva of Kashmīr. Nothing more is known about its date than that its commentator Kallinātha lived about 1450 A.D. A later work is the *Saṃgīta-darpaṇa* of Dāmodara, who not only used the *Saṃgīta-ratnākara*, but took over parts of it word for word; when he differs from his predecessor he probably borrowed from older sources and is to this extent important. There are also monographs on melodies, as the *Rāgavibodha* of Somanātha written in 1609 A.D.

An old science is that of gems, with which Varāhamihira shows familiarity in his *Bṛhat-saṃhitā*. Several works on this subject are extant, but their date is unknown.

Even the art of thieving is mentioned in the *Mahābhārata* and in one of the early dramas as the subject of a treatise, and one such work has actually been preserved. It is entitled *Ṣaṇmukha-kalpa*, or 'Rules of the six-headed One', that is, of the god of war, Kārttikeya, who is regarded as the guardian deity of thieves. Magic is an art in which the chief of a robber gang is required to be well-versed.

This subject is sufficiently dealt with by Winternitz, *Geschichte*, iii. 508–35.

f. KĀMAŚĀSTRA

The literature which is connected with *kāma*, the third object of life, and which goes under the designation of *Kāmaśāstra*, or 'Doctrine of Love', cannot be altogether passed over here. The oldest work on the subject is the *Kāmasūtra* of Mallanāga Vātsyāyana, whose treatise is evidently modelled on Kauṭilya's *Arthaśāstra*, and who analogously to his prototype may be called the Machiavelli of erotics. The contents of this work appear to us for the most part indecent, but it must be borne in mind that the Indian is always much more outspoken on sexual matters than we are. Like other Sanskrit manuals, it contains many pedantic divisions, classifications, and definitions. It cannot in any way be compared with the 'Ars amatoria' of Ovid. The greater part of the work should be of interest to the ethnologist only but its age alone gives it some importance in the history of literature and civilization. The third section contains some valuable supplementary information on the marriage customs described in the Gṛhya- and Dharma-sūtras, and the sixth section, which deals with the position of courtezans, is of the greatest interest for the history of civilization.

Though this is the earliest extant work on the subject, Vātsyāyana himself mentions that he had many predecessors. The *Kāmaśāstra* has a close connexion with the writers of Kāvya, for its study is enjoined on these poets, and the manuals of poetics (*alaṃkāra*) contain many sections that touch upon the subjects contained in the *Kāmaśāstra*. Both Subandhu and Bhavabhūti are thoroughly familiar with the *Kāmasūtra*, the latter even quoting it. This shows that Vātsyāyana's work must have been written before 600 A.D. On the other hand, it is undoubtedly later than Kauṭilya's *Arthaśāstra*. We may therefore conjecture that it dates from somewhere about 450 A.D.

There is a very detailed commentary on the *Kāmasūtra* entitled *Jayamaṅgalā* written by Yaśodhara Indrapāda, who lived in the thirteenth century. A rather extensive literature on erotics flourished in the later period. Of this may be mentioned the *Ratirahasya*, or 'Secret of Love', composed before 1200 A.D., by Kokkoka, who professes to have used as his sources not only Vātsyāyana's teachings, but also those of other exponents of the subject. Another well-known work is the *Anaṅga-raṅga*, 'the Stage of Cupid', by a royal author named Kalyāṇamalla, who probably lived in the sixteenth century.

Winternitz, *Geschichte*, iii. 536–41, gives a brief account of this subject, together with its bibliography.

g. MEDICINE

The beginnings of medical science reach far back into Vedic times. In the magical hymns of the *Atharvaveda* and the magical ceremonies of the ritual literature, especially the *Kauśika Sūtra* belonging to this Veda, we find early acquaintance with the healing art and healing plants. Here as elsewhere the magical physician is the first 'medicine man'. This connexion with magic has never been forgotten in India; for even in scientific medical works demons are recognized as originators of disease, and incantations as remedies. In Vedic texts can be traced the beginnings of anatomy, embryology, and hygiene. Thus the *Atharvaveda* and the *Śatapatha Brāhmaṇa* contain an exact enumeration of the bones of the human skeleton. The old name of medical science is *Āyurveda*, or 'Veda of longevity', regarded as one of the supplements of the *Atharvaveda*. The *Āyurveda* according to tradition consisted of eight parts, among which were included demonology (the doctrine of diseases caused by demons) and toxicology (the science of poisons). The age of medical science in India is attested by its frequent mention in ancient Buddhist literature. In later times, too, the Buddhists showed a partiality for the study of medicine. This is indicated by the detailed account given by the Chinese traveller I-tsing (seventh century A.D.) of the medical science of the Indians. The oldest approximately datable medical texts were also Buddhist. An ancient Sanskrit manuscript containing seven texts was found in 1890 at Kucha in Chinese Turkistan buried in a Buddhist relic-mound (*stūpa*). The palaeographical evidence indicates that it dates from about 350 A.D. Three of the seven texts are medical. One of them deals with garlic, which is said to heal many diseases and to prolong life to one hundred years. Another, entitled *Nāvanītaka* ('Cream'), is an abstract of the best of earlier treatises. The contents include prescriptions of an archaic type, and many medical authorities are mentioned, but none now known except Suśruta. All these manuscripts, which are fragmentary, are in verse, partly even in artificial metres. The language in which they are written is Sanskrit mixed with Prākritisms.

The three ancient authorities on Indian medicine are Charaka, Suśruta, and Vāgbhaṭa. These names are represented by three Saṃhitās, that is, large collections or compendia of medicine which were probably based on older special treatises, no longer extant, of different branches of medicine.

The *Caraka-saṃhitā* is, according to its own statement, an adaptation of an older work by an authority named Agniveśa. The Chinese translation (472 A.D.) of the Pāli *Tipiṭaka* states that Charaka was the court physician of King Kaṇishka. If this statement is correct, Charaka lived in the second century A.D., but the evidence is uncertain. It is, however, clear that the text has not come down to us in its original form. Both the manuscripts and the editions show very divergent readings. Moreover, a Kashmīrian named Dṛiḍhabala, who lived about 800 A.D., supplied about one-third of the text, besides revising and adding to the whole work. But the original part of the book, which, like the *Kauṭilīya-arthaśāstra*, is written in prose, with verse at the end of each chapter, is undoubtedly old, being probably the earliest of the surviving treatises on medicine.

The *Caraka-saṃhitā* consists of eight parts covering the whole field of medical science. One of its statements is that the three mainstays of bodily health are eating, sleep, and abstemiousness. Charaka is a moralist and philosopher as well as a physician. In connexion with hygienic rules and with the doctrine that sin is one of the causes of disease, he also gives many religious and moral precepts. In his discussions about the soul he shows himself familiar with the Sāṅkhya philosophy, as well as with the theory of the syllogism in the Nyāya, and with the categories of the Vaiśeshika system.

The oldest commentary on Charaka is that of Chakrapāṇidatta, which dates from the eleventh century. Long before that time Charaka had been translated into Persian, and thence into Arabic about 800 A.D.

The best known Indian treatise on medicine is the *Suśruta-saṃhitā*, which is composed in prose intermixed with verse; but, both in language and matter, it appears to be later than the original part of Charaka's work. The name of Suśruta was known in the ninth and tenth centuries to the people of Cambodia in Farther India, as well as to the Arabs, as that of a famous physician. Though it cannot be doubted that Suśruta belongs to one of the early centuries of our era and cannot be much later than Charaka, the authenticity of the text of his work in its extant form is guaranteed by the safeguard of commentaries only from the eleventh century onwards. Before that time it was probably subjected to considerable changes. Thus it is said to have undergone a revision at the hands of Nāgārjuna. Suśruta, as contrasted with Charaka, was particularly partial to surgery, which is hardly touched upon by the earlier author. Suśruta requires a high moral standard in the votaries of medical science. Thus he says among other things that priests, friends, neighbours, widows, the poor, and travellers should be treated gratis by the physician as if they were his relations, while to hunters, fowlers, outcasts, and sinners no medical aid at all should be extended.

The oldest commentaries on Suśruta no longer survive; the earliest one extant is the *Bhānumatī* of Chakrapāṇidatta, the commentator of the eleventh century already mentioned.

With the name of Vāgbhaṭa, the last of the medical trio, are associated two famous works, the *Aṣṭāṅgasaṃgraha*, 'Compendium of the Eight Branches', and the *Aṣṭāṅga-hṛdaya-saṃhitā*, 'Collection of the Quintessence of the Eight Branches' of medicine. Even in form, as being composed in a mixture of prose and verse, the former is older than the latter, which is entirely metrical. The difference between the two works is apparent in their matter also. When quoted by later medical writers the former appears as Vṛiddha-Vāgbhaṭa, 'the old Vāgbhaṭa', while the latter is simply called Vāgbhaṭa. On these grounds we are justified in assuming that there were really two writers of the name, and that the elder probably lived about 600 A.D., the younger some two centuries later. The elder was probably the man of whom, without mentioning his name, the Chinese traveller I-tsing says that he had recently written a compendium of the eight parts of medical science. The elder was undoubtedly a Buddhist, and probably the younger also. Both of them quote Suśruta as well as Charaka.

Much about the same time as the younger Vāgbhaṭa, that is, *c.* 800 A.D., was written the *Rug-viniścaya*, 'Investigation of Diseases', by Mādhavakara, the son of Indukara. This work is generally called *Mādhava-nidāna*, or is referred to by the still shorter title of *Nidāna*. This is, indeed, the chief Indian work on pathology, in which the most important diseases are treated in detail, and which has remained an authority to all later treatises on the subject. Its celebrity is attested by the number of commentaries to which it gave rise. It is presupposed by Vṛinda's *Siddhi-yoga* or *Vṛndamādhava*, which gives prescriptions for all diseases ranging from fever to the results of poisoning. The two works are so intimately connected that they have even been supposed to be by the same author. Chakrapāṇidatta, a native of Bengal, already mentioned as a commentator on Charaka and Suśruta, was also an independent medical author. He wrote in 1060 A.D. the *Cikitsā-sāra-saṃgraha*, a large compendium of therapeutics, based chiefly on the *Siddhiyoga*.

Another medical work is the *Śārṅgadhara-saṃhitā*, which cannot have been written later than 1200 A.D., as there is a commentary on it by Vopadeva dating from about 1300 A.D. Preparations of opium and quicksilver are mentioned in it as remedies, and the feeling of the pulse in diagnosis is exactly described, subjects which do not occur in earlier treatises. Many other medical works, including monographs, have been written in later centuries, down to quite modern times, but these it would be superfluous to mention here.

There is a very extensive literature that deals with the miraculous healing powers of metallic preparations (called *rasa*) and that belongs to the lower branch of medicine concerned with magic and alchemy. The most important substance here used is quicksilver, which is recommended as an elixir of life, a means of rejuvenation, and a remedy for all kinds of diseases. As quicksilver was also regarded as a means of transmuting baser metals into gold, works dealing with *rasa* belong to the sphere of alchemy also. Such works were already (*c.* 1030 A.D.) known to Albērūnī, who speaks of them with great contempt.

Medico-botanical glossaries called *nighaṇṭu* were probably known even in ancient times; but the extant dictionaries of this kind are not very old. A Bengal physician named Sureśvara or Surapāla composed in the year 1075 A.D. a vocabulary of medical botany entitled *Śabdapradīpa*. All these medical glossaries are written in verse.

Even in the nineteenth century a number of works on the remedial substances used in the practice of medicine were composed in Sanskrit.

Though there can be no doubt as to the indigenous origin of Indian medicine, it has many resemblances to the Greek science, some of which can hardly be explained except by the influence of the latter. Several remedies, such as opium and quicksilver, and in diagnosis the feeling of the pulse, Indian medicine owes to the Persians and Arabs. On the other hand, Indian works on medicine (Charaka and Suśruta) were translated into (Persian and) Arabic about 800 A.D. In the Middle Ages Arabic medicine became the chief authority of European physicians and remained so down to the seventeenth century. In this way Indian medical writers became known in Europe, Charaka being repeatedly mentioned in the Latin translations of leading Arab medical writers. In modern times European surgery has borrowed the operation of rhinoplasty, or the surgical formation of artificial noses, from India, where Englishmen became acquainted with the art in the eighteenth century.

The medicine of Tibet, Ceylon, and Farther India is altogether dependent on that of India.

Jolly, *Medicin*, in Bühler's *Encyclopaedia*, iii, part 10. Winternitz, *Geschichte*, iii. 541–54. Macdonell, *History*, 435–6.

h. Astronomy

The science of astronomy has almost invariably been associated in India with astrology, its unscientific branch. The same writers are, indeed, often the authors of works on both astronomy and astrology.

The beginnings of Indian astronomy are to be traced in the mythological and cosmological fancies of the Vedic hymns and the Brāhmaṇas. The celestial phenomena of light as subject to an invariable natural law (*ṛta*) are constantly dwelt on by the Vedic bards. Occasionally we find traces of a more scientific conception of the movements of the heavenly bodies. Thus one of the Brāhmaṇas observes that the sun does not really rise or set, but produces day and night on the earth by revolving. The Vedic sacrificers had to make careful chronological calculations with regard to their ritual, having for this purpose to observe accurately the phases of the moon, the course of the sun, the seasons, and especially the zodiac with its twenty-seven or twenty-eight constellations (*nakṣatras*). The origin of this zodiac, which is also found among the Arabs and the Chinese, is still an open question. The attempts to constitute a calendar for sacrificial and ritual purposes reach far back into Vedic times, but actual works on astronomy do not exist in Vedic literature.

Of the supplementary literature attached to the Vedas under the general name of *Vedāṅgas* only one short work survives from among probably many that dealt with astronomy. It is the *Jyotiṣa-vedāṅga*, a brief treatise composed in *ślokas* (forty-three in the recension of the *Yajurveda* and thirty-six in that of the *Ṛigveda*), and concerned exclusively with chronological calculation. Only partially intelligible on account both of its *sūtra*-like style and of the corrupt state of the text, it chiefly describes the five-year *yuga*, or cycle of five years of 366 days, as well as the positions of moon and sun at the solstices and at new- and full-moon in the circle of the *nakṣatras*, or lunar mansions.

To the earlier post-Vedic period of Indian astronomy belong the following works: the *Vṛddha-garga-saṃhitā*, which, however, is chiefly astrological; an extensive astronomical *Upāṅga* of the Jains, the *Sūriyapaṇṇati*, or 'Instruction regarding the Sun'; also some supplementary treatises of the *Atharvaveda*, which are mostly astronomical. There is also an astronomical fragment preserved among the Weber MSS. which were purchased at Leh in Ladakh by the missionary F. Weber. Two other works are known from quotations only. The astronomical-cosmological sections of the *Mahābhārata*, the Purāṇas, and the *Mānavadharmaśāstra* belong to the same age: none of these works show any trace of the influence of Greek astronomy. Here we first come across the doctrine of the four ages called *kṛta*, *tretā*, *dvāpara*, and *kali*, of which each preceding one surpasses in excellence that which follows.

The later post-Vedic period of Indian astronomy is entirely post-Christian. As opposed to the pre-Christian stage, it is scientific in character as well as no longer purely Indian. The system of astronomy here developed, in fact, presupposes knowledge of Greek astronomy. The works belonging to this period may be divided into four classes: 1. *Siddhāntas* or handbooks giving a detailed account of a complete system of astronomy; 2. *Karaṇas* or works serving as guides for rapid and convenient astronomical calculations; 3. Works with astronomical tables facilitating calculations; 4. Numerous commentaries on older works often containing valuable quotations from treatises that have been lost.

1. The oldest and most important complete extant work of this period is the *Sūrya-siddhānta*, which, composed in *ślokas*, is divided into four chapters. The present form of the text is not the original one; but its chief teachings are those of Greek astronomy. There seems even to be an allusion to a foreign source in the introductory verses, where the book is stated to have been revealed in the city of Romaka, which must refer to Rome or Alexandria. The peculiarly Indian impression made by this work is due to the enormous duration of the cosmic ages that it lays down, to conceptions such as that of Mount Meru being situated at the North Pole, by the acceptance of the traditional views as to the conjunctions of the planets with the lunar mansions, and other features. The aim of the author was in fact to retain as many of the old views as was compatible with the new doctrines and to adapt the latter as far as possible to the earlier methods and calculations.

2. The *Sūrya-siddhānta* is one of the five old Siddhāntas described by the famous astronomer and astrologer Varāhamihira in his *Pañcasiddhāntikā*, which gives the doctrines of the five Siddhāntas that were authoritative in his time in the form of a Karaṇa. Internal evidence shows that this work was composed in the year 505 A.D. The account that Varāhamihira here gives of the four Siddhāntas other than the *Sūrya-siddhānta* is all the more important as these four (the *Pitāmaha-*, the *Vāsiṣṭha-*, the *Pauliśa-*, and the *Romaka-siddhānta*) are no longer extant. Judged by the evidence of the *Pañcasiddhāntikā*, the clearest traces of Greek influence appear to have been found in the *Romaka-siddhānta*. The length of the year was here calculated in exactly the same way as it was by Hipparchos (second

century B.C.), and after him by Ptolemy (second century A.D.). The author also took a *yuga*, or cosmic age, to consist of 2,850 solar years, thus departing entirely from the Indian tradition of the duration of such an age. Different from the old *Romaka-siddhānta* is the work with the same title that was revised and alleged to have been improved by Śrīsheṇa after Varāhamihira. Of this work Brahmagupta says it had borrowed so much from Lāṭa, Āryabhaṭa, and others that it had the appearance of a much-patched garment. But though the doctrines of the older *Romaka-siddhānta* are Greek, it nevertheless diverges in essential points from Greek astronomy. It further differs quite considerably from the *Sūrya-siddhānta*, which also shows Greek influence. These two Siddhāntas must therefore go back to different sources. But since the *Sūrya-siddhānta*, though agreeing generally with the astronomy of Ptolemy (140 A.D.), yet also differs from him, it is impossible to answer with certainty the question when and through what works Greek astronomy influenced that of India. The uncertainty is all the greater since we know no more of the date of the five Siddhāntas than that they were regarded by Varāhamihira about 500 A.D. as authoritative works. All therefore we can say is that they must have come into existence in the early centuries after Christ, perhaps in the fourth.

Among some older astronomers mentioned by Varāhamihira is Āryabhaṭa, whose work, the *Āryabhaṭīya*, is of equal importance in the history of mathematics and of astronomy. Written in the *āryā* metre, it consists of four parts. The first of these deals with a system of numeral notation peculiar to Āryabhaṭa and with the fundamental elements of the system; the second gives a brief summary of his mathematical teachings; the third contains the outlines of astronomical calculations of time; while the fourth is concerned with the celestial sphere. Āryabhaṭa was probably the first who concisely summarized the system developed in the Siddhānta, without, however, introducing many improvements. His point of view is much the same as that of the author of the *Sūrya-siddhānta*. There is, however, one point in which he showed great originality: he maintained the daily rotation of the earth round its axis, explaining the daily rotation of the celestial sphere as only apparent. It cannot be proved that this doctrine, which was rejected by the later Indian astronomers, was adopted by him from the Greeks. Both Varāhamihira and Brahmagupta assailed this doctrine, just as the Greek doctrine was long combated in Europe. Āryabhaṭa was, according to his own statement, born in 476 A.D. and wrote his work in 499 A.D.

An extensive astronomical work entitled *Ārya-siddhānta*, by another but later Āryabhaṭa, was known to Bhāskara and has been preserved.

The most famous of the Indian astronomers who lived after Varāhamihira were Brahmagupta and Bhāskarāchārya. The former, according to his own statement, wrote his *Brāhmasphuṭa-siddhānta* in the year 628 A.D. He generally agrees with his predecessors, but his treatment of his subject-matter is more detailed and methodical. The eleventh chapter of his work is exclusively concerned with criticizing his predecessors, especially Āryabhaṭa. Though Brahmagupta is chiefly eminent as a mathematician, some of his chapters are devoted to the solution of astronomical problems.

The last famous astronomer, Bhāskarāchārya, was born in 1114 A.D. and produced the *Siddhānta-śiromaṇi*, written in the *āryā* metre in 1150 A.D. He enjoys a great reputation, especially as a mathematician, and in astronomy his work is regarded as second only to the *Sūrya-siddhānta*. But the high value attached to his work is due solely to the fact that it represents the old system more completely and clearly than earlier works do, and that Bhāskara himself has added a commentary in which the usually concise rules are explained and proved in detail. But Bhāskara teaches nothing new, and is in fact completely dependent on Brahmagupta. His work consists of four parts, of which the first two, entitled *Līlāvatī* and *Bījagaṇita*, form the mathematical introduction, while the other two, the *Grahagaṇitādhyāya* and the *Golādhyāya*, deal with astronomy proper.

A second work by Bhāskara, the *Karaṇa-kutūhala*, was written in 1178.

From the centuries between Brahmagupta and Bhāskara few astronomical books are known.

With the conquest of India by the Muhammedans the Perso-Arabic influence on Indian astronomy began, but it was not strong enough to oust the old indigenous science. In later centuries the last work of any importance on Indian astronomy was the *siddhānta-tattva-viveka* of Kamalākara, written in 1658 A.D. Though borrowing from Perso-Arabic astronomy, it is essentially based on the *Sūrya-siddhānta* and attacks Bhāskara. The old Indian astronomical works have never altogether lost their authority, even since European science has become known.

i. Astrology

Astrology, or the theory of the influence of the stars on human life, has been very intimately connected with astronomy in India. The belief in the importance of celestial phenomena as good or bad omens, and in the possibility of inferring the fortunes of men and of prognosticating future events from the position of the heavenly bodies, is extremely old in India as well as in other eastern countries with an ancient civilization. Even in the Brāhmaṇas we hear of stars that were 'favourable' or 'unfavourable' at weddings and other ceremonies. According to the Dharmasūtras an astrologer is as indispensable to the king as the *purohita* (or domestic chaplain). On the other hand, occupation with astrology, as with magic, is regarded as causing impurity. Buddhist monks, too, were forbidden to have anything to do with astrology, soothsaying, and similar superstitions. The older works on astrology have been almost entirely lost, having been ousted by Varāhamihira, who attained the highest authority as a teacher of the subject. The only one of the earlier treatises that has come down to us is the *Vṛddha-garga-saṃhitā*; but it is very doubtful if even that work has been preserved in an approximately original form. It is interesting to note that here is to be found a verse in which the dependence of Indian on Greek astronomy is acknowledged: 'The Greeks indeed are barbarous, but this science is well established among them; therefore even they are honoured like seers, how much more a Brahmin who is an astrologer.'

According to Varāhamihira, the *jyotiḥ-śāstra*, or 'Science of Stars', which embraces astronomy and astrology, is divided into three branches: *tantra*, which deals with calculating astronomy; *horā*, which is concerned with the horoscope; and *śākhā* or *saṃhitā*, which teaches natural astrology, that is to say, the doctrine of omens derivable from occurrences in nature generally, but especially from celestial phenomena.

The chief work of Varāhamihira, who dealt with all departments of astrology, is the *Bṛhatsaṃhitā*, which is at the same time the most important work on natural astrology. It may even be called one of the most important works of Indian literature in general. For as natural astrology is concerned with all departments of existence, the most diverse aspects of public and private life come to be touched upon in this work, which thus assumes quite an encyclopaedic character. It is of great importance even for the history of religion, in which respect it has not been exploited nearly sufficiently. This astrological work is of appreciable value even as a specimen of artificial poetry, for many passages rise to a considerable level of poetical merit. Thus the author writes: 'As a night without a lamp, as a sky without the sun, so is a king without astrologers: like a blind man he wanders on his path.'

Great importance being attached to the teachings of astrology in the building of a new house, the digging of wells, the laying out of gardens and tanks, the search for underground water, the construction of idols, many chapters deal with those subjects. Some are concerned with jewels, while others have affinity with the *Kāmaśāstra*. Eleven chapters again form a treatise called 'augury' (*śākuna*). Although two chapters of the *Bṛhatsaṃhitā* are concerned with weddings, Varāhamihira also wrote a separate astrological treatise on the auspicious times for marriage. He further wrote another work dealing with the omens on the occasion of a king's marching out to war and entitled *Yoga-yātrā*, 'Expedition at Lucky Conjunctions of Stars'.

While that part of the *Jyotiḥ-śāstra* which is concerned with natural astrology is chiefly a genuine product of Indian pseudo-science, its aspect dealing with the horoscope, and called by the Sanskrit term *jātaka*, 'nativity', or the Greek name *horā*, is entirely under the influence of Greek astronomy. The contents of these horoscopic works, which also contain Greek technical terms, correspond entirely to the Greek books dealing with this subject.

Varāhamihira also devoted to this branch of astronomy a large work entitled *Bṛhajjātaka*, also called *Horā-śāstra*, and a shorter one, the *Laghu-jātaka*, the former of which is the best known and most studied. These works are concerned with foretelling the fortunes of a human being from the positions of heavenly bodies at the time of his birth.

This 'science' probably had its origin among the Babylonians, from whom it was conveyed by the Greeks to other peoples. It is, however, not quite certain when it reached the Indians from the Greeks: the evidence seems on the whole to point to the third century A.D. About 600 A.D., Pṛithuyaśas, the son of Varāhamihira, wrote an astrological work entitled *Horāṣaṭpañcāsikā*. The commentaries of Bhaṭṭotpala, dating from the tenth century, on this and on all the works of Varāhamihira, are important because of the numerous quotations from older works that they contain. He is also himself the author of a *Horā-śāstra* in seventy-five verses.

As regards the extremely extensive astrological literature of later times, mention need only be made of the *Jyotir-vid-ābharaṇa*, 'the Ornament of Astrologers', probably written in the sixteenth century. In this work, the author of which calls himself Kālidāsa, occurs the celebrated verse about the 'nine gems' at the court of King Vikramāditya, on which the theory of contemporaneousness of various authors and the date of Kālidāsa was at one time based. But the value of this evidence is practically none, because this work is late, as it refers to Arabic astrology and is not mentioned till 1661, when it is quoted in a commentary.

After Varāhamihira's time a special type of astrological works came into being under the name of *Muhūrta* (primarily meaning an hour of forty-eight minutes), the object of which is to fix the moment of time (*muhūrta*) favourable not only for religious ceremonies, family festivals, such as weddings, but also for journeys and other undertakings of daily life.

After the beginning of the Arabic conquest, the influence of Perso-Arabian astrology resulted in the rise of a special class of works called Tājik (from the Persian word for 'Arabic'), which are derived from Arabic sources.

Works on omens and portents, soothsaying, interpretation of dreams, and so forth are infinitely numerous. The only one that need be mentioned here is the *Svapna-cintāmaṇi*, 'Thought-gem on Dreams', which is of interest both for religious and for literary history. It is a handbook for the interpretation of dreams, by Jagaddeva, who in writing it made, as he himself states, much use of medical literature. The dreams mentioned by him often show a striking agreement with fairy-tale motives.

j. MATHEMATICS

Mathematical science, as well as astrology, was in India pursued in the closest connexion with astronomy. Thus arithmetic and algebra form parts of the astronomical works of Āryabhaṭa, Brahmagupta, and Bhāskara. The theory that our decimal system is derived from India still holds the field, though the objections raised against this view appear to require a new examination of the question.

The most important mathematical texts are the first two sections of the *Āryabhaṭīya*, the *Gaṇitādhyāya* and the

Kuṭṭakādhyāya in the *Brāhma-sphuṭa-siddhānta* of Brahmagupta, and the *Līlāvatī* on arithmetic, and the *Bīja-gaṇita* on algebra in the *Siddhānta-śiromaṇi* of Bhāskara. The latter remarks at the end of his section on algebra that he had compiled his work from the too diffuse treatises of Brahmagupta and others. In the works of Brahmagupta and of Bhāskara we have the mathematical achievements of the Indians in their most highly developed form. Simple arithmetic is here described as concerned with the 'eight operations' consisting in addition, subtraction, multiplication, division, raising to the square and the cube, and the extraction of the square and the cube root. The methods employed are on the whole similar to our own. Then follow rules about fractions, about the zero, and about the practical applications of arithmetic, comprising the rule of three, the calculation of interest, and so on.

Algebra was also highly developed. Both Brahmagupta and Bhāskara handle a number of simple equations. The following is a sum involving such an equation from Bhāskara's *Līlāvatī*. 'Of a swarm of bees one-fifth settled on a Kadamba flower and one-third on a Śilīndra blossom; one bee remained over, hovering in the air, attracted at the same time by the charming perfume of a jasmine and of a pandanus. Tell me, charming one, the number of the bees.' These treatises also solve equations with more than one unknown quantity, as well as equations of a higher degree. In all these respects Indian algebra rises appreciably above the level attained by Diophantus, the Greek algebraist of Alexandria (*c.* 250 A.D.). The Indian mathematicians had by this time arrived at very advanced results in analysis, and, what represents the highest level of their attainments in the mathematical field, they had discovered a method of solving indeterminate equations of the second degree. This method is by a high mathematical authority (Hankel) declared to be the most delicate operation in the theory of numbers that had been achieved before the time of the great French astronomer Lagrange (eighteenth century).

The beginnings of geometry go back to a period of high antiquity in India, for a considerable amount of geometrical knowledge is to be found in the *Śulva-sūtras*, or 'String Rules', which form a part of the general Vedic ritual (*kalpa*) *sūtra* works. These give the rules for the laying out of the sacrificial ground, for the construction of the fire-altars, and other arrangements necessary for the performance of the single great sacrifices. The design of the sacrificial ground with its most important constituent parts made the construction of right angles, squares, and circles, as well as the transformation of plane figures into others of equal area, a matter of necessity. To sacrificial experts it was of the utmost moment that the measurement of the sacrificial ground by means of cords (*śulva*) stretched between stakes should be carried out accurately according to rule. These practical requirements resulted in a considerable aggregate of geometrical knowledge, including the Pythagorean proposition (worked out in Euclid i. 47). Thus the ritual experts understood how to transform rectangles into squares, squares into circles, as well as vice versa. It is probable that such geometrical knowledge based on practical operations goes back even to the time of the Vedic hymns.

The geometrical attainments of the Indians in later times, however, fell far short of those of the Greeks. Though there are agreements between the former and the Greek mathematician Heron (third century B.C.), it is probable that they acquired independently the geometrical knowledge found in the *Śulva-sūtras.* In the eighteenth century a Sanskrit translation of the elements of Euclid was made from the Arabic by a writer named Samrāḍ Jagannātha.

Trigonometry was known to the Indians in its application to astronomical calculations, and it is to be assumed that they obtained their knowledge of it from the Greeks in connexion with astronomy.

Thibaut, *Astronomie, Astrologie und Mathematik,* in Bühler's *Encyclopaedia,* iii, part 9. Macdonell, *History,* 434–5. Winternitz, *Geschichte: Astronomie, Astrologie und Mathematik,* iii. 555–77.

VIII

VERNACULAR INDIAN LANGUAGES AND LITERATURE

A. Five linguistic families as vernaculars — The Indo-Aryan the most important — Original home and migrations of the Aryans — Their early habitat in India — Māhārāṣṭrī the vehicle of lyrics in the drama — Apabhraṃśas — Modern vernaculars — Three Aryan elements in Indo-Aryan vernaculars — Foreign elements — Statistics of Indo-Aryan vernaculars — Four groups — Non-Aryan languages: the Dravidian group; the Muṇḍā; the intermediate group; the Indo-Chinese group. B. Modern vernacular literature — a. Dravidian: Tamil: Kurraḷ, Nāladiyār, Tiruvāśagam — Vishṇuite religious poetry — Jain epics in Tamil — Translations of Rāmāyaṇa and Mahābhārata — b. Indo-Aryan vernacular literature — Panjābī and Hindī: Kabīr, Nānak — Ādigranth of the Sikhs — Marāṭhī: paraphrase of the Bhagavadgītā; short poems called Abhang; Tukārām, most famous Marāṭha poet — Vidyāpati Ṭhākur's Maithilī allegory — Mīra Bāī, the Braj Bhāshā poetess — Bihāri Lāl — Tulsī Dās, the greatest poet of northern India: the Rām-charit-mānas, a Hindī Rāmāyaṇa — The Kāśmīrian 'Utterances of Lallā' — Rich Jain literature in Gujarātī — Bengali versions of Rāmāyaṇa, Mahābhārata, and some Purāṇas — Mukundrām Kavikankan, great Bengali poet — Chaitanya: his religious influence — Ram Prasād — The reformer Rāmmohan Roy — Influence of English literature on Bengali prose — Michael Madhu Sūdan, famous Bengali poet — Rabīndranāth Tagore's works.

A. Vernacular Groups of India

FIVE main linguistic families have their homes as vernaculars in India. Of these by far the most important, both from the number of its speakers and from being the chief vehicle of Indian civilization, is the Indo-Aryan speech. Representing the language of the people who migrated into India perhaps 1500 B.C., its descendants are now spoken by

233 of the 320 million inhabitants, or about three-fourths of the total population of India. The Indo-Aryan language in its oldest form is highly synthetical in structure, its grammar being even more complicated than that of the

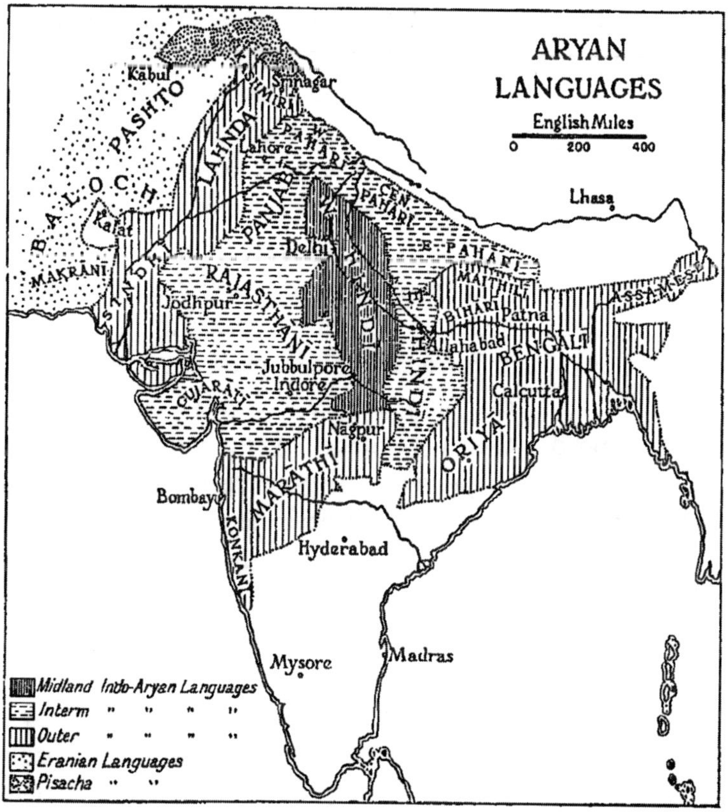

cognate Latin and Greek. The modern Aryan vernaculars, on the other hand, are essentially analytical, the terminals of nouns and verbs having given place to postpositions and to disjointed modern particles for the purpose of indicating time, place, and relation. These tongues are spread over the whole of northern India from the ocean in the west to the extreme east of Assam, and from the Himālaya in the north to the boundary of Kanara in the south of the Bombay Presidency. The speakers of the Aryan languages have lost their ethnical type by intermixture with the numerically predominant aborigines, but the languages themselves have preserved their identity by superseding the indigenous non-Aryan forms of speech. This is to be accounted for by the fact that when an Aryan tongue comes into contact with that of a less civilized people, it tends to displace the latter. It was only in the south of India, where the aboriginal languages were associated with a comparatively high degree of culture, and where the number of their speakers was greatly superior to that of the immigrants, that the indigenous speech held its own.

The original home of the Aryan-speaking people, who later overspread Europe besides parts of western and southern Asia, has long been a debated question. The most probable theory is that they occupied an area in south-eastern Europe, where they were a pastoral people with some knowledge of agriculture, and whence they wandered east and west. Linguistically they first split into the two groups of the *centum* and the *śatem* languages, the speakers of the former travelling westward, those of the latter, including the Aryans (in the narrow sense), mostly to the east. The Aryans then migrated, probably by a route north of the Caspian, into the country on the banks of the Yaxartes and the Oxus, the oasis of Khiva having most likely been one of their ancient seats. They then worked their way to the highlands of Khokand and Badakshān. There they divided into two sections. One, the Indian, moved southward over the Hindu Kush and through the valley of the Kābul into the plains of India. The other, the Iranian, separated into two branches. The Persic, which was employed by Darius I (522–486 B.C.) in the Behistun rock inscription, passing through Pahlavi became modern Persian, which under Musalmān rule played the part of an Indian classical language, the vehicle of some of the most famous Persian books. The Medic branch became the language of the *Avesta* and the parent of the two modern Iranian languages, Pashto and Baloch, which belong to India and extend almost to the Indus as their eastern boundary, reaching from its mouths to a good way north of Peshāwar.

There are several border languages which are neither entirely Iranian nor entirely Indo-Aryan, but have something of both. The tribes that spoke them were in the early centuries of our era nicknamed *Piśāchas*, or flesh-eaters; by the Aryans of India Proper, who had entered the Panjāb by the valley of the Kābul. These dialects have a very archaic character, ordinary words still in use showing forms almost the same as in Vedic hymns, while in India itself they survive only in a corrupt form. These languages are without literatures and have only recently been reduced to writing by European scholars. Yet it is handed down by tradition that the great collection of Indian folklore called the *Bṛhatkathā* (p. 119), which no longer exists, was composed in the language of the Piśāchas.

At the earliest period of which we have any knowledge the Panjāb was inhabited by a number of tribes who had evidently come into the country from the west and who spoke the oldest form of the Indo-Aryan language. Later the *Madhyadeśa* or 'Midland', that is, the Gangetic Doab, with the country immediately to the north and south of it, came to be regarded as the true home of the Indo-Aryan people. The dialect of this region, representing a linguistically more recent phase than that of the Vedic hymns, became fixed as Sanskrit by the labours of grammarians, which culminated in about the fourth century B.C. with the famous work of Pāṇini. It is a polished form of the language developed from the much older Vedic dialects by a process of decay rather than of growth. As an arrested vernacular it became the vehicle of literature, used by the educated as a second and cultivated language, beside their vernacular which was really a later development of itself, much as Latin continued to be used for literary purposes contemporaneously with the spoken dialect derived from its own earlier phase. In this capacity it has remained the literary language of the Hindus, like Latin throughout the Middle Ages in Europe.

Beside Sanskrit the vernaculars, derived from the Vedic stage, developed. They are termed Prākrits, as being their earlier phase. They were still synthetic languages with fairly complex grammars, but phonetically differing considerably from Sanskrit owing to their avoidance of harsh combinations of consonants and to their preference for final vowels. Thus the Sanskrit *sūtra*, 'thread', and *dharma*, 'duty', appear in Prākrit as *sutta* and *dhamma*; while *vidyut*, 'lightning', becomes *vijju*. Prākrit was in full use as a vernacular at a very early period, for we know that Buddha employed it for preaching his gospel in the sixth century B.C., while the earliest Indian inscriptions, from the third century B.C. onwards, were written in Prākrit, not Sanskrit.

After centuries of decay the Prākrits arrived at a condition of almost complete fluidity, each language becoming a collection of vowels only occasionally interrupted by a consonant. This excessive emasculation necessarily resulted in a new stage about 1000 A.D., that of the Tertiary Prākrits or modern Indo-Aryan vernaculars. The hiatus produced by contiguous vowels was removed by contraction into diphthongs, while combinations of consonants, which had disappeared through 2,000 years of attrition, reverted to forms that existed 3,000 years ago. Nominal and verbal endings, consisting of worn-down vowels, disappeared. The old synthetic type of Prākrit has been displaced by one that is now analytic, like English compared with Anglo-Saxon.

The earliest form of Prākrit preserved is called Pāli. Two hundred and fifty years B.C. the edicts of King Aśoka were inscribed on stone in a form of this language. One of the Prākrits in the Pāli stage was stereotyped as a sacred language for use in writing the Buddhist Pāli books.

The term 'Prākrit' is, however, usually restricted to the vernaculars which had developed in a decayed form beyond the stage of Pāli, but had not yet reached the analytic stage of the modern Indo-Aryan vernaculars. We have information about all these secondary vernaculars except that of the Panjāb.

Śaurasenī was the language of Śūrasena, the Sanskrit name of the country round Mathurā (now Muttra), close to the great kingdom of Kanauj, the leading Indian power.

Ardha-māgadhī was the Prākrit spoken in what is now Oudh and Bhagelkhand. Further east was Māgadhī, the vernacular spoken in what is the modern Bihār. To the south of these three lay the territory of Māhārāshṭrī, the dialect of Vidarbha (now Berār), which received early literary culture and in its native land became the vehicle of some of the most charming lyrics ever composed in an Indian tongue. Its popularity carried it over the whole of Hindustān, where it was employed for epic poetry and for the later religious writings of Jainism. But it is best known from the Sanskrit dramas, in which, while most of the vernacular prose is written in Śaurasenī, the songs are usually composed in Māhārāshṭrī.

The last stage of the Secondary Prākrits was that known as 'Literary Apabhraṃśa'. When the Prākrits came to be used as literary languages, the Indian grammarians began to apply the term *apabhraṃśa*, or 'decayed', 'corrupt', to the true vernaculars that were the basis of the literary dialects. In the end these Apabhraṃśas themselves came to be used for literary purposes by the Hindu grammarian successors of those who despised them. While the earlier Prākrits had been reduced to an artificial state by literary pruning, this was much less the case with the Apabhraṃśas, the rather scanty literary remains of which therefore give valuable evidence regarding the actual spoken language when it began to be written down.

The modern vernaculars are the direct descendants of these Apabhraṃśas.

From the Apabhraṃśa of Śaurasenī are derived Panjābī, which is spoken to the east of the Sutlej, and Western Hindī, the home of which is the Doab of the Jumna and Ganges. To the south of these lay Avantī, spoken round Ujjayinī (now Ujjain), from which is descended Rājasthānī. To the south-west of this dialect was spoken Gaurjarī, the mother of Gujarātī.

From the Apabhraṃśa of Ardha-māgadhī is descended Eastern Hindī.

From the Apabhraṃśa to the east of the Indus are derived Kāśmīrī in the north and Lahndā in the south.

From a Vrāchaḍa Apabhraṃśa, spoken on the lower course of the united stream of the Indus, is derived Sindhī.

From the Apabhraṃśa of Māhārāshṭrī, spoken south of the Vindhya in Berār, is descended Marāṭhī.

On the eastern side, four dialects are derived from the

Apabhraṃśa of Māgadhī: Bihārī, north of Patna; Oṛiyā on the south; and on the east, the Bengali of northern and of Central Bengal.

Sanskrit, owing to its prestige as the language of religion and learning, continued to exercise great influence during the development of the Prākrits. Its influence was in earlier times greatest in its special home, the 'Midland'. Thus the vocabulary of Śaurasenī Prākrit, if we make allowance for phonetic change, is practically the same as that of Sanskrit. The farther we move from the 'Midland', the more numerous grow the strange words technically known as 'local' (*deśya*). These, though also Indo-Aryan, are not derived from the particular ancient dialect which is the source of Sanskrit, but from contemporary dialects prevailing in far-off parts of India.

At the same time, literary Sanskrit has, owing to its prestige, exercised a constant influence over all the Indo-Aryan vernaculars. As it is universally believed in India to be the origin of all of them, words from its vocabulary have been freely borrowed by them. This tendency was stimulated by the revival, at the beginning of the nineteenth century, of Sanskrit learning under the influence of English scholars. It then became the fashion, in some of the modern vernaculars, to substitute Sankskrit words for those derived from Prākrit, just as if we were to substitute the Anglo-Saxon *hlāford* for 'lord' in modern English. Such words are by Hindu grammarians called *tatsamas*, 'the same as that' (i.e. as Sanskrit), while those derived from Prākrit are *tadbhavas*, 'originating in that' (i.e. in Sanskrit). Thus the Aryan elements in the Indo-Aryan vernaculars are of three kinds: *tatsamas*, *tadbhavas*, and *deśyas*. The languages especially overloaded with *tatsamas* are Marāṭhī, Hindī, and Bengali. This pedantry has made the literary language unintelligible to the vast mass of the population not educated in Government schools. But besides their predominant Indo-Aryan elements, these languages also contain a good number of foreign words in their vocabulary. The Dravidian tongues, which prevailed in India before the arrival of the Indo-Aryans, have supplied many words, some of them in the most ancient times. The chief contributions have been made during the last thousand years, since the Muhammadan conquest, by Persian and indirectly by Arabic through Persian. In northern India every peasant uses a few of these, while the literary Urdū of Lucknow contains so many that only inconsiderable elements of the true vernacular remain. A few words have also been borrowed from Portuguese, Dutch, and English, sometimes in a curiously disguised form.

The number of people speaking Indo-Aryan languages is, according to the Census Report of 1921, upwards of 233,000,000, or about three-fourths of the total population of India.

The following is a summary of the main Indo-Aryan languages with the respective number of their speakers in round numbers:

1. The languages of the Midland and those allied to them;

(*a*) Western Hindī . .	41,000,000	
(*b*) Eastern Hindī . .	23,000,000	
(*c*) Rājasthānī . . .	13,000,000	
(*d*) Gujarātī . . .	10,000 000	
(*e*) Panjābī . . .	16,230,000	103,230,000

2. The languages of the West:

(*a*) Kāśmīrī . . .	1,250,000	
(*b*) Lahndā . . .	5,500,000	
(*c*) Sindhī	3,372,000	10,122,000

3. The language of the South:		
Marāṭhī	19,000,000	19,000,000
4. The languages of the East:		
(*a*) Bihārī	34,500,000	
(*b*) Oṛiyā	10,000,000	
(*c*) Bengali	49,300,000	
(*d*) Assamese	2,000,000	95,800,000
		228,152,000

We may now proceed to deal briefly with these languages in detail.

1. *The Midland group of vernaculars*

Hindī, strictly speaking, means the 'language of India'; but it is in English specially applied to the speech of the Midland (Western Hindī) and of Oudh (Eastern Hindī), which really represent two distinct languages.

(*a*) *Western Hindī.* This is the vernacular of the region between the Jumna and the Ganges, besides the country to its north. As spoken in Madhyadeśa, the special home of Sanskrit in old times, it is by far the most important of all the modern languages of India.

Hindustānī. The principal dialect of Western Hindī is Hindustānī, the home of which is the upper Gangetic Doab, the country round Meerut, and the southern boundary of which extends close to Delhi. Hindustānī is, however, not only a local vernacular, but one that is spoken over the whole of the north and west of India as a second language, a *lingua franca* used in court and market-place by every one of any education. From Delhi, where it was first in general use, Hindustānī was disseminated all over India by the officials of the Mughal Empire. It has been cultivated as a literary dialect by both Musalmans and Hindus. The former introduced a large number of Persian and Arabic words into its vocabulary. When this process is pushed to an extreme, as in Lucknow, the language can only be understood by Musalmans or by Hindus educated like Musalmans.

Urdū. This Persianized form of Hindustānī is called Urdū, or the language of 'the military bazaar' near the Delhi Palace where it arose. Though Urdū literature is Musalman in origin, the excessive Persian element was first introduced into the language by Hindu scribes who were employed in the Mughal administration. It was not due to Persians or Persianized Mughals, who for many centuries used only Persian for literary purposes. Even in the Dravidian parts of the Deccan Urdū is used by the Muhammadans, for it was in fact here that Urdū literature arose. But the Urdū of the Deccan differs somewhat from that of Delhi and Lucknow, as it retains some archaic features that have disappeared in the north. For several centuries Urdū literature was entirely poetical. Prose Urdū was a result of the British occupation of India, which called forth the need of text-books for the college of Fort William at Calcutta. The Hindī form of Hindustānī was created at the same time by the staff of that College. Being intended for the needs of Hindus, it was purified of all Persian and Arabic words, for which were substituted words borrowed or derived from Ṣanskrit. Since it could be used by Hindus without offending any of their religious prejudices, it was soon widely adopted, and is now accepted as the medium for writing prose in Upper India by all who do not use Urdū. Although the sole difference between the two was one of vocabulary, the Sanskritic Hindustānī has in the course of a century created some idioms of its own. Hence an Indian can seldom be found who is able to write with equal correctness both the Persianized and the Sanskritic form of Hindustānī. Thus a certain well-known Hindustānī book, written by a Muhammadan and containing not a single Persian or Arabic word, is yet considered by strict judges of dialect to be composed in Urdū as exhibiting idioms to be found in that dialect only, and not in Sanskritic Hindustānī. As is to be expected from its origin, Urdū is generally written in a modified form of the Persian script, while for Hindustānī (as for Hindī) the Devanāgarī character, specifically used for Sanskrit, is commonly employed. Urdū is used for writing both poetry and prose, Hindustānī for prose only. For poetry a Hindu employs a naturally-developed dialect of Western Hindī (generally Braj Bhāshā) or Eastern Hindī (usually Awadhī). When 'Hindustānī' is meant to designate a particular form of speech, a language neither excessively Persian nor excessively Sanskritic in vocabulary is intended.

Of the four other dialects of Western Hindī it is only necessary here to mention Braj Bhāshā, which is nearest to the ancient Prākrit Śaurasenī. It is spoken round Muttra and in the Central Gangetic Doab. Its literature, which is considerable, is for the most part poetical. It was the form of Western Hindī chiefly used for literary purposes before Hindustānī was invented.

Western, as well as Eastern, Hindī is very flexible and copious. Both have no very complicated grammar and are capable of expressing abstract ideas of all kinds. The older phases of their literatures contain high flights of poetry and eloquent products of religious devotion.

(*b*) *Eastern Hindī*. Here the influence of the Midland language is far less evident than in Rājputāna and the Panjāb. Being the language of Oudh, it is the vernacular of the native country of Rāma. An earlier form of it, the secondary Prākrit called Ardha-Māgadhī, was used by the Jain apostle Mahāvīra for teaching his disciples, and thus became the sacred language of the Jains. The modern vernacular, Eastern Hindī, on the other hand, came to be the vehicle for celebrating the deeds of Rāma and subsequently the dialect in which nearly all the epic poetry of Northern India has been written. Eastern Hindī has, indeed, probably a greater literature than any other modern Indo-Aryan vernacular. This literature, being founded on the genuine language of the people and free from the obscuring influence of Sanskrit additions, is familiar to every peasant of Oudh. Eastern Hindī, as well as Oṛiyā, meets Marāṭhī in the Central Provinces, shading off into it through mixed dialects. These two are the only dialects that are not sharply divided from Marāṭhī. This is an indication of the close kinship which existed 2,000 years ago between the Ardha-Māgadhī and the Māhārāṣṭrī Prākrits.

Eastern Hindī has three main dialects. The standard one, which is spoken in Oudh, is called Awadhī.

(*c*) *Rājasthānī*, the modern language of Rājputāna, has close affinities with the speech of the Midland. It has four main groups of dialects. The westernmost of these is Mārwāṛī, which is by far the most important. One of the places in which it is spoken is Bīkānēr. Its speakers are enterprising merchants and bankers, who have carried it all over India. It has an extensive literature, written in a peculiar character belonging to the same group of alphabets as the Laṇḍā of the Panjāb and the Śārada of Kashmīr.

Naipālī, the language of the ruling classes of Nepāl, is an offshoot of Rājasthānī, imposed on the inhabitants some centuries ago by bands of Rājputs who invaded and conquered their hills.

(*d*) *Gujarātī*. This dialect lies to the south-west of

Rājasthānī, and is the most western of the vernaculars over which the influence of the Midland language extends. Its basis is the old Saurāshṭrī, the Prākrit of Surāshṭra (perhaps the modern Surat). Its printed character is modelled on Kaithī, the current form of Devanāgarī used all over India. As several of its old grammars survive, the history of this language can be studied from its beginning as a vernacular 900 years ago. The literature goes back to early times.

(*e*) *Panjābī.* This vernacular, closely akin to the modern language of the Midland, is spoken in the Central Panjāb and is the dialect used by the Sikhs and Hindus. Its proper script is related to that used in Mārwār. Called *Laṇḍā*, or 'clipped', it is noted for its illegibility. An improved form of it is known by the name of *Gurumukhī*, which was invented about three centuries ago for writing the Sikh scriptures. The standard Panjābī is spoken around Amritsar. Of all the Midland group of languages, Panjābī is the purest, being freest from both Persian and Sanskrit borrowings. Nevertheless it is capable of expressing all kinds of ideas.

2. *The Western group of vernaculars*

(*a*) *Kāśmīrī* is the most northern, being the language of the state of Kashmīr. Owing to the peculiarity of its vowels, it is somewhat difficult to pronounce. It has an extensive old literature; but as the modern vernacular has borrowed very freely from Persian and Arabic, books written two or three centuries ago are hardly intelligible to the people of the country at the present day. It seems to be a Dardic language very heavily impregnated with borrowings from the Apabhraṃśa of the north-west of India. The bulk of the population being Muhammadans, only a few Pandits preserve the memory of the old language.

(*b*) *Kohistānī.* This is the name of the old language spoken on the Indus and in the valley of its tributary, and is another belonging to the Western group. At the present day, however, it is spoken by only a few tribes, having been nearly superseded by Pashto, the Iranian dialect of Afghānistān.

(*c*) *Lahndā.* This is a third language belonging to the Western group. Its name means 'the West'. It is spoken as far east as Panjābī (and thus touches the Midland group), but there is no dividing line between these two languages. Lahndā is spoken west of the Indus up to the Afghān frontier by Hindus, while the Pathān Musalmans speak Pashto. Lahndā has two dialects, the one extending to the north, the other to the south, of the Salt Range. It has no literature.

(*d*) *Sindhī.* This, the language of Sindh and its neighbourhood, is the fourth and last of the Western group. It is nearly related to Lahndā. As it occupies an isolated area, it has retained many archaic phonetic and flexional peculiarities. It has no literature of any account. As the population speaking it is largely Musalman, it has borrowed much from Persian. An adaptation of the Persian character has been employed for writing it by Moslems since about the seventeenth century. Hindus use and have used the Laṇḍā alphabet in the Panjāb.

3. *Marāṭhī*

South of Gujarātī and spoken along the coast of the Arabian Sea from near Daman to some way beyond Goa, lies the home of the southernmost Indo-Aryan vernacular, Marāṭhī, the descendant of Māhārāshṭrī Prākrit.

The Saurāshṭrī dialect of Māhārāshṭrī, which once occupied Gujarāt, has been ousted by a language belonging to the

Midland group; but traces of it seem to be found in the Marāṭhī area. The home of Marāṭhī comprises the north of the Deccan plateau, the strip of country between the Ghāts and the Arabian Sea, and the territory of Berār within the Bombay Presidency, as well as a good part of the north-west of Hyderābād State. It is bounded on the north by Gujarātī, Rājasthānī, Western and Eastern Hindī, till it reaches the boundary of the Eastern group in Oṛiyā.

Marāṭhī, which has a copious literature, is a true vernacular. The later phase of the language has indeed been to a considerable extent Sanskritized, but has not been exposed to this process in the same degree as the literary speech of Bengal. As the Marāṭha country was not invaded till a comparatively late date by the Muhammadans, who were also ultimately expelled, the number of words the language borrowed direct from and through Persian is inconsiderable.

Marāṭhī is printed in the Devanāgarī character, but a form of script called *mōḍī*, or 'twisted', is used for writing the language in a current hand.

Of its three dialects, the standard one called Deśī Marāṭhī is spoken in its purest form around Poona.

4. *The Eastern group.*

The eastern Indo-Aryan linguistic group consists of four languages derived from the old Māgadhī dialect.

(*a*) *Bihārī.* This language occupies the original home, Magadha, of the parent speech in which Buddha preached. Here lay the capital of King Aśoka, Pāṭaliputra (the modern Patna). Magadha corresponds to the present districts of Patna and Gayā. To the north across the Ganges lies the country of Tirhut, the ancient Mithilā. To the west is the district of Bhojpur, comprising the west of modern Bihār and the east of the United Provinces. To the south of the ancient Magadha lie the two plateaux of Chotā Nāgpur. All this territory forms the area of the present Bihārī, of which there are three dialects: Maithilī, Māgadhī, and Bhojpurī.

Maithilī has a limited literature going back to the fifteenth century. When written by Brahmins it has a character of its own resembling that used for Bengali. The language is full of archaic expressions. The original Indo-Aryan speech of Nepāl, before its invasion by Rājputs, was an old form of Maithilī.

Māgadhī, the language of the ancient Magadha, or South Bihār, resembles Maithilī in its general character. Although directly derived from the tongue in which Buddha preached, it has no literature and no traditions.

Bhojpurī differs considerably from the other two dialects: it is a flexible speech, free from grammatical complexity.

All the dialects of Bihārī, except that of the Tirhut Brahmins, are written in 'Kaithī', a current form of Devanāgarī used all over India.

(*b*) *Oṛiyā.* This is the language spoken in Orissa and the adjacent parts of Madras and of the Central Provinces. Occupying an isolated area of India, it has changed but slightly since the fourteenth century, when it first appears in inscriptions. It has a literature of inconsiderable extent but some merit. It is written in a peculiar script in which the long horizontal straight line of Devanāgarī is replaced by short curves, because the stylus with which it was written on talipot palm-leaves tended to split the leaves if the lines were straight. Phonetically the Oṛiyā language has a musical sound, while its grammar is simple, but adequate. The vocabulary of its literary style, however, suffers from being overloaded with Sanskrit.

(*c*) *Bengali.* This language is spoken by a larger population than any other Indian vernacular, the number being, according to the census of 1921, 49,000,000. The main dialectical division of the language is to be found in the difference between the literary and the spoken speech. The written dialect is the same in the whole province, except on the eastern side of the delta of the Ganges, the inhabitants of which are Muhammadans. The literary language is never used in conversation, which is always carried on in the colloquial dialect, even by the most highly educated Bengalis. It differs from the colloquial language both in its vocabulary, which is highly Sanskritized, and in its grammar, which keeps the obsolete forms of three centuries ago artificially alive. The origin of this literary form of Bengali goes back to the beginning of the last century, when a revival of learning arose in Calcutta under English influence. Before that epoch Bengal had produced a poetical literature written in a purified form of the spoken vernacular. But with the establishment of the English in Calcutta the want of a Bengali prose literature arose, a want which was easily supplied by pedants who have been styled 'Sanskrit-ridden Pandits'. 'Anything more monstrous', says Sir George Grierson, 'than this prose dialect, as it existed in the first half of the nineteenth century, it is difficult to conceive. Books were written, excellent in their subjects, eloquent in their thoughts, but in a language from which something like ninety per cent. of the genuine Bengali vocabulary was excluded, and its place supplied by words borrowed from Sanskrit which the writers themselves could not pronounce.' Since the middle of the nineteenth century there has been a somewhat unsuccessful attempt to reduce the enormous Sanskritization of literary Bengali. This is the official language of Government and of missionaries, generally taught in the Bengali grammars meant for English students.

There are three groups of spoken Bengali: the Western, the Eastern, and the Northern. The first, which is the standard dialect, is spoken in the area occupying both sides of the Hūgli and extending farther west. The centre of eastern Bengali is the city of Dacca. Northern Bengali is spoken north of the Ganges and at the lower end of the Assam valley. In derivation it is intermediate between Bihārī and Assamese.

Bengali and Assamese are written in very nearly the same script, which is akin to that used by the Brahmins of Tirhut. Though of the same origin as Devanāgarī, it has been an independent script since about 1000 A.D.

(*d*) *Assamese.* This is the language of the middle and upper parts of the Assam valley. It is nearly related to colloquial Bengali; but its claim to be regarded not as a dialect of Bengali, but as an independent language, rests mainly on the fact that it possesses an important literature, besides having several characteristic features of pronunciation. Its literary style does not suffer like Bengali from the excessive use of Sanskritisms. The literature goes back to an early date, is varied in character, and especially abounds in historical works. Assamese cannot be said to have any real dialects.

Non-Aryan languages

Besides the Indo-Aryan languages of northern India, there are also non-Aryan languages spoken by about eighty-six millions.

The most important group here is the Dravidian. Linguistically it occupies a much more restricted area than the

Dravidian race. For the latter have in the north of India been for the most part completely Aryanized, adopting the Indo-Aryan language of their conquerors, though they have retained their ethnic characteristics. They have also

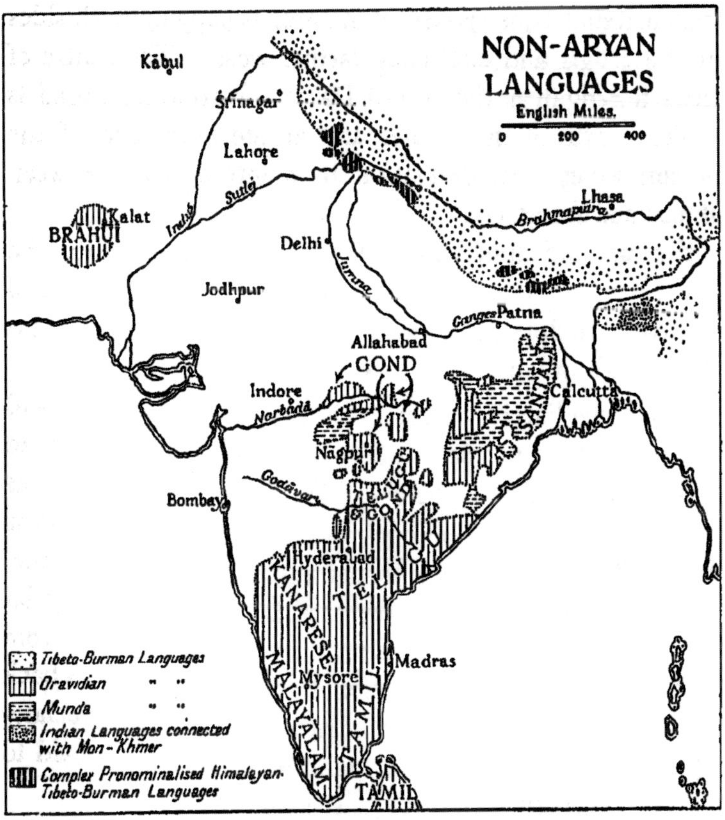

adopted the speech of another race of the same physical type, who spoke a language which was different from their own, being unrelated in phonetics, in inflexion, and in vocabulary—the Muṇḍā tongue.

The Dravidian group was spoken in 1921 by about sixty-four million people. Its home is the south and the hills of central India. One small branch, Brāhūī, with fewer than 200,000 speakers, is found in the north-west, in Balochistān. The Dravidian languages have various peculiarities distinguishing them from the Indo-Aryan. Among them the following may be mentioned: All nouns denoting inanimate objects and irrational beings are of the neuter gender. Nouns are inflected not by means of case-terminations but by means of prepositions and separable particles suffixed. The verbal system, while lacking a passive voice, possesses a negative as well as an affirmative voice. Instead of clauses introduced by relative pronouns, relative participial nouns are used: thus 'the man who came' would in Dravidian be 'the who-came' literally. This use of the relative participle occurs also in the Muṇḍā languages and in Tibeto-Burman.

The Dravidian group comprises nine vernaculars, but the lesser ones need not be mentioned here.

(*a*) *Tamil.* By far the most important is Tamil, which is spoken by nineteen millions and the area of which covers the whole of the country south of a line drawn from Mysore on the west to Madras on the east, including the northern half of Ceylon. It is the Dravidian language which has undergone a literary cultivation from a very early period and has assimilated many Sanskrit words along with Brahmin civilization. Its copious literature is written in a somewhat artificial dialect, distinguished by the term 'perfect' (*shen*) from the colloquial, called 'rude', much in the same way as in Aryan India Sanskrit ('the purified') is contrasted with Prākrit ('the vulgar'). The terms 'Tamil' and 'Drāviḍa' are both derived from the same original word 'Drāmiḍa'. The Tamil language has a script of its own.

(*b*) The language called *Andhra-bhāṣā* by Sanskrit writers is Telugu, which is spoken by twenty-four millions and is the chief language in eastern India, extending from Madras northwards to near Orissa. It is also spoken in the east of the state of Hyderābād and in the extreme south of the Central Provinces, reaching southwards into Berār. It has an extensive literature written in a script of its own, which is allied to Devanāgarī, but, being written on palm-leaves, it is, like Oṛiyā, characterized by numerous curves.

(*c*) *Malayālam*. This language is spoken by seven millions along the west coast from Mangalore southwards. It separated from Tamil in the ninth century A.D. Characteristic features of it are, generally speaking, that it has dropped all its personal verbal endings, and that it has borrowed a conspicuous number of Sanskrit words. It has an extensive literature, which is written in the old script, called *grantha*, used in southern Malabar for Sanskrit writings.

(*d*) *Kanarese*. This language is spoken in the Mysore State and some neighbouring British territory by nearly ten and a half million people. It has an ancient literature written in a script closely allied to that used for Telugu.

(*e*) *Tuḷu*. A quite small Dravidian language is Tuḷu, spoken by over half a million of the inhabitants of the south Kanara district of the Madras Presidency.

If the Dravidians entered India from the north-west, the speakers of Brāhūī in Balochistān and Sindh seem to represent an isolated remnant of their rear-guard.

2. *The Muṇḍā languages*

This tongue, which is quite distinct from the Dravidian group, is known under this name to Sanskrit writers. Often wrongly called 'Kolarian', it probably represents the aboriginal speech of India.

The Muṇḍā languages are of an agglutinative type. There is a fundamental difference between the Muṇḍā and the Dravidian verb.

The most important branch of the Muṇḍā language is Kherwari, which has three and a half million speakers who form a collection of tribes inhabiting a compact area of country on the Chotā Nāgpur plateau. One of the dialects is Santālī, spoken to the east of Calcutta. Another dialect is that of the Savaras, which is spoken by over 150,000 people. They are an ancient tribe known in Vedic times, mentioned in one of the Brāhmaṇas, and spoken of by Pliny and Ptolemy. None of these Muṇḍā languages have any script of their own, nor any literature.

3. *An intermediate group*

Besides these two main groups of non-Aryan speech, there is an intermediate group in central India north of the Telugu area spoken by about 3,000,000. The three chief languages are the speech of the Gonds, spoken by a million and a half in the hill country of central India ; Kurukh or Oraon, the tongue of nearly a million ; and Khandī or Kui, that of half a million in the Orissa hills. This group has had no literary cultivation.

4. *The Indo-Chinese group*

The languages of Farther India are usually grouped under the general name of Indo-Chinese, spoken by about 13,000,000. Their original home seems to have been north-western China. Hence they spread down river valleys into Burma and down the Brahmaputra into India proper in the hill country south of the central Assam valley. Here Khāsi is spoken by fewer than 200,000 speakers.

A century ago it was a rude, unwritten language. But now it has a literature, created by the missionaries who worked among them. It is written in the Roman character, and is recognized as one of the Indian vernaculars that are a subject of examination in the University of Calcutta.

Grierson, *The Imperial Gazetteer of India*, vol. i, ch. 7, pp. 349–401, Oxford, 1907; *Linguistic Survey of India*, 11 vols., Calcutta, 1903–1926.

B. Modern Vernacular Literature

The concluding phase of the long history of Indian literature is that of the modern vernaculars. It appears in Hindustān written in the latest descendants of the ancient Aryan tongue that entered the north-west of India some 3,500 years ago; and in the Deccan in the unallied languages of the south. The extent of modern Indian literature being very great, only its chief products can here be described in outline. Neither the ancient influence of Greece, nor the medieval rule of Islām, nor the modern dominion of Christian Britain have essentially altered the civilization and mentality of the Hindus. Persian models are followed entirely by the Urdū literature resulting from the Muhammadan conquest, and largely by Sindhī writings. The literature of all the other modern vernaculars has, moreover, in recent times been variously affected by Arabic-Persian and by English writings. But the literary influence of ancient Sanskrit works has been much deeper. The great epics, *Mahābhārata* and *Rāmāyaṇa*, have by translations become the common property of all Indians. So too the *Pañcatantra* and other story books in various versions continue to live among the people. As in Sanskrit literature the religious and moral element greatly predominates, so the poetry of modern India is uniformly fertilized by the teachings of Brahmanism, Hinduism, Buddhism, and Jainism.

The vernacular literatures, like the languages in which they are written, may be divided into the two groups of the Indo-Aryan in the north and the Dravidian in the south.

Though genealogically unconnected with Sanskrit, Dravidian literature is permeated by Sanskrit linguistic and literary elements. Its older phases can be traced back to an earlier time than the modern Indo-Aryan literatures. For, owing to the fundamentally different character of the Dravidian languages, an independent literature was here able to develop sooner than in the north, where Sanskrit dominated intellectual life to such an extent that there was no room for a separate vernacular literature to grow up. The view now generally accepted is that the flourishing period of Tamil literature lay between about 100 and 300 A. D. The most famous Tamil work supposed to go back to this ancient period is the *Kurraḷ* of the weaver Tiruvaḷḷuvar, which is a collection of 1,330 aphorisms on the three aims of life (in Sanskrit *dharma*, *artha*, *kāma*). Tiruvaḷḷuvar is not a personal name, but a title by which the religious teachers of the Pariahs of southern India were known, while *Kurraḷ* designates a short aphoristic stanza. Hence we really know neither the title of this celebrated anthology nor the name of its author. The contents of the work represent the general aphoristic wisdom of India, and do not belong to any particular sect. This is indicated by the fact that Buddhists, Jains, Vaishṇavas, and Śaivas, who successively prevailed in southern India, equally claimed Tiruvaḷḷuvar as one of their own teachers. The poet, in fact, stands above all races, castes, and sects, inculcating a general human morality and worldly wisdom. Not only the ethical content of the book but the skill with which the author gives his aphorisms a poetical setting in a difficult metre have evoked admiration. This is one of his sayings:

> 'Note that all men are equals born;
> For works alone cause grades of rank.'

Another famous collection of aphorisms in Tamil is the *Nāḷadiyār*. Consisting of 400 stanzas, it embraces teachings on rebirth, retribution, and salvation, on *dharma*, *artha*, and *kāma*, in the general manner of Indian aphoristic poetry. The author was probably a Jain, as may be gathered from a miraculous legend told about the collection, though the verses themselves are not Jainistic, nor even religious in character.

Religious lyrical poetry forms the content of the third Tamil classic, the *Tiruvāśagam*, 'the Sacred Utterance', of Māṇikka-Vāśagar, who was an enthusiastic votary of Śiva and a bitter opponent of the Jains and Buddhists. His father was a Brahmin at the court of the Pāndya king Arimarṭana, and became the minister of the king who reigned at Madura about 800 A.D. Songs from the *Tiruvāśagam* are sung in every Śiva temple in the Tamil country at the present day. The Tamils say: 'He whose heart is not melted by the *Tiruvāśagam* must have a heart of stone.' An eminent authority on Tamil, the late Dr. G. U. Pope, who was long a missionary in southern India, admired the deeply religious spirit of these songs, comparing the poet to St. Paul and to St. Francis of Assisi. Māṇikka-Vāśagar regards Śiva as a personal deity; but, with the curious mixture of theistic and pantheistic ideas so often found in medieval and modern India, he nevertheless identifies the god with the universe.

Another famous Śivaite poet is Tiru-nāna-sambandhu, whose image is still daily worshipped in south Indian temples.

Contemporaneous with the religious poetry of the Śivaites is that of the Vishṇuites in south India. A sacred book of this sect is the *Vaiṣṇava-prabandha* in 4,000 verses, by the twelve Ālvars or saints, who were at the same time singers of divine love (*bhakti*). The author of the majority of these verses was Tiru-mangai, who is supposed to have lived in the first half of the eighth century. The Ālvars included a woman, the Saint Aṇḍāḷ, to whom 107 of these songs are attributed. She sang of Kṛishṇa and dreamt of being wedded to the god, like the female saints of medieval Christianity. Prominent among the successors of Rāmānuja was Pillai Lokāchārya (born in 1213 A.D.) who, in a popular form of Tamil largely admixed with Sanskrit, wrote eighteen Rahasyas or 'secret texts', which were also translated into Sanskrit.

Jain writers composed the Tamil epics *Sindāmaṇi* (Skt. *cintāmaṇi*) and its imitation *sūḷāmaṇi* (Skt. *cūḍāmaṇi*) in which Jain legends were presented in a poetical garb.

The old Sanskrit epics were of course translated into Tamil. Famous is the version of the *Rāmāyaṇa* by the poet Kamban, who is said to have lived in the eleventh century. Tamil versions of the *Mahābhārata* belong to a later date. There are also Tamil historical poems and a considerable philosophical literature, especially on the Vedānta system. A Vedāntic poem is the *Kaivalya-navanīta*, or 'Cream of Spiritual Isolation'.

Less important than the literature of Tamil is that of the three other non-Aryan languages of the south—Telugu, Malayālam, and Kanarese.

In all the modern Indian vernaculars, Dravidian as well

as Indo-Aryan, there is a rich popular literature of songs and tales. Among the beautiful Dravidian folk-songs, there are many of an artificial rather than of a popular type. In the various collections of fairy-tales and stories there is much old and well-known material derived from Sanskrit literature.

The earliest literature in the Indo-Aryan vernaculars of northern India is represented by the poetical chronicles of Rājputāna, in which the heroic conflicts of the Rājputs with the Muhammadan conquerors are celebrated by contemporary bards. The oldest of these chronicles that are extant date from the twelfth century. These, however, made use of earlier sources, many of which may go back to perhaps 800 A.D. They are often of considerable poetical merit. The most famous is the epic *Pṛthī Rāj Rāso* of Chand Bardāī. Here the heroic fights of Pṛthī Rāj are extolled by his friend, the Court bard, Chand.

Panjābī. A wealth of popular poetry prevails in the Panjāb at the present day. In these ballads much very ancient material survives, as the story of Nala and the legend of the fight between Kṛishṇa and Śiśupāla. These are sung and heard with as much pleasure as songs relating to the events of the last hundred years. There are bards at the courts of native princes in the Panjāb who, besides celebrating the warlike deeds of the heroes of ancient times, also preserve and often modify arbitrarily the family history of the princes of to-day.

Hindī. Far more extensive is the religious literature in Hindī beginning in the fourteenth century. The great founders of Indian sects were for the most part poets as well as religious leaders. All of them were inspired by *bhakti*, or mystical devotion to the deity.

About 1500 A.D. Rāmānanda, a follower of Rāmānuja

(p. 149), founded a new sect teaching that the way to salvation was to be found in *bhakti.* He was the first to teach with great emphasis that for the votaries of Vishṇu there existed no differences of caste. A disciple of Rāmānanda was the famous Benares weaver Kabīr, who wished to abolish not only caste, but religious and sectarian barriers. In praiṣing God he made no difference between Allah and Rāma, calling himself 'the child of Allah and Rāma'. By birth a Muhammadan, he became an enthusiastic theist of the type of a *bhakti* worshipper of Rāma. The formalities and ceremonies of both Hindus and Muhammadans were equally hateful to him. Here are some of his words:

'There is nothing but water in the sacred bathing-places; and I know that they are useless, for I have bathed in them. Lifeless are all the images of the gods: they cannot speak; I know it, for I have called aloud to them.'

He seems to have died about 1518. At his funeral, Hindus and Moslems, according to legend, vied for the honour of disposing of his body, as that of one who belonged to themselves. Kabīr's adherents at the present day number only about 8,000 to 9,000 in Northern and Central India. But his influence can be traced in other sects, especially in the religion of the Sikhs, which was founded by Nānak (1469–1538), the most famous disciple of Kabīr. He sought to blend Hindu and Moslem theology into a unit to an even greater degree than his teacher Kabīr. His poems and those of his successors, the later saints and teachers, were collected in the time of the Guru Arjuna (1581–1604) in the *Ādi-granth*, the sacred book of the Sikhs. Songs of Kabīr have also been incorporated in this work, which for the Sikhs is a hymn-book, a prayer-book, and a manual of theology, all in one. The hymns are chiefly composed in old Hindī, with a certain number in Panjābī. The tenth Guru,

Govind Singh (1675–1708), turned the Sikhs into a great military organization. After his death his hymns were added to the *Ādi-granth* in 1734.

The Moslem Fakir Malik Muhamad came under the influence of Kabīr, and about 1540 composed a famous romantic and half-historical epic entitled *Padumavatī*. At the end the poet himself gives an allegorical religio-philosophic interpretation of the poem.

Marāṭhī. Famous poets inculcating the doctrine of *bhakti* arose in the Marāṭha country. Here at Paṇḍharpur there was a temple of Vishṇu under the name of Viṭhobā or Viṭṭhal, in whose cult the singing of short songs called *Abhaṅg* played a great part. The oldest of the Marāṭhī singers is Jñāneśvar, whose chief work entitled *Jñāneśvarī* was completed in 1290. It is a free paraphrase of the *Bhagavadgītā* (p. 90) in Marāṭhī verse.

His friend Nāmdev (1270–1350), who is said to have been a tailor, devoted himself entirely to the service of Viṭhobā as a singer of Abhaṅgs. The following version of one of his songs may serve as a specimen:

The One indeed pervades all things, wherever our glances wander;
But veiled by Māyā's magic spell, by scarce one is comprehended.
Govinda is the All, without him nothing is, he is the One.
For he is like the cord on which one hundred thousand gems are strung.
As sea and wave, bubble and foam, are naught but shapes of water, so
The Universe is nothing else but varied forms of Brahma's sport.

It is remarkable that these Marāṭhī singers, in order to give their divine love more intense expression, often conceive the divinity as a female.

There was a Śūdra female slave named Janabāī, a devotee and handmaiden of Nāmdev and the god Viṭhobā, who was able to express a real mystic divine love and the experience of complete union with God in her hymns.

Tukārām. But by far the most famous of all Marāṭhī poets was Tukārām. He was born in a village near Poona about 1608, and died in 1649, being according to the legend translated to the heaven of Vishṇu. He had early learnt the poems of Nāmdev by heart, and felt himself called upon to continue his work. No fewer than 4,621 Abhaṅgs are attributed to him in the collections handed down by tradition. He had grown so accustomed to celebrate his god in metre that he almost spoke in verse. His songs are in the mouth of all Marāṭhī speakers, educated and uneducated alike. People of all castes and sects sing his verses in the fields and by lamplight in their homes.

Maithilī. The doctrine of divine love (*bhakti*) naturally furnished a suitable atmosphere for the enthusiastic worship of Kṛishṇa. Thus about 1400 A.D. Vidyāpati Thākur sang, in the Maithilī dialect of Bihār, of the yearning of the soul for God in the form of the allegory portraying the love of Rādhā and Kṛishṇa.

Braj Bhāshā. This mystical divine love found its most tender expression in the hymns of the poetess Mīra Bāī (*c.* 1420), who wrote in the Braj Bhāshā, the dialect of Mewār in Western Hindustān. She composed a commentary on the *Gītagovinda* and on songs that were widely diffused in her native land. She was a princess and married a king. But according to the legend her devotion to Kṛishṇa was so great that one day as she stood before his image praying for his love, the idol opened and closed around her, so that she was no longer seen on earth.

At the Court of the Emperor Akbar lived the blind poet

of Agra, Sūr Dās (born in 1483), who translated the *Bhāgavata Purāṇa* into the vernacular, and whose collection of hymns, the *Sūr Sāgar*, is said to embrace 60,000 verses.

About these and many other poets and saints of Kṛishṇa worship much information is furnished in the *Bhakt Mālā*, a collection of legends of the saints by Nābhādās, who lived about 1600 A. D.

The chief seat of Kṛishṇa worship is the neighbourhood of Mathurā (Muttra), where the adventures of Kṛishṇa are believed to have taken place. In the Braj Bhāshā, the central dialect of Western Hindī, Bihāri Lāl (*c.* 1603–63) wrote his *Sat sai* (Skt. *sapta śatī*), a collection of 700 verses, most of which describe the love of Kṛishṇa and Rādhā, but at the same time serve as illustrations of the figures used in poetics.

A translation of the tenth chapter of the *Bhāgavata Purāṇa* in the Braj Bhāshā was turned into Hindī prose by Lallū Jī Lāl in the *Prēm Sāgar*, or 'Ocean of Love'. This work, begun in 1806 under the supervision of the Orientalist John Gilchrist (1759–1841) and printed in 1809, gave rise to a new literary language.

Eastern Hindī. The greatest poet of Northern India was without doubt Tulsī Dās (1532–1624), the writer of the *Rām-carit-mānas*, the 'Lake of the deeds of Rāma'. This poem, which is the Hindī *Rāmāyaṇa*, is not a translation of Vālmīki's epic, but an independent poem, of which the latter work was only one of several sources. Tulsī Dās was not the founder of a sect, but only taught that Rāma dwelt as a benevolent father in heaven, and that all men were brothers. The religious and moral influence of his poem can hardly be over-estimated. The Eastern Hindī dialect, in which the epic is written, is understood throughout an extensive area of Hindustān. It therefore constitutes a kind of Bible for the ninety millions of Hindus who inhabit the vast tract lying between Bengal and the Panjāb, the Himālaya and the Vindhya ranges. 'Pandits', remarks Sir George Grierson, 'may speak of the Vedas and the Upanishads, and a few may even study them, others may say that their beliefs are represented by the Purāṇas; but for the great majority of the people of Hindustān, learned and unlearned, the *Rāmāyaṇa* of Tulsī Dās is the only standard of moral conduct.'

It is, however, not only owing to its high moral standard that this work is so greatly esteemed. It is also a perfect *kāvya*, which only differs, to its advantage, from other works of Indian artificial poetry, by containing beautiful descriptions of nature based not on the rules of the manuals on poetics but on the poet's own personal observation.

Kāśmīrian. The Śaivism of Kashmīr also had its poets. The *Lallā-vākyāni*, the 'Utterances of Lallā', a female ascetic, who composed hymns in the oldest Kāśmīrian dialect of the fourteenth century, long enjoyed great popularity. The memory of this poetess still survives in Kashmīr as that of a prophetess of Śaivism.

Gujarātī. Little is as yet known of the rich Jain literature written in the Gujarātī dialect. Quite recently (1922) a work belonging to the *Pañcatantra* cycle, the *Pañcākhyāna-varttika*, written in Old Gujarātī, has been published. Gujarātī is to-day also the language of the Parsis, the adherents of Zoroastrianism, who have exercised a special influence on journalism in India. Thus the first monthly journal in Gujarātī was founded by a Parsi. As a poet and author in Gujarātī (as well as English), and still more as a courageous champion of social reforms, the Parsi Behramji M. Malabari (born in 1853) made a good name for himself in India.

Bengali. In Bengal, ballads glorifying the kings of the Pāla dynasty were much sung in the tenth century. For hundreds of years, epic and Purānic tales had through Bengali versions become the common property of the people. Such versions, especially of the *Rāmāyaṇa*, the *Mahābhārata*, the *Bhāgavata Purāṇa*, and episodes of the *Mārkaṇḍeya Purāṇa*, were partly read aloud and partly produced in semi-dramatic recitations by professional bards. Such performances are still to be met with in Bengal villages.

From about 1370 A.D. the Bengali translation of the *Rāmāyaṇa* by Kṛittivāsa (born in 1346) has been one of the most popular books of Bengal. The oldest Bengali version of the *Mahābhārata* by Sañjaya is said to date from about the same time. But the best-known translation of the epic is that of Kāśīrām (*c.* 1645). Between 1473 and 1480 the *Bhāgavata Purāṇa* was translated into Bengali by Mālādhar Vasu. From about 1400 A.D. religious poetry was also cultivated in Bengal. A contemporary of Vidyāpati Thākur was the Bengal poet Chaṇḍī Dās, who composed nearly a thousand love-songs in which celestial and human love are combined in celebrating the divine love of Rādhā and Kṛishṇa. Mukundarām Kavikaṅkan is accounted one of the greatest poets of Bengal. He wrote his panegyric of the goddess Chaṇḍī (that is, Durgā) in his *Chaṇḍī-maṅgal* which was completed in 1589. Although the scene of this poem is chiefly laid in the heaven of Śiva, the author describes the actual life of Bengal in accordance with reality.

Chaitanya. This sage, who was an ecstatic and ardent worshipper of Kṛishṇa, and is more closely associated with the history of religion than that of literature, exercised a profound influence on the spiritual life of Bengal. His real name was Bisambhar (Skt. Viśvam-bhara) Miśra (1486–

1534). He became an ascetic (*Sannyāsin*) in 1509, and as such received the name Chaitanya Deva. In the course of his extensive wanderings he gained numerous adherents. Even during his lifetime he was regarded by the people as an incarnation of the god Kṛishṇa, and his image is even at the present day worshipped by the Vishṇuites of Bengal and Orissa. He himself always rejected divine adoration of his person, and it was only when he was in a state of trance that he sometimes exclaimed 'I am He'. Biographies of Chaitanya form quite an essential component part of Bengali literature. The first records of his life were taken down by the smith Govinda, who accompanied the master on his wanderings. He describes Chaitanya as an ecstatic lover of God, who lapsed into tears on hearing any one cry 'Kṛishṇa, Kṛishṇa'. The *Caitanya-bhāgavata* of Vṛindāvan Dās (1507–89) and the *Caitanya-caritāmṛta* of Kṛishṇa Dās (born 1517) and other works are partly poems and partly biographical sketches.

Rām Prasād. The saint and poet Rām Prasād (1718–75), who wrote hymns addressed to Durgā and other religious songs, has been greatly revered in Bengal. D. C. Sen, the historian of Bengali literature, says there is no peasant, no old man, and no woman, who has not derived consolation and edification from the songs of this writer.

From about 1800 A.D. dramatic literature, which had long carried on a feeble existence in the modern vernacular, began to revive. Certain poets, like Kṛishṇa Kamala (1810–88) in his *Svapna-vilāsa*, endeavoured to refine the old popular *Yātrās*, while other poets composed dramas with a political tendency. The first Bengali drama, performed in 1856, the *Kulīna-kula-sarvasva*, of Rāma Nārāyaṇa Tarkaratna, was directed against the Kulin Brahmins, who make a business out of marriages. In 1860 Dīna

Bandhu Mitra wrote the *Nīl Darpan*, which severely criticizes the exploitation of the indigo industry by the British.

Rāmmohan Roy. This author (1774–1833), famous alike as a social and religious reformer as well as a scholar and writer, bore the greatest share in the development of Bengali prose. He was a man who made himself widely acquainted with religious systems other than his own. Born and bred in a distinguished Brahmin family, he was from youth upwards familiar with the Brahmin religion and its sacred books. Having in his early years learnt Persian and Arabic, he used this knowledge for the study of the Qur'an, and made himself acquainted not only with the monotheism of Islām, but with the mystical doctrines of the Persian Sūfis. Later he became acquainted with Buddhism in Tibet, and with Christianity from missionaries in India itself. In order to be able to read the Old and the New Testament in the original text, he even devoted some time to learning Hebrew and Greek. Dissatisfied with Indian polytheism, he set before himself the task of studying all the religions of the world, in order to extract what was best in all of them and to combine this residue into a purified religion. He ended, however, in believing the monotheism of the Upanishads to be the sum of all wisdom. As a result of his study of the sacred books of foreign religions on the one hand, and of the Upanishads on the other, he desired to reform the old Brahmanic religion. He thus became the founder of the Brahmo Samāj, 'the Society of the believers in God'. He regarded himself not as founding a new sect or Church, but only as purifying the old Indian national religion of all that was false. He included in what was false the caste system and the custom of widow-burning, against which as a social reformer he both spoke and wrote. He came to Europe in 1830, when he was hailed by Jeremy

Bentham as a fellow-worker in the service of humanity. Rāmmohan Roy was also a writer of no inconsiderable merit. His book on the worship of idols among the Indians (1790) was the first work written in Bengali prose. In 1815 he wrote an account of the Vedānta philosophy. He was also the author of essays on widow-burning and other social questions both in Bengali and in English. Besides being a prominent prose-writer, he was also a poet who composed songs that are still sung in Bengal.

He was followed by two prose-writers and essayists who dealt with subjects of social reform. These were Akkhay Kumār Datta (1820–86) and Īśvara Chandra Vidyāsāgara (1820–91).

In the nineteenth century English literature began to exercise great influence on the development of Bengali writing, especially in prose. The first important Bengali novelist, Bankim Chandra Chatterji (1838–94), came so much under the influence of Scott that he has sometimes been called the 'Indian Walter Scott'. A number of novels were also written by Romesh Chander Dutt, otherwise known as a writer on ancient Indian civilization and literary subjects.

One of the most highly esteemed poets of the nineteenth century, and according to many the greatest Bengali poet of modern times, was Michael Madhu Sūdan, a convert to Christianity.

The Tagores. An attached friend and adherent of Rāmmohan Roy and promoter of his work was Dvārkanāth Tagore (the anglicized form of his Bengali name Thākur). His son, Devendranāth Tagore (1818–1905), joined the Brahmo Samāj and became its first organizer. In 1848 he compiled a collection of texts from the Upanishads, Manu's Law-book, the *Mahābhārata*, and some other books, in order to serve as the foundation of the confession of faith of the Brahmo Samāj. This creed represents the belief in Brahma as the only eternal and perfect God and creator of the world, by whose worship alone salvation can be obtained in this world and the next. Such worship consists in the love of God and the performance of works that God loves, being a genuinely Indian compromise between the monism of the Upanishads and the theism of the *Bhagavadgītā*. It is a conservative and national faith. The branch of the Brahmo Samāj that arose under the guidance of Keshub Chunder Sen was more radical. Though Devendranāth Tagore did not, like the orthodox Brahmins, regard the Upanishads as revealed, he yet revered them as sacred books that are receptacles of profound wisdom.

Rabīndranāth Tagore. A son of Devendranāth Tagore is the poet Rabīndranāth Tagore, born in 1861. He had long been famous in India, when in the year 1912 a small volume of his poems entitled *Gītāñjali*, 'a Handful of Songs', in an English translation, drew attention to him in Europe also, so that only a year later, in the autumn of 1913, the Nobel prize for literature was awarded to him. Since then his poems, dramas, tales, romances, and prose writings have become known all over the world in English and German translations. At the present day Rabīndranāth Tagore occupies the position of a world-poet in whose works the purely human elements appeal to us with all the vividness of our own experience. But his appeal is by no means that of a colourless cosmopolitan poet. He is thoroughly Indian, and the spirit of India breathes throughout all his poetry. His tales represent true Indian life, and ancient Indian wisdom reappears in his religio-mystical poems and in his religio-philosophical addresses. The outlook of his father and the spirit of the Brahmo Samāj meet us in his addresses, and have found their complete expression in his poems. Just as in the case of Kabīr and the other poets of mystical devotion to God, the pantheistic doctrine of the Upanishads is by him combined with the theism of the *bhakti* conception of the *Bhagavadgītā.* But like his father in recent times and like Kabīr some centuries ago, Rabīndranāth is also a free-thinker who does not blindly take over all the doctrines of the ancients. The old Indian sages taught that the highest goal, salvation, could be reached only by renunciation of the world, that only the *sannyāsin*, the ascetic, could attain to God. With this ideal Tagore has decidedly nothing to do. Neither by renunciation of the world, nor by asceticism (*yoga*), nor by ceremonies, does he wish to reach God, but in his home and at his work. That he lives in the world and takes a lively interest in all human and terrestrial affairs is proved by his songs for children and his love songs, in which he shows that he is one of the few world-poets able to identify himself with the soul of the child and of woman. This is proved by his novels and stories, in which he depicts true to nature the Indian life of to-day, draws men and women to the life, and lays bare their mental struggles in a way that only a poet can do who loves this world of the great and the small.

He shows a deep understanding of the problems of female life in his drama of *Chitra.* On the basis of a rather rough legend of the *Mahābhārata* he has here produced a dramatic poem, that in its high conception of wedlock as a true community of life rises far above the marriage ideal of most of the poets of Hindustān. He shows no trace of that contempt of woman and of family life which appears in the old Indian ascetic poetry, especially in the songs of the Buddhist monks.

Combining old Indian wisdom with the modern progressive spirit, he does not regard the world-stirring questions of our time with the eyes of the Indian Yogī. The problem of war he handles in the drama called the *Sacrifice*, that of religion in the play entitled *Mālinī*. That the subject of nationalism moves him deeply is shown by his novel *The Home and the World*, as well as in his addresses collected under the title of *Nationalism* (1917). Both here and in his recent work *Creative Unity* (1922) he has given expression to his views on the relations between India and the West. Regarding Western culture and its ideals the poet manifests a balanced judgement. He says, for instance: 'It is only by really knowing the Europe that is great and good that we can effectively guard ourselves from the Europe that is base and greedy.' He acknowledges that Europe has introduced to the East, 'through the smoke of cannon and the dust of markets', the idea of freedom in all directions: the ideal of moral freedom, freedom of conscience, freedom of thought and action, freedom from bondage in literature and art. But he stigmatizes as a deadly poison, from which he wishes to preserve the East, the worship of power and the 'boundless greed' that characterize the West. He is in full sympathy with national feeling and the preservation of national peculiarities; but he condemns national conceit, boastfulness, and all national hatred; for he places humanity above the nation.

Tagore would be no Indian if his poetry did not rise to heights of mysticism, to which ordinary mortals are incapable of following him. But those whom mysticism does not attract can hardly fail to admire the moral elevation that is here revealed.

Grierson, *The Modern Vernacular Literature of Hindustan*, Calcutta, 1889; *The Popular Literature of Northern India*, in *Bulletin of the School of Oriental Studies*, i, part 3, London Institution, 1920. Winternitz, *Geschichte*, iii. 578-604. Macauliffe, *The Sikh Religion*, six vols., Oxford, 1909. Temple, *The Legends of the Panjab*, 3 vols., Bombay, London, 1893-1901. Keay, *A History of Hindī Literature*, London, 1920. Rabīndranāth Tagore, *One Hundred Poems of Kabīr*, London, 1915. Macnichol, *Psalms of Marāṭhī Saints*, London, 1919. Pincott, tr. of the Hindī version of the *Prem Sāgar* (10th ch.) into English, Westminster, 1897. Growse, tr. of the *Rām-carit-mānas* of Tulsī Dās into English, Allahabad, 1877. Temple, tr. of *Lallā-vākyāni*, London, 1924. Dinesh Chundra Sen, *History of Bengal Language and Literature*, Calcutta, 1911. Rabīndranāth Tagore, *Gitanjali*, Eng. tr., London, 1912; *The Home and the World*, 1919; *The Sacrifice*, 1917; *Nationalism*, 1917.

IX

THE RECOVERY OF INDIA'S PAST

Dawn of European knowledge of early India — Abraham Roger's 'Open Door' (1651) — First European Sanskrit grammar (1790) — First English book based on Sanskrit original (1776) — Foundation of Asiatic Society of Bengal (1784) — The three first English Sanskrit scholars: Wilkins, Jones, Colebrooke — Bhagavadgītā first Sanskrit book translated (1785) — First Sanskrit text printed (1792) — Jones first asserted relation of Sanskrit to European languages — Colebrooke's great services to Sanskrit learning — Alexander Hamilton — F. Schlegel — A. W. v. Schlegel first professor of Sanskrit in Europe — F. Bopp founder of comparative philology — Anquetil Duperron makes known the Upanishads — Rāmmohan Roy founds the Brahmo Samāj — Rosen publishes part of Ṛigveda (1838) — Eugène Burnouf founds Vedic scholarship in Europe — Rudolf Roth — Max Müller — Th. Aufrecht — Foundation of Pāli and Buddhist scholarship — James Prinsep eminent decipherer of inscriptions — Great advance in Indian studies (1850-80) — Böhtlingk and Roth's great Sanskrit Dictionary (1852-75) — Aufrecht's great catalogue of Sanskrit MSS. published (1891-1903) — Pāli text society founded by Rhys Davids (1882) — Sacred literature of Jainism made known by Weber's great essay (1883-5) — Bühler's Encyclopaedia of Indo-Aryan Research (1896-1925).

Early chronological information derived from Greek, Chinese, and Persian visitors to India — Paucity of indigenous historical information — Rājataraṅgiṇī (1148) — Historical chapters of the Purāṇas — Harṣacarita and Vikramāṅkacarita — Untrustworthiness of chronicles — Importance of archaeology in historical reconstruction — India particularly rich in inscriptional material — Languages in which inscriptions recorded — Predominance of inscriptions on stone — Published lists of Indian inscriptions — Number of known inscriptions very large — Forged inscriptions — Best method of utilizing inscriptions — Great advance of historical knowledge likely by improved archaeological research — Importance of studying Indian coinage — Its history — Early period — Influence of Roman coinage — Indo-Roman coinage of Kushān dynasty — Date of Kaniṣka — Rise of Gupta dynasty (320 A.D.) — Characteristics of its coinage — Disappearance of Greek alphabet — New type of Hindu coinage after 900 A.D. — Muhammadan coinage — Dravidian coinage — Historical value of South Indian coinage — Modern uniform currency established throughout British India in 1835.

THE preceding chapters describe the intellectual inheritance of India as represented in various forms of literature. It now remains to show how, as a consequence of the discovery of the sea route to India four centuries ago, not only this aspect of India's past has gradually become known to the West, but also another phase that could only have been reconstructed in a fragmentary way from literary sources has been revealed in far greater detail by the labours, during little more than a century, of a small band of workers in another branch of research.

The process by which European investigators became acquainted with India's past was by working backwards from its latest to its earliest phase. Thus they came to know the oldest period last of all. From about 1600 A.D. Europeans began to learn some of the Indian vernaculars spoken at the time, such as Gujarātī and Bengali. Then the later stage of the ancient period known by the name of Classical Sanskrit first came within the ken of English scholars about 150 years ago. Last of all, the oldest and most important phase, the Vedic language, became accessible to European research not more than eighty-five years ago.

Some fragmentary knowledge of the Sanskrit language and literature, besides the religious ideas embedded in them, had begun to be acquired from the seventeenth century onwards by a few stray travellers and by some missionaries, but without exercising any influence on European thought. The first who published any account of such knowledge was Abraham Roger, a Dutchman who lived in the neighbourhood of Madras, and who in 1651 brought out at Amsterdam in Dutch a book entitled 'Open Door to Hidden Heathendom'; it not only describes the customs and religion of the Brahmins, but was also the first European work to make known an actual specimen of Sanskrit literature by the translation of some of the sententious poetry of the Sanskrit writer Bhatṛihari. The first mention of the Veda occurs in this work also.

The writings of two Frenchmen, Bernier (1671) and Tavernier (1677), resident in India for several years, give an account not only of the geography, the political conditions, and social customs, but also of the religious beliefs and practices of the country in the second half of the seventeenth century. A more advanced knowledge of the religion and literature of the Brahmins is shown in an important record, left in 1740 by a missionary named Père Pons, about the ancient literary records of the Indians. He must have possessed some knowledge of Sanskrit. He seems to have been the first to describe correctly the native system of grammar; he also mentions the Sanskrit dictionaries, among them the famous *Amara-kośa*, or 'Thesaurus of Amara', as well as the native system of poetics called *alaṃkāra* or 'Ornament'. He further describes the six orthodox systems of Hindu philosophy, besides mentioning the heterodox systems of the Jains and the Buddhists. In 1778 was published a work representing the knowledge of Sanskrit literature prevalent among the missionaries of the seventeenth and eighteenth centuries, under the title of *L'Ezour Vedam*. It created a sensation in the West, because it attracted the attention of and produced a deep impression on Voltaire. He believed it to date from before the time of Alexander the Great. But it was later shown to be the work of a European compiled for the purpose of converting the Hindus, its whole tendency being to criticize the worship then prevailing in India. The doctrines and legends described by it are post-Vedic, its account of the real Vedas being quite incorrect. The original, found in the possession of the missionaries at Pondicherry, was probably composed about the middle of the eighteenth century by one belonging to the school of a missionary named Robertus de Nobilibus, who died at Mylapore near Madras in 1656. Some time before 1750 a Danish missionary produced a book purporting to reproduce the chief contents of the *Yadzur Vedam*; but the title does not correctly describe the real *Yajurveda*, for it is used as a general term connoting an encyclopaedic account of modern Brahmanism. But its statements regarding sacrifice represent the actual subject-matter of the *Yajurveda*.

Somewhat earlier a German Jesuit named Hanxleden (1699–1732) had written in Latin the first Sanskrit grammar. Though this was never published, it was utilized by the Austrian missionary Fra Paolo Bartolomeo, who worked in Malabar from 1776 to 1789 and published two Sanskrit grammars at Rome (1790), the first place in Europe where such works were printed. Their author approaches the standard of a scholar more nearly than any of his predecessors.

Though the Sanskrit language had not become known in Europe before this date, specimens of the Sanskrit alphabet had appeared in a few books printed in the latter half of the previous century. In Kircher's *China Illustrata* (Amsterdam, 1667) five tables of the Sanskrit alphabet had been printed; single words engraved in the Sanskrit character had been reproduced in the *Hortus Indicus Malabaricus*

(1678); and in Thomas Hyde's *Historia Shahiludii* (Oxford, 1694), the names of several chessmen had appeared in Sanskrit letters with their anglicized phonetic equivalents, as *curry* (i. e. *karī*), 'elephant'. Though these works had attracted the attention of scholars to India, they had no direct influence on the development of Sanskrit philology. But the dawn of Sanskrit scholarship in the English world was heralded by the publication in 1776 of the earliest English work on Indian law. The desire of the Governor-General, Warren Hastings, to rule Indians in accordance with their own laws, induced him to commission certain Pandits to compile the original form of this book from the Sanskrit sources known to them. This Sanskrit original was first rendered into Persian, from which Halhead made a translation into English entitled *Code of Gentoo*[1] *Law* (London, 1776). This second-hand translation led to the study of Sanskrit philology by an association of Englishmen, who founded the Asiatic Society of Bengal in 1784. The new science was inaugurated by the works of three Englishmen, Sir Charles Wilkins, Sir W. Jones, and H. T. Colebrooke.

Wilkins is described by his contemporaries as the first European who really understood Sanskrit. His earliest work was his translation of the famous religious philosophic poem *Bhagavadgītā*, 'Song of the Adorable One' (1785), published in London, which was thus the first place in Europe where a translation from Sanskrit was printed. Wilkins also published the first translation of the well-known collection of fables called *Hītopadeśa* (1787), and later (1808) a Sanskrit grammar. He was also the first who took up the study of Indian inscriptions, some of which he translated into English.

[1] The Portuguese form of *Hindu*.

Sir William Jones (1746–94), who was a Fellow of University College, Oxford, went to India in 1783 as a Puisne Judge of the Supreme Court at Fort William in Bengal. In the following year he founded the Asiatic Society at Calcutta and was its President till the end of his life ten years after. He was the first translator of the famous play *Śakuntalā* (Calcutta, 1789) by Kālidāsa, India's greatest poet, as well as of the lyrical drama *Gītagovinda*, 'the Cowherd in Song', and of the *Lawbook of Manu* (1794). He also edited at Calcutta in 1792 the lyrical Sanskrit poem *Ṛitusaṃhāra*, 'the Cycle of the Seasons'. This was the first Sanskrit text ever printed. Sir W. Jones was, moreover, the first scholar who definitely asserted the genealogical connexion of Sanskrit with Greek and Latin, and its probable affinity with Persian, German, and Celtic.

H. T. Colebrooke, the founder of Indian philology and archaeology, continued Jones's work. He arrived at Calcutta in 1782, but did not trouble about Sanskrit for the first eleven years of his stay in India. By the time of Jones's death (1794) he had only just learned Sanskrit for the purpose of translating a compilation made by Pandits, at Jones's instigation, from the Sanskrit law-books on inheritance and contracts. This translation appeared in 1797 and 1798 under the title of 'A digest of Hindu Law on Contracts and Succession', in four volumes. From this time onward Colebrooke devoted himself with indefatigable zeal to the study of Sanskrit literature, though rather to its technical than its poetical side. Thus he produced not only further works on Indian law, but epoch-making essays on the philosophy, religion, grammar, astronomy, and arithmetic of the Indians. He was the first to give an accurate and trustworthy account of the Vedas, in 1805. He also edited some native Sanskrit dictionaries, the grammar of

28. SIR WILLIAM JONES

Fellow of University College, Oxford

Pāṇini, the *Hitopadeśa*, and the epic *Kirātārjunīya*, 'the combat of the Mountaineer and Arjuna'. He further wrote a Sanskrit grammar, besides working at and translating a number of Sanskrit inscriptions. Finally, he made an extensive and valuable collection of Sanskrit manuscripts which, on his return to England, he presented to the East India Company's library, now in the India Office.

Till the beginning of the nineteenth century the only Europeans who had any real knowledge of Sanskrit were a few Englishmen. One of these was Alexander Hamilton, who, on his return from India, was travelling about France when, on the renewal of hostilities with England, he was detained as a prisoner of war at Paris in 1802. By a coincidence which turned out to be highly fortunate for the advancement of Sanskrit studies in Europe, the German poet Friedrich Schlegel, one of the leaders of the Romantic School, happened to arrive at Paris in the same year. The Romantic School was particularly attracted by the literature of India, which was, however, at that time known only through translations of the works of Sir William Jones. Schlegel became acquainted with Hamilton, who taught him to read Sanskrit, and whom he speaks of as the only man in Europe, except Wilkins, familiar with Sanskrit. A result of this acquaintance was the publication by Fr. Schlegel, in 1808, of his work entitled 'On the Language and Wisdom of the Indians', and constituting the foundation of Indian philology in Germany. His brother, August Wilhelm von Schlegel, became, at the University of Bonn in 1818, the first professor of Sanskrit in the West. Sanskrit research has since been pursued in Germany with more zeal and success than in any other European country.

A contemporary of A. W. v. Schlegel was Franz Bopp (1791–1867), who, having studied Sanskrit in Paris and

London, published in 1816 his work 'On the Conjugational System of the Sanskrit language in comparison with that of the Greek, Latin, Persian, and Germanic languages'. By this work he became the founder of a new Science, Comparative Philology, which long remained combined with the study of Sanskrit, and in a few universities is still officially taught by the holder of the Sanskrit Chair.

Till 1830 European scholars had paid attention only to 'Classical' Sanskrit. The works that had been specially studied were *Śakuntalā*, the *Bhagavadgītā*, the *Code of Manu*, the sententious poetry of Bhartṛihari, the *Hitopadeśa*, and some episodes of the great epics. About the Vedas no trustworthy information was available except what was contained in Colebrooke's Essay. Of the extensive Buddhist literature nothing at all was known. Of Vedic literature itself, the Upanishads, the philosophical treatises forming the latest works of that period, had become to some extent directly accessible. These had in the seventeenth century been translated into Persian, from which they were rendered into Latin at the beginning of the nineteenth century by the French Orientalist Anquetil Duperron under the title of *Oupnek'hat* (Paris, 1801–2). Though full of inaccuracies, this work exercised considerable influence on the German philosophers Schelling and especially Schopenhauer. About the same time the Indian Rāmmohan Roy, the founder of the new sect called the Brahmo Samāj, in which his purpose was to combine what was best in European and Hindu religion, had been studying the Upanishads as a source of the purest theism. In 1816–19 he published an English translation of several of the Upanishads, besides editing the Sanskrit text of several of them.

It was not, however, till about eighty-eight years ago that

29. H. T. COLEBROOKE
Founder of Sanskrit philology

30. F. MAX MÜLLER
Fellow of All Souls College, Oxford

the actual philological investigation of the Vedas was inaugurated by the publication of the first eighth part of the *Ṛigveda* by F. Rosen in 1838. But it was the great French Orientalist Eugène Burnouf who, by his lectures in the early forties of the nineteenth century, laid the foundations of Vedic scholarship in Europe. He gathered around him several students who later became great scholars. One of these was Rudolf Roth (1821–95), who by his short but epoch-making work 'On the Literature and History of the Veda' (1846) became the founder of Vedic philology in Germany. Another pupil was F. Max Müller (1823–1900), who produced the first edition, in six volumes, of the *Ṛigveda*, with the great Sanskrit commentary of Sāyaṇa, in the course of a quarter of a century (1849–75). While this edition was in course of publication, Theodor Aufrecht (1822–1907), who was Professor of Sanskrit at Edinburgh from 1862 to 1875, published an edition of the complete text of the *Ṛigveda* in Roman characters (1861–3).

Burnouf, by the publication, with Ch. Lassen, of his 'Essay on Pāli' (1826) and his 'Introduction to the History of Indian Buddhism' (1844), further laid the foundation of the study of Pāli (the oldest daughter of Sanskrit) and of the investigation of Buddhist literature.

With the opening up of the Vedic language and literature as well as of Pāli and the Buddhist religion, Indian philology had completed its period of infancy about the middle of the nineteenth century. In this early period the foundations of the history of Ancient India were laid by Englishmen who were resident in the country and who accumulated archaeological facts that could not be extracted from the literature, by describing the antiquities they excavated and the ancient coins they collected, and by deciphering the old alphabet on coins and in inscriptions.

The years 1834 to 1838 were the most glorious years of research on Indian antiquities. The man who in this brief space accomplished most in deciphering coins and inscriptions was James Prinsep (1799–1840), a genius whose early death was a grievous blow to the advance of archaeological study in India.

From about 1850 Indian studies entered upon a period of such development among Western scholars in all directions that within thirty years all the important Vedic and many classical Sanskrit texts had been critically edited in trustworthy editions; all the achievements in the sphere of Indian archaeology had been summed up in Christian Lassen's 'Indian Antiquities' (1843–62); a very detailed History of Indian Literature had been published (1852) by Albrecht Weber (second edition, 1876); and a very large Sanskrit Dictionary in seven volumes, which itself contributed very considerably to the rapid advance of Indian philology, had been brought out (1852–75) by the two great German Sanskritists Böhtlingk and Roth. An essay written by A. W. v. Schlegel in 1819 enumerated hardly more than a dozen Sanskrit books known either in editions or translations. Only thirty-three years later, Weber describes in 1852 nearly 500 works of Indian literature. In the years 1891 to 1903 Theodor Aufrecht published his *Catalogus Catalogorum*, which contains an alphabetical list of all the Sanskrit manuscripts existing in the larger Indian and European libraries. The number of Sanskrit books represented by these manuscripts already amounts to many thousands, though the whole of Buddhist literature and all works written in other Indian languages are excluded.

Meanwhile, the foundation of the Pāli Text Society in 1882 by the late Prof. T. W. Rhys Davids had immensely stimulated the investigation of the extensive Buddhistic literature. Very soon after, in 1883 and 1885, Prof. Weber made another branch of Indian literature accessible to scholars by his great essay on the sacred writings of the Jains, a sect which, as we have seen, very nearly contemporary in origin with Buddhism, arose in the sixth century B. C.

By the end of the nineteenth century the progress of Indian studies had covered so vast an area that it became impossible for any single scholar to master the whole field. The necessity therefore began to be felt for an encyclopaedia of Indo-Aryan research giving a comprehensive survey of all that had been done in the various branches of the subject. Such a work was planned by the late Prof. Georg Bühler, of Vienna. Some thirty scholars of various countries having agreed to collaborate under his direction, its parts began to come out in 1897, and twenty-two of them have appeared till now (1925). It is still in progress, for about fifteen parts have yet to be published. This work shows better than anything else the enormous advance made in this domain during the sixty-two years that have elapsed since the publication of the last volume of Lassen's 'Indian Antiquities'.

By the researches of the above and many other scholars, the whole of India's intellectual past has been very fully opened up in the various stages of its literature, and can be read from its very beginnings by the modern world. The literature, the languages, the religions, and the social institutions of the country can here be followed without a break throughout a period of some 3,000 years. The civilization thus revealed well deserves study both in itself and for the light it throws on the present. Its history has been gradually and laboriously pieced together, at first only by Englishmen, but afterwards predominantly by Germans, and to some extent by scholars of other nationalities, French, Dutch, American, Danish, Italian, and Indian. But as far as described in the preceding chapters it is largely a history of mental development extracted from literature, which supplies hardly any of the chronological framework of Indian civilization. Nearly all such literary information as we have is derived from the records of a few foreigners down to somewhat later than 1000 A.D. These authorities are the Greek Megasthenes (*c.* 300 B.C.), the Chinese Buddhist pilgrims Fa Hian (399–415 A.D.) and Hiouen Tsiang (629–45 A.D.), and the Persian writer Albērūnī (1031 A.D.). Without their aid the periods illustrated by their records would still be obscure. If we had to rely on literature alone, our knowledge of the early history of India would be very imperfect. For rich though Indian literature is in other respects, the Hindus did not compose any historical works till the Middle Ages. They appear never to have produced works setting forth genuine history on broad critical lines as Thucydides did for Greece in the fifth century B.C.

The historical chapters of the Purāṇas, though sketchy and meagre, are clearly based on ancient archives, but they are quite untrustworthy. They can be shown to omit some dynasties altogether, and to be sometimes inaccurate even in the names of the kings recorded by them. They also commit the fault of treating contemporaneous dynasties as successive. Their statements cannot therefore be treated as historical without a good deal more corroborative evidence than has yet been forthcoming.

The only other attempt at anything like a general history is the *Rājataraṅgiṇī* (1148–9 A.D.). The author says he has consulted charters of kings, laudatory inscriptions on stones, and manuscripts. His work seems to be fairly reliable for his own time and perhaps for a century or so before; but for any earlier period it soon shows itself to be imaginative. Thus he places Aśoka (the real initial date of whose reign was 264 B.C.) towards the close of the period 2448–1182 B.C., and Mihirakula, the great invader of India, whose actual period was about 530 A.D., he assigns to 704–630 B.C.; he was therefore obliged to allot to one of his kings a reign of 300 years to make his dates come right.

With these two exceptions, the *Rājataraṅgiṇī* and the historical chapters of the Purāṇas, the Hindus never made any real attempt to deal with history on general lines. The historical matter found in their ordinary literary works is only quite incidental and secondary. The names of historical persons interwoven in the plots of plays, in classical poems, and collections of stories, supply us with very little knowledge, and naturally enough give no dates. The geographical names thus occurring afford little more information. Thus when Kālidāsa (who we know from other evidence flourished before 634 A.D.) mentions Gokarṇa, which lies in north Kanara, his statement at least indirectly proves that in that locality there existed a famous shrine of Śiva at any rate as early as *c.* 600 A.D.

Mention has already been made of the two literary works that aim at being historical chronicles, but are really only historical romances. The *Harṣacarita* of Bāṇa (p. 131) deals with the career of the great northern king Harsha of Thānesar, and the *Vikramāṅka-carita* (ed. G. Bühler) treats of the life of the noted southern king Vikramāditya VI of Kalyāṇi. Both these works deal with their subject in prose, but according to the rules of poetics, and are full of mythical and supernatural matter. The historical facts they contain are given without dates and could be summed up in a few sentences. Bāṇa mentions the month and the day, as well as the position of the moon, when King Harsha was born, but not the year; and Bilhaṇa does not even mention the month or the day of Vikramāditya's birth, but only tells us that 'flowers fell from the sky, Indra's drum resounded, and the gods rejoiced in heaven'. Thus if we did not know from other sources the date of these two kings, we should not be able to tell from these would-be biographies when they lived.

The literature is undoubtedly of great importance for the investigation of manners and customs, details of domestic, social, public, and religious life, trade and commerce, allusions to geography and methods of travel, but the information it furnishes is of little chronological value, for the writer tells us nothing about his own date. We sometimes obtain rather more historical data in the introductions and colophons of literary works; but even these are scanty, referring mostly to the writers themselves and not to their patrons, whose chronological importance is usually much greater. Thus, regarded as a whole, the historical information to be gleaned from literary works is extremely imperfect. Even the date of Aśoka would be at least 1,000 years too early, if we had to depend solely on the statements of literature. The royal pedigree (*vaṃśāvalī*) of Nepāl, which purports to give an unbroken list of the rulers of that country from 1768 A.D. back to six or seven centuries before the beginning of the Kali age in 3102 B.C., would even place him at least 1,500 years before his real date. Such pedigrees are exposed to the further risk of the inventions of quite modern bards having been worked into genuinely historical material. Had it not been for the discovery of Chandragupta by Sir William Jones as early as 1793, the chronology of ancient India might have been placed on an utterly fictitious basis, varying 1,000 to 2,000 years from the truth.

31. BUDDHIST INSCRIBED RELIC VASE, PESHĀWAR

It is thus clear that India more than any other country with an ancient civilization must rely for the reconstruction of its past history on other than literary sources. Fortunately such are to be found in the evidence of India's own archaeology in the shape of inscriptions, coins, and architectural art. As a compensation for the conspicuous lack of historical matter in its literature, India happily supplies a vast field from which the zeal of researchers for more than a hundred years, but especially since the end of the last century, has been extracting in ever increasing quantity historical data not otherwise obtainable.

a. EPIGRAPHY

India is particularly rich in inscriptional treasures, of which there are doubtless still far more underground than those already unearthed. They are the only sure basis of historical research, because they in fact control chronologically all that we can learn from tradition, literature, or art. These records were not written for the direct purpose of conveying the historical information that we seek, but only incidentally and in a purely secondary manner. On this very account they are peculiarly trustworthy; for their evidence is free from bias. Much time and patience are, however, required for extracting and piecing together that evidence.

Often a large amount of epigraphical material must necessarily be combined in order to attain a single result, as for instance the refutation of the legend of the Vikramāditya era, which at one time dominated the history of Sanskrit literature. The theory that the year 58 B.C. was invented as an era by a king named Vikramāditya who lived at that time was by such aggregate evidence thus proved to be untenable. Sometimes, however, a single inscription has established an important fact, such as that which locates the birthplace of Buddha, or that which settles the epoch of the Gupta dynasty.

Inscriptions became known and began to be studied by English scholars in India soon after some of the earliest Sanskrit books with which they became acquainted engaged their attention. The most important epigraphical event was the decipherment by James Prinsep of the inscriptions of Aśoka; for this laid the real foundations of the superstructure of Indian chronology that has since been erected.

The inscriptional material available includes the legends on coins and gems; but as these form a special class in archaeology, it is preferable to treat of them separately under the head of numismatics.

The inscriptions are generally meant to be permanent records of an official and public character. They are almost always engraved: sometimes on monolith pillars, as the moral and religious edicts of Aśoka, or Yaśodharman's panegyrics of victory at Mandasor in Mālwā; but usually on the walls and columns of caves and temples, and stone tablets, on metal plates, on images and statues, and on relic caskets. They also sometimes appear painted, written in ink, or stamped on clay or bricks. They embrace all sorts of information that can be utilized to extract historical facts.

The languages of the inscriptions are Sanskrit, Pāli, some Prākrits, mixed Sanskrit, Marāṭhī, as well as the south Indian Dravidian tongues Kanarese, Malayālam, Tamil, and Telugu. They are either entirely in prose, entirely in verse, or in a mixture of prose and verse.

It must be evident that on a minute examination of the inscriptions, begun more than a century ago, the ancient political history of India is almost entirely based. Nearly

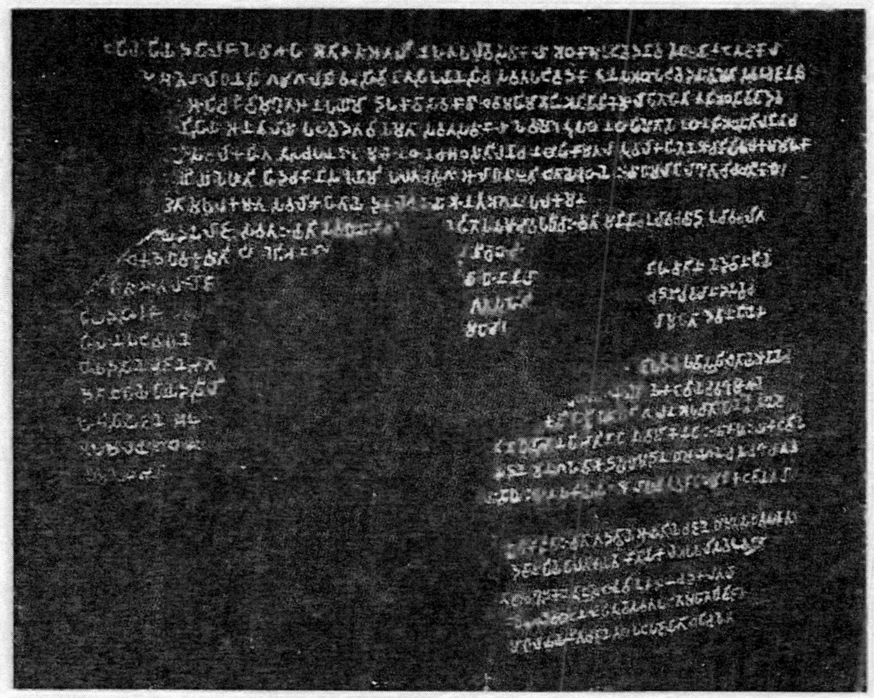

32. EARLY INSCRIPTION IN BRĀHMĪ WRITING

every other line of research, such as literature, religion, and art, ultimately owe much of their chronological framework to this source. Hence it is of the utmost importance that the Indian government's archaeological department, which has been more scientifically organized in the present century than ever before, should not only be maintained, but systematically developed, because from its work must be derived nearly all the light that can in the future be shed on India's past.

Among the inscriptions engraved on metal, the most important one on iron is a short poem forming an epitaph on the Gupta king Chandragupta II, composed *c.* 415 A.D. and incised on an iron column at Meharaulī near Delhi. An ancient record on brass engraved on a relic vase comes from a *stūpa* at Vardak in Afghānistān dating from 6 B.C. An old inscription on bronze has been found which is of great palaeographical value, because its legend appears in three classes of characters, Brāhmī, Kharoṣṭhī, and Greek. Most metal inscriptions are, however, incised on copper. Some of these are commemorative, having been found in relic mounds, but most of them are grants or title-deeds.

A few inscriptions were written with ink on earthenware, the earliest coming from Central India, and probably dating from the second or third century B.C. Even painted inscriptions have been discovered accompanying frescoes in the Buddhist caves of Ajantā.

Copper-plates have often been found in localities other than those to which they originally belonged. This is naturally seldom the case with records on stone; but two lithic columns with inscriptions of Aśoka, now at Delhi, are known to have been removed there, the one from Meerut, the other from the Ambāla District, in the fourteenth century.

Many small inscribed clay or terra-cotta tablets have turned up in different parts of India. The best-known are Buddhist, inscribed with the formula or creed proclaimed by Assaji, one of the earliest followers of Buddha. A large collection of clay seals was also found at Basārh, in the Muzaffarpur District of Bengal. The inscriptions on them are connected with officials, corporations, temples, and private individuals.

Bricks were never in general use for inscriptions in India, but several such have been discovered referring to one of the Gupta kings of the fifth century A.D. There have also been unearthed in the Gorakhpur District some brick tablets with Buddhist *sūtras*, one of which is a version, in Sanskrit, of a short sermon preached by Buddha at Śrāvastī.

By far the greatest number of inscriptions appear on some form of stone. The most famous of these are the rock and pillar edicts of Aśoka scattered over all parts of India. They are proclamations on religion and morality meant for the guidance of his subjects and placed in conspicuous localities. The idea of inscribing them on rock surfaces was in all probability suggested by the similar records of the Persian king Darius at Behistun. The most noteworthy is on the rock at Girnār, which, besides the edicts of Aśoka, contains dated inscriptions of the Mahākṣatrapa Rudradāman (150 A.D.) and the Gupta king Skandagupta (455–8 A.D.). Among the many rock inscriptions of Aśoka may be mentioned one that was inscribed when the king had gone into religious retirement at Songīr (Suvarṇagiri) in Magadha. Another, written in duplicate Brāhmī and Kharoṣṭhī characters, is found in the Kāngra District of the Panjāb. A third is the epitaph, in the Chandragiri Hills, Mysore, of the Jain teacher Prabhacandra, which commemorates the migration of the Digam-

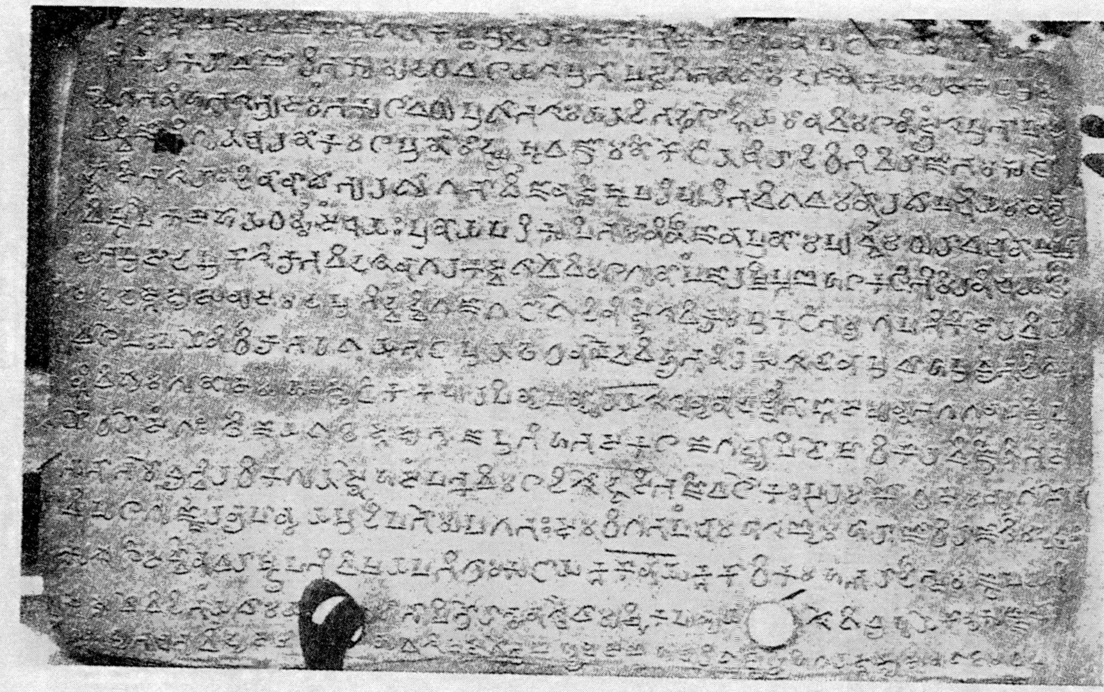

33. COPPERPLATE INSCRIPTION IN BRĀHMĪ SCRIPT

bara sect to Southern India, and their settlement at Śravaṇa Belgola.

There are, moreover, the seven 'pillar edicts' of Aśoka situated at Allahābād, Delhi, and other places. One of the historically most interesting is the column at Rummindēī within the Nepāl frontier, in which the king identifies the Lumbinī grove as the birthplace of Buddha. Another is the column at Allahābād, which in addition to two pillar edicts has two short Aśoka edicts known as the Queen's edict and the Kōsambī edict, as well as a record of Samudragupta of about 375 A.D. At Eran, in the Central Provinces, is a pillar record of Budhagupta of 484 A.D. which is of great importance because it helps to fix the beginnings of the Gupta era. At Mandasor in Mālwā there are two columns recording the victory of Yaśodharman, who defeated the great foreign invader Mihirakula and swept away the last remnant of the Gupta dynasty.

Of the relic receptacles from the interior of Buddhist *stūpas* the soapstone vase from Piprahwa bears the oldest known Indian inscription, which locates Kapilavastu as the home of Buddha. In one of the *stūpas* at Sānchī were found two soapstone caskets recording in ink that they contained the relics of Sāriputta and Moggallāna, the two chief disciples of Buddha.

Other soapstone vases from the same locality corroborate statements in Buddhist books about missionaries sent out to border countries in Aśoka's time. An inscription on a pillar of one of the gateways of the *stūpa* of Bhārhut is noteworthy as containing the only known epigraphical reference to the dynasty of the Śungas, which by the Purāṇas is placed immediately after that of the Mauryas. An inscription on the southern gateway of the Sānchī *stūpa* mentions Siri-Sātakarṇi, one of the early kings of the

Deccan and Central India. On other parts of the same *stūpa* are several short records that mention the donors' residences, the names of which are identical with those of cities and towns still in existence. Some of the donative inscriptions also show that as early as the second or first century B.C. the Buddhist canon already had divisions known by the titles of *Piṭaka*, *Sūtrānta*, and the *Five Nikāyas*.

Other inscriptions describe the sculptures to which they are attached, such as representations of the Jātakas or previous existences of Buddha. Three of them mention ancient kings: Janaka, Pasenaji of Kosala, and Ajātasatru depicted as worshipping Buddha. One of them indicates the *bodhi* tree under which Buddha was seated when he attained enlightenment. Others refer to the *bodhi* trees of previous Buddhas whose names they mention. One explains a sculpture as Mahādeva rescuing Vasugutta and two companions from a sea monster that is disgorging a boat containing them. Another describes a medallion as the dream of Māyā, Buddha's mother, about a white elephant representing her future son. A rail of the Sānchī *stūpa* bears an inscription specifying 412 A.D. as a date in the reign of the Gupta king, Chandragupta II, in whose reign Kālidāsa probably lived.

On the walls and other parts of caves there are important inscriptions in some six localities in eastern and western India. Such are records of Aśoka in the Barābar Hills in the Gayā District of Bengal; the inscription of Khāravela of Kalinga (Orissa) apparently dating from 156–5 B.C.; and in the cave-temples of Nāsik, Junnar, and Kārli are noteworthy inscriptions throwing much light on the history of Western India in the first and second centuries A.D.

There are also inscriptions on pedestals and other parts

of statues and images. One is of a king or prince named Turāmala, dated 7 or 8 A. D., on the base of a colossal statue of Buddha at Bodh Gayā. Another, dated 22 A. D., is inscribed on the base of a Jain image at Muttra; a third, dated 328 A. D., is found on the pedestal of a statue of Buddha at Hastnagar in the Peshāwar District; an inscription, dated 448 A. D., on an image of Buddha at Mankuwār in the Allahābād District, from the time of Kumāragupta I; one of the Mahārāja Bhīmavarman, dated 458–9 A. D., on the base of a group of Śiva and Pārvatī at Kosam near Allahābād; and one, dated 672 A.D., of the time of Ādityasena, on the pedestal of an image of the Sun at Shāhpur in the Patna District. A colossal statue near Kasiā in the Gorakhpur District, United Provinces, of the dying Buddha, bears an inscription referring to the fifth century A. D.; while at Śravaṇa Belgola in Mysore, a gigantic inscribed figure of the Jain Saint Gummaṭa or Gomateśvara dates from the period 977 to 984 A. D.

The subjects of the inscriptions are of various kinds. A few are of a literary type. Two are fragments of otherwise unknown Sanskrit plays found at Ajmīr; one represents the first two acts of a play as yet untraced elsewhere, on a stone at Dhār in central India; other stones at the same place are inscribed with two Prākrit poems in honour of Vishṇu. Some present purely historical narrative, as the Hāthigumphā cave inscription, which summarizes the first thirteen years of the reign of King Khāravela of Kalinga. One, inscribed on the Aśoka column at Allahābād, is a eulogy of King Samudragupta. A short poem in duplicate describes the triumphs of King Yaśodharman on two columns of victory at Mandasor. Two rock inscriptions at Junāgarh record the repairing of the embankment of a great lake. Of a similar type are epitaphs, as that on the iron pillar at Meharaulī commemorating King Chandragupta II. A subdivision of this class are pillars and tablets in memory of those who died in battle. These, called *vīrgals* or 'hero stones', are found chiefly in Central India, Bombay, and Madras. More miscellaneous are those that record the construction of tanks, the setting up of boundary marks, or specifying the spot where a man was killed by a tiger, an ascetic had immolated himself in the fire, or a wife had burned herself with her dead husband. The great majority are the result of the general religious taste of the Hindus for constantly making endowments. The purely religious motive is particularly striking in the inscriptions of Aśoka, though these incidentally mention much contemporaneous matter relating to internal history, geography, ethnography, administration, and other subjects. The same motive accounts for the commemoration of saints by inscribed relic caskets and monumental pillars like those of Piprahwa and Rummindēī. A similar reason explains the inscriptions commemorating the building of the gateways of *stūpas*, the erection of monasteries, the celebration of sacrifices, the building or restoration of temples, visits to sacred sites, endowments made to gods, temples, religious institutions, and communities. There are, however, also a good many inscriptions relating to secular grants, chiefly of land.

Donative inscriptions are by far the most numerous. They chiefly constitute title-deeds of real property or certificates of rights or privileges. In this group the records of royal donations, whether for religious or for other purposes, form the greatest number. This was probably the result of gifts taking the place of sacrifices that the kings of India used to perform for the purpose of acquiring religious merit or obtaining other objects. These inscriptions con-

34. ENGRAVED AND INSCRIBED MEMORIAL SLAB (VIRGAL)

sequently contain more genealogical and political information than would otherwise be the case. Thus, without the express object of preserving history, but generally with the intention of emphasizing the religious importance of the event, there grew up the great mass of inscriptions from which the early history of India is in process of being pieced together.

These inscriptions come from all parts of India. But there are also others of importance for its history that have been found beyond the frontiers of India proper. Thus there are such from Afghānistān written in the mixed dialect that is neither exactly Sanskrit nor exactly Prākrit; others in Sanskrit are derived from Nepāl. In Central Asia have been found inscriptions as well as manuscripts composed in a mixed dialect and written not only in the Kharoṣṭhī characters chiefly limited to the north-western parts of India, but also in the usual ancient Indian Brāhmī script. From Ceylon come many Sanskrit, Pāli, and Singhalese inscriptions that are useful both historically and palaeographically. Farther India furnishes from Cambodia, in Indo-China, Sanskrit inscriptions from soon after 600 A. D., and Java from 732 A. D. downwards. Valuable inscriptional records have also been found in Burma.

Some sixteen years ago the list of inscriptions, large and small, before 400 A.D., already numbered between 1,100 and 1,200. For Northern India (i. e. the country north of the Narmadā and the Mahānadī), the late Prof. Kielhorn had given a list of 700 with names and dates from 400 A.D. onwards; and for South India another list of nearly 1,100 after 500 A.D. New records are coming to light every year, and the mass of material awaiting discovery is incalculable. To show how much may be expected, the statement suffices that, a good many years ago, 9,000 had already been reported from Mysore alone, and ink impressions of nearly 1,000 inscriptions had been collected from not even the whole of the Belgaum and Dhārwār districts in the Bombay Presidency.

From the first century B.C. onwards, the inscriptions are datcd in various ways. As the initial years of all the eras are now well known, there is not much difficulty in stating the equivalent European dates. Explanations of the various eras are to be found in the epigraphic journals, especially the *Indian Antiquary*.

Research has to guard against epigraphical as well as numismatic and literary forgeries, by which erroneous matter has been introduced into Indian history, and which it is the task of critical study to remove. An account of how such matters can be detected is to be found in the *Indian Antiquary*.[1] A very fair knowledge has already been gained of the ancient history of India from 58 B.C. to 320 A.D., and a comparatively extensive knowledge of it from the latter date onwards. Almost all this is derived from inscriptions.

Much more is to be hoped from the results of such excavations as have been going on for years at sites like Taxila, for the earlier period; and judiciously selected sites are sure to supply for the whole period important inscriptional evidence, as those of Sārnāth, Kasiā, and Basārh have already yielded to the labours of Sir John Marshall, the Director-General of Archaeology in India.

Considerable advance in historical knowledge of ancient India is, moreover, bound to result from the systematic chronological co-ordination of material already found by arranging it in separate volumes according to dynasties. Already published matter will have to be revised and

[1] Vol. xxx, pp. 201 ff.

brought up to date; for the wider experience and knowledge gained in the course of time will enable mistakes to be removed and historical points to be brought out that could hardly have been detected at an earlier stage.

The increasing evidence of epigraphy will be able to control to a greater degree the value of tradition as a subsidiary source of history, since without its aid tradition can supply only very uncertain results.

Hand in hand with the revision of inscriptions must go the revision of palaeography, which owes so great a debt to the labours of the late Prof. Bühler. More perfect texts of records already handled must be produced and real facsimiles furnished instead of the touched-up and sometimes misleading lithographs that were occasionally issued in earlier days.

Simple palaeographic evidence is in any case insufficient to fix within a century, or even more, the time of an undated inscription lacking a clue such as the name of a well-known king or some other outside chronological test. Thus on the strength of the characters, a certain coin was at one time not unjustifiably asserted to date from about 900 A. D., but the name of a king subsequently deciphered in the legend proved that the coin could not date from earlier than 1150. It must be remembered that the script of workmen varies according to their skill as well as the material on which the record is inscribed. Hence undated inscriptions may seem to belong to widely different periods, whereas they may be really about contemporary. Again, the imitation of a previous model may produce the effect of identical age, whereas the dates really lie far apart. Thus the importance of decisive facts to regulate the chronology of undated inscriptions is evident. Similar considerations apply in estimating the age of undated coins.

We have seen that even for the political history of India

the data available have not yet been fully exploited. Much less is this the case in other directions of inquiry into India's past. Thus geographical research has been mainly confined to the identification of places, countries, and tribes mentioned by Greek, Chinese, and Arabic writers. Many errors here have been committed by ignoring the fact that towns disappear, coast-lines shift, rivers alter their courses or dry up, place-names change in an arbitrary manner even though the places themselves still exist, and distances recorded by travellers are inaccurate, because often stated at second hand. Thus few of the names mentioned by those who actually visited India with Alexander the Great have been identified with certainty. Many of the places named by the author of the *Periplus*, who wrote about 70 A.D., and who had personal knowledge of the Indian coast, cannot be identified. The position of inland places is rendered doubtful by the vagueness of the information supplied.

Ptolemy, who wrote about 150 A.D., and whose information is second-hand, can only be utilized in a very general way for the reconstruction of early Indian geography. Though he knew the importance of observing latitude and longitude, the positions laid down by him were nearly always the results of computations from itineraries and travellers' statements. His longitudes were less than they should be, and his conception of the shape of India was utterly erroneous. The impossibility of adjusting his data so as to frame a map of India at all accurate in its details is thus obvious. Much still remains to be done with the help of inscriptions even in identifying the sites visited by the Chinese pilgrim Hiouen Tsiang, though his travels all over India covered a period of sixteen years (629–45 A. D.) and were very carefully recorded by him.

Albērūnī's *India* supplies a fair amount of geographical

information; but much investigation is still necessary before it can all be utilized.

Extensive research on the indigenous sources must be carried out before the additional material to be derived from them can be filled in. All geographical data thus extracted will have to be indexed and an atlas of Ancient India compiled from this material, with a series of maps to illustrate successive periods. Only then will it be possible to utilize properly the information derived from early foreign sources. Many a wrong identification will then be eliminated, and correct new ones added as a result of the very preparation of such a work. Only in the present century has it been shown by the late Dr. Fleet that the ancient and famous town of Tagara still exists under its old name in the form of Tēr in the State of Hyderābād, and that the ancient city of Śākala or Sākala, the She-ka-lo of Hiouen Tsiang, is the Siālkot of to-day in the Panjāb.

One of the difficulties to be overcome is the ascertainment of the real forms of the modern place-names. Compilations will have to be prepared in a thoroughly skilled and critical manner for the various territorial divisions of India, giving in native characters as well as transliteration the actually correct forms of the modern names of all the principal towns, villages, rivers, and mountains.

It is thus evident that much original research as well as revisional work still remains to be done. It can only be carried out comprehensively by co-operation in other lines of study, resulting in a more accurate understanding of the records. This means a compilation of the historical, geographical, and cognate matter to be extracted from the epics, plays, classical poems, collections of stories, and historical romances. For this purpose editors and translators should always make a point of collecting such matter in an introduction or appendix, so as to reach the hands of scholars concerned with such researches.

Geographical indexes to some of the Purāṇas, like the topographical lists extracted from the *Bṛhatsaṃhitā*[1] and the *Bhāgavata Purāṇa*,[2] would be serviceable. Many of the works in praise of special localities, entitled *Māhātmya* or *Sthala-purāṇa*, would be of use for local geography or the identification of places. Thus the *Mahākūṭa-māhātmya* enabled Dr. Fleet to identify the Vātāpi of the inscriptions, the capital of the Chālukyan dynasty of Western India, with the modern Bādāmi.[3] Indexes, like Sörensen's, of the names of the *Mahābhārata* will be required, as well as others, bringing together all information that can be collected concerning social customs, trade and commerce, arts and industries, administration, and other subjects. Indexes are wanted for the *Rāmāyaṇa*, for the dramas, the prose romances, the *Rājataraṅgiṇī*; for the Jātakas, the *Lalita-vistara*, the *Divyāvadāna*, the *Dīpavaṃsa*, the *Mahāvaṃsa* and the writings of Buddhaghosa; for the Jain and other Prākrit works a certain knowledge of Sanskrit is advisable for the purposes of such research. For though most of the records are not in Sanskrit, it is more or less the key to the languages in which they are written, and a general knowledge of Sanskrit literature and mythology is essential to an adequate understanding of many of the allusions contained in the inscriptions.

b. NUMISMATICS

Indian coins have been in use for some 2,600 years. Having been studied for nearly a century by many scholars, they have contributed their share towards the reconstruction

[1] *Indian Antiquary*, vol. xxi, p. 169.
[2] Op. cit. xxviii, p. 1.
[3] Op. cit. v. 68; viii. 238.

of the history of ancient India. For some periods coins are the only evidence. Their employment seems to have been introduced with foreign maritime trade and alphabetical writing, probably about 700 B.C. The earliest kind of currency seems to have taken the form of punch-marked coinage, which in accordance with its origin was struck not by governments, but by traders as private persons. Coins of this type are in the *Code of Manu* called *purāṇas* or 'ancient pieces'. They were probably copied from Babylonian originals after the opening of maritime trade with the west coast of India. The oldest-looking coins of this kind are copper pieces found at very ancient sites near Benares. The punch-marks are very numerous and varied, consisting of rude outlines of men, animals, trees, the sun, and many other objects; but legends are always absent. These coins are usually rectangular, but roughly circular examples occur, being probably a later development. The best specimens of the silver coins have a weight of about 55 grains, equal to 32 *ratī* seeds. The whole system of the ancient Hindu coinage of Northern India is founded on the weight of this seed (1·8 grains).

Cast coins, generally of copper or bronze, were largely used in Northern India alongside of the punch-marked type. A few specimens are inscribed with characters dating from about 300 B.C. Sometimes these cast coins, while still in a half-fused state, were stamped with a die that produced a square or circular hollow. Such coins were often struck in the second century B.C. Many of these found at Taxila in the Panjāb show how from them were developed the single-die, and finally the double-die stages of coining. The adoption of the double-die type was undoubtedly due to Greek and Roman examples. Alexander's invasion (326–325 B.C.) did not affect the indigenous coinage any more than other Indian institutions; for immediately after his death the region east of the Indus was reconquered by Chandragupta and administered according to Indian methods. But after the Bactrian Kingdom had become independent of Syria, several Bactrian rulers, especially Eucratides and Menander, in the second century B. C., made incursions into India, where their coins are now found. Princes of the royal Bactrian house established themselves in what are now Afghānistān, Balochistān, and the Panjāb, largely Hellenizing those territories. They issued an abundant coinage of a Greek type, which down to about 150 B. C. showed great artistic merit. They bear bilingual legends owing to the mixture of population at the time, as well as devices representing familiar Indian objects. The later Indo-Greek coins are degenerate in style. The populations of the interior of India remained unaffected by the coinage of these countries in the north-west, and continued to use the indigenous private currency. This is indicated by the fact that no coins bearing any name of the Maurya dynasty are known. But it may be due to Greek influence that the names of kings, such as Agnimitra, belonging to other dynasties appear. The coins of the Andhṛabhṛitya dynasty (90–220 A. D.) often bear the name of the reigning king. But the old system of private coinage remained in many localities and still prevailed in Central India at the time of the English conquest.

The subjugation of Afghānistān and the Panjāb by the Kushān clan of the Yueh-chi horde, about the middle of the first century A. D., brought India into contact with the Roman Empire of Augustus and his successors, as it extended eastwārds. Kadphises I (*c.* 45–85 A. D.), who annexed the Kābul valley to the Kushān Empire, issued copper coins which, on the obverse, show a king's head obviously

35. GREAT STONE WHEEL ON THE TEMPLE OF THE SUN AT KONĀRAK NEAR PURĪ, ORISSA

(*for Indo-Aryan architecture see p. 83*)

imitating that of Augustus, and on the reverse the figure of a king seated on a curule chair. His son Kadphises II, who conquered Northern India, went further in imitating the coinage of imperial Rome; for he struck an abundance of gold pieces exactly corresponding to the Roman *aurei* in weight. Pliny's statement that in his time (77 A.D.) a stream of gold flowed eastward is corroborated by the many hoards of Roman coins that have been found in both Northern and Southern India. The Kushān coins, though Roman in weight, are for the most part Indian in style. The device of Kadphises II's coins is on the reverse constantly the god Śiva accompanied by his humped bull Nandī. The legends giving the name and titles are bilingual as on the Bactrian coins. The obverse is in Greek, both language and script, while the reverse legend is in Prākrit, and the characters in Kharoṣṭhī, read from right to left. The copper coins of Kadphises are found in great numbers as far east as Benares. The Indo-Roman coinage of the Kushān dynasty, usually called Indo-Scythian, marks an epoch in India's numismatics. Though many Oriental features in device were retained, the European type of coin was in essentials adopted. Henceforward the main coinages of Northern India were double-die pieces, issued by the authority of the sovereign, and usually bearing his effigy or his name on both sides.

Kanishka seems to have succeeded Kadphises II in 125 A.D.[1] He conquered Kashmīr and regarded Kābul and Peshāwar as his capital cities. He was the convener of the last Buddhist council, and was a zealous patron of the Mahāyānist or newer form of Buddhism. He issued vast quantities of

[1] The exact date of Kaniṣka's accession is still somewhat uncertain: he may possibly have preceded the two Kadphises kings; in that case his date (as the foundation of the Śaka era) would be A.D. 78.

gold and copper coins. His *aurei* agree with those of Kadphises II in weight and purity, but differ greatly in design and legend. The obverse, as in the coins of Kadphises II, bears the device of the king as a sacrificer at a fire-altar. The reverse displays various gods, some being clearly Zoroastrian, besides the Indian Buddha, and the Greek sun and moon. This seems to indicate that he was a fire-worshipper first and became a Buddhist afterwards. The legends on both sides are in Greek characters only, but the title 'King of Kings' is generally translated into a form of Old Persian.

His successor Huvishka, who succeeded in 153 A.D., is represented on his bronze coins as riding an elephant, sitting cross-legged, or perched on the edge of a throne, with one leg hanging down and the other tucked up. On the reverses various gods appear, Greek, Persian, and Indian, as on the coins of Kanishka. The legends are in the Greek character.

Under his successor Vāsudeva, the coinage began to deteriorate, the gold of the *aurei* being much less pure. The obverse, as is usually the case on Kanishka's coins, shows the king standing at an altar sacrificing, and the reverse, Śiva with his bull, as in Kadphises II's coins. The miscellaneous gods no longer appear. The execution is semi-barbarous, and the only survival of Hellenic influence is the use of Greek characters in the legends. Vāsudeva died in 225 A.D. In 320 A.D. the new imperial dynasty of the Guptas arose, with Pāṭaliputra as its capital. The second of the line, Samudragupta, extended his conquests, about 330 A.D., to nearly the southernmost point of the peninsula, and his successor annexed Gujarāt and Kathiāwār up to the Arabian Sea. But under its fifth ruler the dynasty was destroyed about 480 A.D. by the White Huns. India was then thrown back to the normal condition of a seething mass of states engaged in unceasing warfare, uncontrolled by any paramount power.

The gold coinage of this dynasty was a continuation of that of the Kushān, the weight of the Indo-Roman *aurei* remaining the same under the first three emperors. The devices, which are very varied, are sometimes more artistic than anything seen since the time of Graeco-Bactrian kings. The variety of the earlier gold devices was gradually narrowed down to the single type, the standing king on the obverse, and a goddess seated on a lotus on the reverse. These two designs prevail in the coinage of Northern India for hundreds of years. They are found in the provincial coinage of Kashmīr as late as 1339 A.D. The artistic merit of the best Gupta coins seems to be contemporaneous with the literary revival of Sanskrit, as distinguished from Prākrit, that took place between 350 and 450 A.D., culminating in the poetry of Kālidāsa. The position that Sanskrit then held is illustrated by the legends on the coins. These are no longer expressed in either Greek or Prākrit, but in strictly grammatical Sanskrit. The White Hun invasion, however, eclipsed the artistic and literary glory of this period.

The last trace of the use of the Greek alphabet had disappeared by 400 A.D.; but 'drahma' in the form of *dramma* as the designation of a coin, as well as the weight-standard, survived in certain localities till at least 1100 A.D.

After the collapse of the Gupta Empire, the coinage of the innumerable native states, as well as of the Hun invaders themselves, shows great degradation; nor does the partial restoration of the paramount power under Harshavardhana (606–48 A.D.) improve matters much. The type prevailing from about 600 to 900 A.D. was a barbarous imitation of the Sassanian coinage of Persia, the characteristic device of which is a fire-altar with supporters. Introduced into India by the Huns, it is often unrecognizable except to the trained eye.

About 900 A. D. several Hindu dynasties arose: the Chandels of Mahoba, the Tomars of Delhi, the Rāthors of Kanauj, and the Haihayas of Chedi or Central India, who soon after 1000 A.D. introduced a new type of coinage, due probably to Muhammadan influence. The king's name and title here appear instead of his effigy on the obverse, while the seated goddess on the lotus of the Gupta coins occupies the reverse. The latest specimen of this type known is a Chandel coin issued about 1250 A.D.

A second new style was invented by the Brahmin kings of Ohind (*c.* 860 to 950), known as the 'Bull and Horseman' type, because a horseman is the device on the obverse and a bull on the reverse. It was copied by the Chauhan kings of Delhi and Ajmīr and by the early Muhammadan Sultans of Delhi till 1265, and by the Rājas of Kāngra till about 1600 A.D.

The earliest Muhammadan coins were struck in India after the conquest, in 712 A.D., of Sindh, by Muhammad the son of Kāsim. The influence, however, of this first Muslim invasion did not extend beyond Sindh and the Indus valley.

The first Muhammadan who may be accounted an Indian sovereign is Mahmūd of Ghazni (998–1030 A.D.), who was engaged during the greater part of his reign in making plundering raids into India. His coins are noteworthy as having a marginal legend in Sanskrit which explains the Arabic inscription. His son and grandson struck coins copying the 'Bull and Horseman' type, and thereby breaking the strict rule of the Qur'an that forbids the making of images. These appear to be the earliest Muhammadan coins in India bearing effigies. The Muhammadan kings of Ghazni and North-western India continued this forbidden practice till 1265 A.D. Their Indian coins are very numerous and are of the 'Bull and Horseman' type. The use of the native scale of weights and of bilingual legends was a concession to Hindu prejudices. On some of the gold coins the image of the Hindu goddess Lakshmī actually appears. Effigies on Muhammadan Indian coinage then disappeared till they were to some extent revived by Akbar (1556–1605) and his son Jahāngīr.

Altamsh (1210–35), the most noteworthy ruler of the Turkish Slave dynasty of Delhi, the creator of the Kutb Minar near that capital, was the issuer of an abundant coinage. His daughter Razīa (1236–9), the only queen who ever ruled at Delhi, also issued some coins. Balban (1265–87) was the last sovereign of Delhi to use the 'Bull and Horseman' device, though he also issued many coins of the orthodox type.

Alā-ud-dīn Muhammad Shāh (1295–1315), the conqueror of Southern India, issued very numerous coins chiefly of silver and copper, besides not a few gold ones. His son, Kutb-ud-dīn Mubārak Shāh (1310–20), introduced an innovation into Muhammadan coinage by reverting to the old Hindu square form, which continued to be occasionally used till the reign of Shāh Jahān (1627–58).

Muhammad, son of Tughlak (1324–51), who gained the throne by parricide, was a learned and religious, but merciless and mad, despot. He issued coins of great variety and beauty, superior to those of all other Indian sovereigns in the artistic merit of their Arabic legends. He perpetrated the unsuccessful numismatic eccentricity of trying to replenish his treasury by coining brass in vast quantities and (unsuccessfully) commanding its acceptance as silver.

In 1526 Bābar (1483–1530) founded the dynasty of the

'Great Mughals' by the decisive victory of Pānīpat. The Afghān rival of his son Humāyūn (1508–56) was Sher Shāh, who established the reformed system of currency that lasted throughout the Mughal period and was adopted and maintained by the East India Company down to 1835, and is the basis of the present British currency in India. He caused well-executed pieces to be struck in gold, silver, and copper, with a fixed standard of both weight and purity. His silver rupees weigh 180 grains, containing 175 grains of pure silver, practically equal in value to the modern rupee. They have often the king's name in Nāgarī characters in addition to the usual Arabic inscriptions.

The great Akbar (1556–1605) closely followed the example of Sher Shāh in his coinage. Like his son Jahāngīr (1605–27) and his grandson Shāh Jahān, he disregarded the prohibition of Moses and Muhammad against making the likeness of anything that is in heaven or on earth, for he freely used pictorial art in the decoration of his palaces; but he employed image devices very sparingly on his coins.

Jahāngīr's coins are remarkable for their beauty and for various curiosities introduced into them. His great affection for his wife Nūr Jahān is attested by the coins of his later years bearing her name as well as his own. His disregard of orthodoxy and his addiction to intoxicants are indicated by his gold coins, which represent his effigy seated cross-legged on his throne, with a goblet in his hand. He was the only Muhammadan ruler of India who placed his portrait on his coins.

Shāh Jahān did not repeat his father's eccentricities in his very numerous silver and gold coins; but some of his gold pieces were enormously large.

The coinage of the fanatical Aurangzib (1659–1707) is of

course free from all unorthodox features and is monotonous in character. In spite of the disorder and disintegration of the empire under his successors, the weight and purity of the imperial coinage were maintained. It gradually passed into an Anglo-Indian coinage. The East India Company, which had long been copying the imperial currency, formally received the right, in 1717 A.D., to coin at Bombay, and, in 1742, to copy the rupees of Arcot near Madras. In 1757 the Company's mint was legally established at Calcutta. Other mints were later set up at Benares and elsewhere. The coins issued by all these mints were copies of Mughal currency, differentiated merely by the introduction of certain emblems.

This system disappeared in 1835-6, when an English coinage was established with the head of William IV replacing the name of the Mughal emperor. All other issues were suppressed. Since 1835 the currency of India has been a branch of that of the British Empire.

The Dravidian Deccan was, except in prehistoric times, far less affected by foreign influences than the plains of Hindustān. Its political history is obscure, and little light is shed on it by the coinage. Really ancient coins are rare; besides, their devices are crude and indistinct; legends are either absent or enigmatical; and dates, except on some late Muhammadan coins, are always wanting. The dearth of old coins is perhaps due to plundering invasions from the north. The earliest known raid was that made about 330 A.D. by Samudragupta, who penetrated almost to Cape Comorin, and returned north with vast spoil. Nearly a thousand years later the south was raided by Malik Kāfūr, who returned to Delhi with gold estimated at three millions sterling. Later, Muhammadan invaders, in 1565 A.D., sacked the vast Hindu city of Vijayanagar on the Tungabhadra and carried off untold hoarded treasure.

In ancient times rectangular punch-marked coins circulated in the south as well as the north. Such have been found associated with *denarii* of Augustus, who died in 14 A.D. When the silver and copper punch-marked coins ceased to circulate in the south is unknown, but it was probably not earlier than 200 A.D. Die-struck silver coins, which may have been introduced from the north with Buddhism, are very rare and of little importance at anything like an early date. The principal coinage in historical times has been gold, not silver. The earliest known gold coins of the south are supposed to date from the first two centuries of the Christian era. They consist of slightly flattened globules of gold, without any device except an indistinct punch-mark.

The weight of the southern coinage was, like the northern, based on that of an indigenous seed, which was, however, not the same. It was the *kalañju* or 'Molucca bean', weighing about 50 grains. The *purāṇa*, or silver punch-marked coin, was equal in weight to one of these seeds. The standard coins, later known to European settlers as 'pagodas', usually weighed about 52 grains. This type lasted practically unchanged till 1833. The boar device characteristic of the Chālukyan coinage is the origin of the vernacular designation *varāha* or *varāgan* ('boar') universally applied to the peculiar gold coins of Southern India, the 'pagodas' of Europeans in later times. The Chālukyan boar, as well as the fish of the Pāndyas of the extreme south, continued to appear during the eleventh century on the coins of the Chola dynasty of Tanjore after it had absorbed those two lines. The famous King Rājarāja, who ascended the throne in 985, was the first to adopt on the obverse the device of a standing figure which the Pāndyas had borrowed from the 'standing king' of the Guptas of Northern India. This in its turn was imitated by the Ceylonese king Parākrama Bāhu, who succeeded in 1153 A.D.

The powerful dynasty of Vijayanagar (1340–1565) issued a coinage, chiefly in gold, which weighed about 52 grains, or half that amount. After the destruction in 1565 of Vijayanagar, this coinage was imitated by innumerable native chieftains, in particular by Haidar Alī, Tipū Sultān, Kṛishṇa Rājā of Mysore, as well as by the European factories. The Travancore State still issues the Southern style of coinage, but Mysore has adopted the imperial British currency. The various Muhammadan states of the south have followed the style of the ordinary Delhi coinage, unaffected by the southern system.

During the eighteenth century the currency of the Deccan had become so confused that in 1806 English officials found thirty-two kinds of gold pagodas and fifteen kinds of silver rupees in circulation. This chaos was removed in 1833 by legislation that made the rupees of Madras, Bombay, and Upper India equal in value. Acts passed in 1835 and subsequent years introduced the modern uniform currency prevailing throughout British India.

E. J. Rapson, *Indian Coins*, in Bühler's *Encyclopaedia*, 1898. V. A. Smith, *Catalogue of the Coins in the Indian Museum, Calcutta*, Oxford, 1906; *Imperial Gazetteer of India*, vol. ii, pp. 135–154. C. J. Brown, *The Coins of India*, Oxford University Press, 1922.

INDEX